The Librarian's Companion

The Librarian's Companion

A HANDBOOK OF THOUSANDS OF FACTS AND FIGURES ON LIBRARIES / LIBRARIANS, BOOKS / NEWSPAPERS, PUBLISHERS / BOOKSELLERS

Vladimir F. Wertsman

Second Edition

Greenwood Press
Westport, Connecticut • London

Library of Congress Cataloging-in-Publication Data

Wertsman, Vladimir, 1929–
  The librarian's companion : a handbook of thousands of facts and
figures on libraries, librarians, books, newspapers, publishers,
booksellers / Vladimir F. Wertsman.—2nd ed.
      p. cm.
  Includes bibliographical references and index.
  ISBN 0–313–29975–7 (alk. paper)
      1. Library science—Handbooks, manuals, etc.   2. Libraries—
Handbooks, manuals, etc.   3. Books and reading—Handbooks, manuals,
etc.   4. Book industries and trade—Handbooks, manuals, etc.
  I. Title.
  Z670.W39   1996
  011'.02—dc20   96–5802

British Library Cataloguing in Publication Data is available.

Library of Congress Catalog Card Number: 96–5802
ISBN: 0–313–29975–7

First published in 1996

Greenwood Press, 88 Post Road West, Westport, CT 06881
An imprint of Greenwood Publishing Group, Inc.

Printed in the United States of America

The paper used in this book complies with the
Permanent Paper Standard issued by the National
Information Standards Organization (Z39.48–1984).

10 9 8 7 6 5 4 3 2

Libraries are as forests, in which not only
the cedars and oaks are to be found, but bushes
too and dwarfish shrubs, and as in apothecaries'
shops all sorts of drugs are permitted to be,
so many sorts of books be in a library.

—William Drummond of Hawthornden
(1585–1649), Scottish poet
(*On Libraries*, 1631)

Keepers of books, keepers of print and paper
on the shelves, librarians are keepers also of the
records of human spirit—the records of men's watch
upon the world and upon themselves. In such a time as
ours, when wars are made against the spirit and
its works, the keeping of these records
is itself a kind of warfare.

—Archibald MacLeish (1892–1982),
American poet, lawyer, Librarian of Congress
(*A Time to Speak*, 1941)

Contents

Acknowledgments

An author once remarked that a book cannot afford to be more than ten percent new. Even if this percentage is relative and subject to debate, the truth is that any book owes its existence, at least in part, to other books, with the sole difference that fiction authors don't have to mention their sources, while for nonfiction authors, the bibliography is a must.

In this context, I would like first to acknowledge all authors and publishers of those books cited after each entry and in the bibliography following each section. Without these books I never could have gotten the documentation and, subsequently, the inspiration for this volume.

Special thanks are expressed to Philip Gerrard, Coordinator of Donnell Library Center, New York Public Library, and the following unit heads: Burt Abelson (Reference), James Peters (Adult Lending), and Bosiljka Stevanovic (Foreign Language) for their encouragement and fine cooperation.

My appreciation also goes to Lester Annenberg (Time, Inc.), Patricia F. Beilke (Ball State University), and the following staff members of the Donnell Library Center: Osman Bayazid, Erwin Buttler, Hung Yun Chang, Anthony Fichetti, Earl Gladden, Sylvia Goldberg, Millie Bulion, Lee Johnson, and Nelida Kahan; as well as to Roger Giordano (Andorra), Patricia Moore (New York Public Research Libraries), Elizabetta Righi Iwanejko (San Marino), Linda Soper (World Literature Today), and George Wolf (Brooklyn Public Library) for their assistance during various phases of research and preparation of the book.

Additional thanks are expressed, for assistance during various phases of preparing this book and for inspirational suggestions, to the following colleagues and friends: Irina Kuharets and Nelida Kahan, Donnell Library Center, World Languages Collection, The New York Public Library; Ewa Jankowska and Marzena Pasek-Hamilton, Research Libraries, General Reference, The New York

Public Library; Rita E. Bott and Joseph Paladino, Mid-Manhattan Library, Reference Section, The New York Public Library; Anna Sheets and Robyn Young, editors, Gale Research Company; Valentina G. Mytko, Minsk Polytechnic Academy, Belarus; and Susan Vince, Technology Generation and Training Company, Bethesda, Maryland.

Introduction
to the First Edition

This volume is a compact and handy reference work that brings together a wealth of information on books, libraries, librarians, and publishers from all over the world in a unique arrangement of topics, with facts and figures of interest to virtually any reference librarian (public, academic, special, school, etc.) as well as to the teacher, student, or other interested researcher. This work also represents a tribute to librarianship as a profession, and a homage to the 100th anniversary of library education in the United States.

This book has 644 entries encompassing thousands of facts and figures—easily accessible, digestible, and retrievable—and referring to almost 200 countries, 300 book and periodical titles, and 338 noted people from all over the world. The use of foreign reference sources in Bulgarian, French, German, Hungarian, Polish, Romanian, Russian, and Spanish, in conjunction with American and British materials, brought to light several pieces of information little known or unknown to librarians at large, with a considerable part rendered in English for the first time. In the process of research; information was culled not only from standard reference works, but also from touristic brochures or local telephone directories (for example, Cook Islands, Dominica) as well as from correspondence with representative institutions (for entries of Andorra and San Marino, for example) to locate information that could not be found otherwise.

The structure of the entire book, the selections found in each section, the multifaceted approach, reflect the universality of the book's, library's and librarian's role and, consequently, include examples from all continents, various countries and nations, and their religious and political beliefs. In this way, the librarian from any country and any field of work has the opportunity to learn about his own country's place in the world, to compare it to other countries, and eventually learn from other countries. The division of the book into two parts has been designed to acquaint the reader first with the librarian's macro-cosmos (part I, The Librarian's World Digest), and then proceed to the librar-ian's microcosmos (part II, The Librarian's Special Interests), which encompass together five sections.

Each section consists of explanatory notes regarding its structure, a selective bibliography, followed by entries arranged in alphabetical order. All sources of reference mentioned twice or more—at the end of entries in sections two to five—are given in abbreviated form (see symbols in list of abbreviations). For singular items, the citation consists of name of the author, book title, place and year of publication, except the well-known titles issued in many editions, in which case the place of publication is irrelevant. In the event of missing dates for individuals, they could not be ascertained despite my best efforts. I will be pleased to be advised of any corrections.

It is my hope that this book will indeed become a companion to all librarians and provide not only knowledge but also instill in them pride in their profession.

Introduction
to the Second Edition

The most satisfying reward of the first edition was its inclusion in Eugene Shee-hy's prestigious *Guide to Reference Books* (10th ed.) published by the American Library Association in 1992, as well as the positive feedback from both American and foreign readers. In the meantime, new statistical data regarding library holdings appeared in 1990 and affected several dozens of countries, including new independent states that appeared after the fall of Communism in the former Soviet Union. In addition, new research materials suitable for inclusion in our handbook were brought to our attention by colleagues and friends suggesting a new and improved edition. Consequently, the present second edition offers almost 1,000 entries compared to the 644 entries of the first edition. In addition to revising, updating, and enlarging old sections of the book, two new sections (Librarian's Latin Expressions and Librarian's Job Finding Sources of Information) were added. Also added were new appendixes (Librarian's and Library Supervisor's Ten Golden Rules, Library Awards and Grants, UNESCO Public Library Manifesto, and others) and, of course, an updated index and supplementary bibliographies to each section of the book.

Readers should keep in mind not to overlook the introduction to the first edition since the structure, methodology, and objectives of the book remain the same as during the publication of the first edition. It is hoped that this edition will be appreciated as much as the first edition, and, as in the past, we remain open to constructive criticism and suggestions that may eventually inspire a third edition, if warranted.

Vladimir F. Wertsman
January 1996

Abbreviations

General

B.P. (*Boite Postal*)	Postal Box (French)
C.P. (*Caixa Postal*)	Postal Box (Portuguese)
GNP	Gross National Product
ILL rate	Illiteracy rate
LHO ratio	Library holdings (in volumes) ratio per inhabitant
n.d.	no data available

Titles

ABTD	*American Book Trade Directory*
AL	*American Libraries*, periodical
ALA	*ALA World Encyclopedia of Library & Information Science*
BDZ	*Buch der Zitate*
BPA	*Book Publishing Annual*
CAD	*Canadian Almanac and Directory*
CE	*Columbia Encyclopedia*
CTRQ	*Crown/Treasury of Relevant Quotations*
D	*The Discoverers*
DDC	*Diccionario de Citas*
DES	*Diccionario Enciclopedico Salvat*
EDC	*Encyclopedie des Citations*
EUI	*Enciclopedia Universal Illustrada, Espasa*

GB	*Der Grosse Brockhaus*
GER	*Gran Enciclopedia Rialp*
GLE	*Grand Larousse Encyclopedique*
GQ	*Great Quotations*
ILMP	*International Literary Market Place*
KES	*Knigovedenie: Entsiklopedicheskil Slovar*
LOC	*Libraries and Our Civilizations*
NCCN	*New Century Cyclopedia of Names*
NCE	*New Catholic Encyclopedia*
NDT	*New Dictionary of Thoughts*
PK	*Pokhvala Knige*
RP	*Racial Proverbs*
S	*Scott's Standard Postage Stamp Catalogue*
SJE	*Standard Jewish Encyclopedia*
SOK	*Slovo o Knige*
SYB	*Statesman's Yearbook*
TDE	*Tesoros de España*
TGAQ	*Treasury of Great American Quotations*
TJQ	*Treasury of Jewish Quotations*
TT	*Topical Time*, periodical
UN	*Unesco Statistical Yearbook*
WBD	*Webster's Biographical Dictionary*
WD	*Writer's Digest*, periodical
WGL	*World Guide to Libraries*
WIJ	*Wit of the Jews*
WW	*Who's Who*
WWA	*Who's Who in America*
WWWA	*Who Was Who in America*

I
THE LIBRARIAN'S
WORLD DIGEST

— 1 —
Library and Publishing Information, by Country

This section contains 194 entries covering countries from all continents. In-cluded are United Nations members and nonmembers, independent states as well as different forms of dependencies (for example, British colonies or French overseas departments) which, nevertheless, have their own library networks and publishing activities, and figure as independent units in official statistical records.

Each entry shows the name of the country, followed by five subdivisions:

General Background

Includes the location of the country, its capital, form of government, population, GNP per capita, Illiteracy rate (ILL rate—persons over the age of 15, in percent), and Library holdings (in volumes) ratio per inhabitant (LHO ratio).

Sources

UN, for population and ILL rate; SYB, for GNP per capita; LHO, computed by the author.

Library Network

Includes the number of libraries (serving units) and their holdings in volumes (physical units of printed works or manuscripts in binding portfolio, rounded to one decimal place for cases in which total volumes exceed one million) arranged by categories: *national*—exercises country's bibliographic control and copy-rights, serves as depository; *public*—serves local and regional communities and population at large; *university*—serves students and teachers of post-secondary—educational institutions; *school*—serves students and teachers of elementary, junior- and senior-high schools; *special*—serves needs of research institutions, museums, archives, etc.; *nonspecial*—used for general research on local levels; *government agency*—serves courts, ministries, postal offices, etc.; *religious*—serves clergy and parishioners of ecclesiastic institutions, in addition to its other functions.

Sources

If no source or year is listed with specific data, the reader is to presume the source is WGL and the year 1982. All other sources and dates are listed with the information.

Publishing Output and Distribution

Lists the number of book publishers, number of book titles, and volumes produced for a specific year; number of daily and nondaily newspapers and other periodicals; with their respective circulations for a specific year, and the number of major booksellers.

Sources

ILMP, uses as basis for computation of number of book publishers, all presumed for 1982; UN, for book titles, number of volumes produced, newspapers, and other periodicals including their circulation; ILMP, for computation of number of major booksellers, all presumed for 1982.

Noted Libraries

Lists national libraries and their addresses. In the case of a country without a national library, their most important library is listed.

Librarians' Organization

In all but one case a national organization equivalent to the American Library Association and its address are listed. The one exception is Belgium, for which two organizations are listed due to the absence of a single national organization. For countries without a library organization, this subdivision has been omitted.

In this second edition, 79 entries (countries) were updated with the latest (1990) data regarding library holdings, number of libraries, and LHO per capita of the respective countries. However, for the bulk of countries included in the first edition, the statistical data on libraries and library holdings as well as the LHO ratio remain the same because new data had not yet been provided or did not reflect substantial changes. It is hoped that as soon as new data are researched and verified, they could be incorporated in an eventual third edition of this handbook. Finally, we should mention that four new entries (Bhutan, Estonia, Lithuania, and Ukraine) were added to the second edition, and the entry on Yemen was restructured as a result of the unification between North and South Yemen, which were listed as separate countries in the first edition.

Bibliography

The Book Publishing Annual: Highlights, Analysis and Trends, 1985. New York: R.R. Bowker, 1985.

International Literary Market Place, 1983–84. New York: R.R. Bowker, 1983.

Knigovedenie: Ėnt́siklopedicheskiĭ Slovar'. Moskva: Sovetskaiâ Ėnt́siklopedîâ, 1981.

Paxton, John, ed. *The Statesman's Year-Book: Statistical and Historical Annual of the States of the World for the Year 1984–85.* New York: St. Martin's Press, 1984.

Statistical Yearbook/Annuaire Statistique 1984. New York: UNESCO, 1984.

Statistical Yearbook/Annuaire Statistique 1985. New York: UNESCO, 1985.

Statistical Yearbook/Annuaire Statistique 1990. New York: UNESCO, 1990.

Steele, Colin. *Major Libraries of the World: A Selective Guide.* New York: R.R. Bowker, 1976.

Wedgeworth, Robert, ed. *ALA World Encyclopedia of Library and Information Services.* Chicago: American Library Association, 1980.

Wedgeworth, Robert, ed. *ALA World Encyclopedia of Library and Information Services.* 3d ed. Chicago: American Library Association, 1993.

World Guide to Libraries/Internationales Bibliotheks Handbuch. 6th ed. München: K.G. Saur, 1983.

AFGHANISTAN

General Background
Location: Central Asia; capital: Kabul; form of government: republic (socialist state); population: 16.7 million (1980); GNP per capita: $168 (1982); ILL rate: 80% (1980); LHO ratio: 1 volume per 33 inhabitants.

Library Network
1 national library/30,000 volumes; 37 public libraries/200,000 volumes (UN 1980); 14 university libraries/140,000 volumes (ALA, 1976); 4 school libraries/ 30,000 volumes (ALA, 1976); 5 special libraries/150,000 volumes (ALA, 1976). Total: 61 libraries/550,000 volumes.

Publishing Output and Distribution
9 publishers; 415 book titles/5.9 million volumes (1981); 13 daily newspapers/ 71,000 circulation (1982); 5 booksellers.

Noted Library
Kabul University Library, Pohantoon, Kabul.

Librarians' Organization
Anjuman Kitab-Khana-I-Afghanistan, P.O. Box 3142, Kabul.

ALBANIA

General Background
Location: Southeast Europe; capital: Tirana; form of government: republic (socialist state); population: 2.85 million (1982); GNP per capita: $840 (1979); ILL rate: n.d.; LHO ratio: 3.1 volumes per inhabitant.

Library Network
1 national library/803,000 volumes (UN, 1980); 3,631 public libraries/5.7 million volumes (UN, 1980); 2 university libraries/606,000 volumes (UN, 1982); 32 nonspecial libraries/1.8 million volumes (UN, 1980). Total: 3,666 libraries/ 8.9 million volumes.

Publishing Output and Distribution
4 publishers; 1,149 book titles/4.6 million volumes (1982); 2 daily newspapers/ 145,000 circulation (1982); 2 booksellers.

Noted Library
Biblioteka Kombetare, Tirana.

Librarians' Organization
Council of Libraries, Rruga Abdi Toptani 3, Tirana.

ALGERIA

General Background
Location: Northwest Africa; capital: Algiers; form of government: republic; population: 20.2 million (1982); GNP per capita: $2,140 (1981); ILL rate: 55.3% (1982); LHO ratio: 1 volume per almost 7 inhabitants.

Library Network
1 national library/920,000 volumes; 8 public libraries/174,000 volumes; 24 university libraries/1.3 million volumes; 55 special libraries/603,000 volumes; 7 school libraries/42,000 volumes; 5 government agency libraries/30,000 volumes. Total: 100 libraries/3.1 million volumes.

Publishing Output and Distribution
1 publisher (state owned); 504 book titles/1.3 million volumes (1982); 4 daily newspapers/448,000 circulation (1982); 15 other newspapers/309,000 circulation (1982); 27 periodicals/476,000 circulation (1982); 3 booksellers.

Noted Libraries
Bibliothèque Nationale, Avenue du Docteur Fanon, Algiers; Archives Nationales, Palais du Gouvernment, Esplanade d'Afrique, Algiers.

Librarians' Organization
Institute de Bibliothéconomie et de Sciences Documentaires, Université d'Alger, Rue Didouche Mourad, Algiers.

ANDORRA

General Background
Location: Southwest Europe; capital: Andorra la Vella; form of government autonomous principality; population: 40,000 (1982); GNP per capita: n.d.; ILL rate: n.d.; LHO ratio: 1 volume for less than 4 inhabitants.

Library Network
1 national library/9,000 volumes (UN, 1980).

Publishing Output and Distribution
n.d. publishers; 5 daily newspapers/n.d. circulation (1979); 4 periodicals/n.d. circulation (1979).

Noted Library
Biblioteca Nacional d'Andorra, Edifici Prada Casadet, Andorra la Vella.

ANGOLA

General Background
Location: Southwest Africa; capital: Luanda; form of government: republic (socialist state); population: 7.4 million (1982); GNP per capita: $470 (1980); ILL rate: n.d.; LHO ratio: 1 volume per 50 inhabitants.

Library Network
1 national library/45,000 volumes (ALA, 1978); 19 public libraries/15,000 volumes; 1 university library/75,000 volumes; 6 special libraries/28,000 volumes; 34 school libraries/n.d. volumes (ALA, 1978); 1 government agency library/ 20,000 volumes. Total: 62 libraries/183,000 volumes.

Publishing Output and Distribution
3 publishers; 57 book titles/n.d. volumes (1979); 1 daily newspaper/50,000 circulation (1982); 5 booksellers.

Noted Library
Biblioteca Nacional Doutor Antonio Augustinho Neto, C.P. 2195 Luanda.

ANTIGUA AND BARBUDA

General Background
Location: West Indies; capital: St. John's; form of government: independent state, British monarch is its nominal chief; population: 76,000 (1981); GNP per capita: $1,270 (1980); ILL rate: 11.3% (1960); LHO ratio: 2 volumes per over 3 inhabitants.

Library Network
1 public library/50,000 volumes.

Publishing Output and Distribution
n.d. publishers; 1 daily newspaper/6,000 circulation (1979).

Noted Library
St. John's Public Library, St. John's, Leeward Islands.

ARGENTINA

General Background
Location: South America; capital: Buenos Aires; form of government: republic; population: 29.1 million (1982); GNP per capita: $2,560 (1981); ILL rate: 7.4% (1970); LHO ratio: 5 volumes per inhabitant.

Library Network
1 national library/1.8 million volumes (UN, 1977); 1,528 public libraries/9.5 million volumes (UN, 1977); 183 university libraries/130 million volumes; 17 professional school libraries/100,000 volumes; 164 special libraries/4.1 million volumes; 30 government agency libraries/1.2 million volumes. Total: 1,923 libraries/146.7 million volumes.

Publishing Output and Distribution
155 book publishers; 4,216 book titles/13.5 million volumes (1983); 191 daily newspapers/3.3 million circulation (1982); 27 booksellers.

Noted Libraries
Biblioteca Nacional, México 564, Buenos Aires; Universidad de Buenos Aires, Bibliotecas, Azcuenaga 280, Buenos Aires.

Librarians' Organization
Asociación de Bibliotecarios Graduados de la Republica Argentina, Cassila de Correo 68, Buenos Aires.

AUSTRALIA

General Background
Location: Oceania; capital: Canberra; government form; self-governing dominion, British monarch is its nominal chief; population: [17.3 million (1990)]; GNP per capita: $11,080 (1981); ILL rate: n.d.; LHO ratio: 7.7 volumes per inhabitant.

Library Network (ALA, 1990)
1 national library/4.8 million volumes; 1,400 public libraries/27.6 million volumes; 67 university libraries/30 million volumes; 10,000 school libraries/65 million volumes; 1,100 special libraries/1.7 million volumes (1987); 8 state libraries/6.7 million volumes. Total: 12,576 libraries/135.8 million volumes.

Publishing Output and Distribution
156 publishers; 2,358 book titles/n.d. volumes (1982); 63 daily newspapers/4.8 million circulation (1979); 470 other newspapers/8.9 million circulation (1979); 3,534 periodicals/n.d. circulation (1978); 12 booksellers.

Noted Library
National Library of Australia, Canberra.

Librarians' Organization
Library Association of Australia, 473 Elizabeth Street, Surry Hills.

AUSTRIA

General Background
Location: Central Europe; capital: Vienna; government form: republic; population: 7.5 million (1982); GNP per capita: $10,210 (1982); ILL rate: n.d.; LHO ratio: over 10 volumes per inhabitant.

Library Network
1 national library/2.3 million volumes (UN, 1980); 2,321 public libraries/5.5 million volumes (UN, 1977); 796 university libraries/18.9 million volumes (UN, 1981); 5,600 school libraries/9.5 million volumes (UN, 1977); 1,434 special libraries/26 million volumes (UN, 1983); 66 nonspecial libraries/17.3 million volumes (UN, 1980). Total: 10,218 libraries/79.5 million volumes.

Publishing Output and Distribution
137 publishers; 6,736 book titles/n.d. volumes (1982); 30 daily newspaper/2.6 million circulation (1982); 2,108 periodicals/n.d. circulation (1982); 29 booksellers.

Noted Library
Österreichische National Bibliothek, Joseph Platz 1, Vienna.

Librarians' Organization
Vereinigung Österreichischer Bibliothekare, Josef Platz 1, Vienna.

BAHAMAS

General Background
Location: West Indies; capital: Nassau; government form: independent state, British monarch is its nominal chief; population: 253,000 (1990); GNP per capita: $3,620 (1981); ILL rate: 10.3% (1963); LHO ratio: 2.2 volumes per inhabitant.

Library Network (ALA, 1990)
1 national library/440,000 volumes; 1 university library/30,000 volumes; 3 special libraries/6,000 volumes (1987). 1 public library/200,000 volumes. Total: 6 libraries/676,000 volumes.

Publishing Output and Distribution
2 publishers; n.d. book titles/volumes; 3 daily newspapers/34,000 circulation (1982); 8 booksellers.

Noted Library
Nassau Public Library, P.O. Box 3210, Nassau.

BAHRAIN

General Background
Location: Persian Gulf; capital: Manama; government form: independent sheikdom; population: 503,000 (1990); GNP per capita: $8,960 (1981); ILL rate: 20.9% (1981); LHO ratio: 1.1 volumes per inhabitant.

Library Network (ALA, 1990)
3 university libraries/190,000 volumes; 1 public library/199,000 volumes; 170 school libraries/186,000 volumes; 65 special libraries/14,000 volumes. Total: 239 libraries/589,000 volumes.

Publishing Output and Distribution
n.d. publishers; 78 book titles/843,000 volumes (1982); 5 booksellers.

Noted Library
Bahrain Historical and Archeological Society Library, P.O. Box 5087, Manama.

BANGLADESH

General Background
Location: South Asia; capital: Dacca; form of government: republic; population: 92 million (1982); GNP per capita: $140 (1981); ILL rate: 74.2% (1974); LHO ratio: almost 1 volume per 70 inhabitants.

Library Network
1 national library/20,300 volumes (ALA, 1976); 14 public libraries/293,000 volumes; 6 university libraries/673,000 volumes; 12 special libraries/275,000 volumes; 2 government agency libraries/53,000 volumes. Total: 35 libraries/1.3 million volumes (ALA: 124 public, 379 university, 16,784 school, 102 special libraries/n.d. volumes).

Publishing Output and Distribution
14 publishers; 542 book titles/n.d. volumes (1980); 3 daily newspapers/542,000 circulation (1982); 14 booksellers.

Noted Library
Dacca University Library.

Librarians' Organization
Directorate of Archives and Libraries, 106 Central Road, Dacca.

BARBADOS

General Background
Location: West Indies; capital: Bridgetown; form of government: independent state, British monarch is its nominal chief; population: 255,000 (1990); GNP per capita: $3,661 (1981); ILL rate: 0.7% (1970); LHO ratio: 2.3 volumes per inhabitant.

Library Network (ALA, 1990)
1 national library/159,600 volumes; 1 university library/215,000 volumes; 2 public libraries/131,135 volumes; 23 school libraries/26,194 volumes (1987); 13 special libraries/66,125 volumes (1987). Total: 40 libraries/598,054 volumes.

Publishing Output and Distribution
4 publishers; 139 book titles/n.d. volumes (1982); 2 daily newspapers/39,000 circulation (1982); 1 other newspaper/28,400 circulation (1979); 5 booksellers.

Noted Libraries
Public Library, Coleridge Street, Bridgetown; University of West Indies, Main Library, Cave Hill Campus, Bridgetown.

Librarians' Organization
Library Association of Barbados, P.O. Box 827, E. Bridgetown.

BELGIUM

General Background
Location: Northwest Europe; capital; Brussels; form of government: kingdom; population: 9.8 million (1982); GNP per capita: $11,920 (1982); ILL rate: n.d.; LHO ratio: over 4 volumes per inhabitant.

Library Network
1 national library/3.3 million volumes (UN, 1980); 2,351 public libraries/24 million volumes (UN, 1980); 57 university libraries/11.1 million volumes; 16 professional school libraries/1.1 million volumes; 96 special libraries/3.4 million volumes; 14 government agency libraries/2.4 million volumes. Total: 2,535 libraries/45.3 million volumes.

Publishing Output and Distribution
245 publishers; 8,065 book titles/n.d. volumes (1983); 26 daily newspapers/2.2 million circulation (1982); 2 other newspapers/32,000 circulation (1982); 12 booksellers.

Noted Library
Bibliothèque Royale Albert I, Boulevard de L'Empereur 4, Brussels.

Librarians' Organizations
Association Nationale des Bibliothécaires d'Expression Française, 56 Rue de la Station, Havelange; Vlaamse Vereiniging van Bibliothek, Archief en Documentation Personeel, Frans van Heymbeecklaan 4–6, Postbus 59, Deurne.

BELIZE (BRITISH HONDURAS)

General Background
Location: Central America; capital: Belmopan; form of government: independent state, member of Commonwealth of Nations; population: 188,000 (1990); GNP per capita: $1,080 (1981); ILL rate: 8.8% (1970); LHO ratio: 1.6 volumes per inhabitant.

Library Network (ALA, 1990)
1 national library/130,000 volumes; 2 university libraries/6,000 volumes; 1 public library/125,000 volumes; 200 school libraries/35,000 volumes; 17 special libraries/14,000 volumes. Total: 221 libraries/310,000 volumes.

Publishing Output and Distribution
2 daily newspapers/6,000 circulation (1979); 6 other newspapers/45,000 circulation (1981); 4 booksellers.

Noted Library
National Library Service, Bliss Institute, P.O. Box 990, Belmopan.

BENIN (DAHOMEY)

General Background
Location: West Africa; capital: Porto Novo; form of government; republic; population: 4 million (1990); GNP per capita: $320 (1982); ILL rate: 72.1% (1980); LHO ratio: 1 volume per over 11 inhabitants.

Library Network (ALA, 1990)
1 national library/11,000 volumes; 1 university library/100,000 volumes; 16 public libraries/99,000 volumes; 3 school libraries/12,000 volumes; 10 special libraries/95,000 volumes; 4 other libraries/40,000 volumes. Total: 35 libraries/357,000 volumes.

Publishing Output and Distribution
2 publishers; 13 book titles/n.d. volumes (1978); 1 daily newspaper/1,000 circulation (1982); 4 periodicals/8,500 circulation (1976); 10 booksellers.

Noted Library
Bibliothèque Nationale du Benin, B.P. 526, Cotonou.

BERMUDA

General Background
Location: Atlantic Ocean; capital: Hamilton; form of government: British colony; population: 55,000 (1982); GNP per capita: $12,910 (1981); ILL rate: 1.6% (1970); LHO ratio: almost 4 volumes per inhabitant.

Library Network
4 public libraries/140,000 volumes (UN, 1980); 1 university library/18,000 volumes (UN, 1982); 22 school libraries/52,000 volumes (UN, 1982); 3 nonspecial libraries/2,000 volumes (UN, 1977). Total: 30 libraries/212,000 volumes.

Publishing Output and Distribution
3 publishers; 2 daily newspapers/14,000 circulation (1982); 3 booksellers.

Noted Library
Bermuda Library, Par-la-Ville, Hamilton.

BHUTAN

General Background
Location: Himalayan Mountains; Capital: Thimphu; government form: monarchy; population: 600,000 (1990); GNP per capita: $180.00 (1990); ILL rate: 68%; LHO ratio: 1 volume per 160 inhabitants.

Library Network (ALA, 1990)
1 national library/12,000 volumes; 1 public library/6,000 volumes; 1 school library/10,000 volumes.; 1 special library/10,000 volumes. Total: 4 libraries/38,000 volumes.

Publishing Output and Distribution
n.d.

Noted Library
n.d.

Librarians' Organization
n.d.

BOLIVIA

General Background
Location: South America; capital: La Paz; form of government: republic; population: 5.9 million (1982); GNP per capita: $600 (1981); ILL rate: 36.8% (1976); LHO ratio: 1 volume per over 4 inhabitants.

Library Network
2 national libraries/135,000 volumes (UN, 1980); 70 public and school libraries/ 345,000 volumes (ALA, 1976); 17 university libraries/220,000 volumes (UN, 1983); 7 professional school libraries/48,000 volumes; 27 special libraries/ 317,000 volumes; 7 government agency libraries/183,000 volumes; 3 nonspecial libraries/220,000 volumes. Total: 133 libraries/1.4 million volumes.

Publishing Output and Distribution
8 publishers; 301 book titles/n.d. circulation (1982); 12 daily newspapers/ 275,000 circulation (1980); 20 other newspapers/7,000 circulation (1980); 20 periodicals/24,500 circulation (1980); 8 booksellers.

Noted Libraries
Biblioteca y Archivo Nacional de Bolivia, Calle Espana 25, Casilla 338, Sucre; Instituto Boliviano de Cultura, Biblioteca, Avenida 6 de Agosto 2424, Casilla 7846, La Paz.

Librarians' Organization
Associación Boliviana de Bibliotecarios, Casilla 992, Cochabamba.

BOTSWANA (BECHUANALAND)

General Background
Location: Southcentral Africa; capital: Gaborone; form of government: republic; population: [1.3 million (1990)]; GNP per capita: $1,010 (1981); ILL rate: 59% (1971); LHO ratio: less than 1 volume per 2 inhabitants.

Library Network (ALA, 1990)
1 national library/21,640 volumes; 1 university library/150,000 volumes; 10 college libraries/75,000 volumes; 1 public library/18,500 volumes; 147 school libraries/328,692 volumes; 1 archival library/13,236 volumes. Total: 161 libraries/ 607,068 volumes.

Publishing Output and Distribution
1 publisher (state owned); 97 book titles/n.d. volumes (1980); 1 daily newspaper/
19,000 circulation (1982); 2 booksellers.

Noted Library
Botswana National Library Service, P.O. Box 0036, Gaborone.

Librarians' Organization
Botswana Library Association, P.O. Box 1310, Gaborone.

BRAZIL

General Background
Location: South America; capital: Rio de Janeiro; form of government: republic;
population: 126 million (1982); GNP per capita: $2,220 (1981); ILL rate: 23.9%
(1978); LHO ratio: over 2 volumes per 5 inhabitants.

Library Network
1 national library/3.5 million volumes; 3,342 public libraries/14.4 million volumes (UN, 1979); 1,029 university libraries/11.4 million volumes (UN, 1979);
9,479 school libraries/14.4 million volumes (UN, 1979); 357 special libraries/
7.2 million volumes; 116 government agency libraries/2.1 million volumes; 781
nonspecial libraries/2.1 million volumes (UN, 1979). Total: 15,105 libraries/55.1
million volumes.

Publishing Output and Distribution
152 publishers; 19,179 book titles/396 million volumes (1982); 322 daily news-
papers/6.1 million circulation (1982); 1,049 other newspapers/n.d. circulation
(1982); 2,419 periodicals/3 million circulation (1981); 23 booksellers.

Noted Library
Biblioteca Nacional, Avenida Rio Branco 219–239, Rio de Janeiro.

Librarians' Organization
Federação Brasileira de Associaçoẽs de Bibliotecarios, Rua Avanhadava 40, Sao
Paulo.

BRUNEI

General Background
Location: South Asia; capital: Bandar Seri Begawan; form of government: sul-
tanate (monarchy); population: 200,000 (1982); GNP per capita: $17,380 (1981);
ILL rate: 20.2% (1981); LHO ratio: over 2.5 volumes per inhabitant.

Library Network
8 public libraries/97,000 volumes (UN, 1980); 5 university libraries/48,000 volumes (UN, 1981); 15 school libraries/191,000 volumes (UN, 1981); 2 special

libraries/6,000 volumes (UN, 1977); 2 nonspecial libraries/176,000 volumes (UN, 1980). Total: 32 libraries/518,000 volumes.

Publishing Output and Distribution
2 publishers; 72 book titles/360,000 volumes (1982); 1 daily newspaper/45,000 circulation (1982); 3 periodicals/60,500 circulation (1977); 4 booksellers.

Noted Library
Language and Literature Bureau Library, Jalan Elizabeth II, Bandar Seri Begawan.

BULGARIA

General Background
Location: South Europe; capital: Sofia; form of government: republic (socialist); population: 9.1 million; GNP per capita: $4,150 (1980); ILL rate: 7.8% (1980); LHO ratio: 12 volumes per inhabitant.

Library Network (ALA, 1990)
1 national library/6.5 million volumes; 29 university libraries/6.6 million volumes; 3,820 public libraries/48.3 million volumes; 3,268 school libraries/17.3 million volumes; 866 special libraries/21 million volumes; 1,563 other libraries/ 9.5 million volumes. Total: 9,547 libraries/109.2 million volumes.

Publishing Output and Distribution
18 publishers; 4,924 book titles/5.9 million volumes (1983); 12 daily newspapers/2.1 million circulation (1982); 37 other newspapers/955,000 circulation (1982); 1,662 periodicals/8.8 million circulation (1982); 1 bookseller (state owned).

Noted Library
Natsionalna Biblioteka Kiril i Metodiĭ, Boulevard Tolbukhin 11, Sofia.

Librarians' Organization
Sektsiia na Bibliotechnite Rabotnitsi pri Tsentralniia Komitet na Profesionalnîa Soîuz, Boulevard Tolbukhin 11, Sofia.

BURKINA FASO (UPPER VOLTA)

General Background
Location: West Africa; capital: Ouagadougou; form of government: republic; population: 6.3 million (1982); GNP per capita: $240 (1981); ILL rate: 91.2% (1975); LHO ratio: 1 volume per 70 inhabitants.

Library Network
1 university library/30,000 volumes; 3 school libraries/8,500 volumes; 11 special libraries/37,000 volumes; 4 government agency libraries/7,000 volumes; 1 religious library/15,500 volumes. Total: 20 libraries/98,000 volumes.

Publishing Output and Distribution
2 publishers; 4 book titles/n.d. volumes (1980); 1 daily newspaper/1,500 circulation (1982); 3 periodicals/5,200 circulation (1976); 4 booksellers.

Noted Library
Université de Ouagadougou, Bibliothèque Universitaire, B.P. 7021, Ouagadougou.

Librarians' Organization
Association Voltaique pour le Development des Bibliothèques, des Archives et de la Documentation, address above.

BURMA

General Background
Location: Southeast Asia; capital: Rangoon; form of government: republic (socialist); population: 34.1 million (1980); GNP per capita: $190 (1981); ILL rate: 34.1% (1980); LHO ratio: almost 2 volumes per inhabitant.

Library Network
1 national library/920,635 volumes (ALA, 1976); 5,961 public libraries/40.3 million volumes (ALA, 1976); 27 university libraries/2.4 million volumes (ALA, 1976); 3,714 school libraries/13.3 million volumes (ALA, 1976); 704 special libraries/6.1 million volumes (ALA, 1976). Total: 10,407 libraries/62.3 million volumes.

Publishing Output and Distribution
10 publishers; 1,164 book titles (KES)/volumes; 6 daily newspapers/502,000 circulation (1982); 12 booksellers.

Noted Library
National Library, Town Hall, Rangoon.

Librarians' Organization
Burma Library Association c/o International Institute of Advanced Buddhistic Studies, Kaba Aya, Rangoon.

BURUNDI (RUANDA-URUNDI)

General Background
Location: Eastcentral Africa; capital: Bujumbura; form of government: republic; population: 4.4 million (1982); GNP per capita: $230 (1981); ILL rate: 73% (1980); LHO ratio: 1 volume per 20 inhabitants.

Library Network
2 national libraries/121,000 volumes; 1 public library/24,000 volumes; 4 university libraries/92,000 volumes (UN, 1978); 6 special libraries/16,200 volumes; 1 government agency library/n.d. volumes. Total: 14 libraries/253,200 volumes.

Publishing Output and Distribution
1 publisher; 2 daily newspapers/1,500 circulation (1977); 3 periodicals/54,500 circulation (1975); 3 booksellers.

Noted Library
Université de Burundi, Direction des Bibliothèques, 29, Avenue de l'Uprona, B.P. 1320, Bujumbura.

CAMEROON

General Background
Location: Westcentral Africa; capital: Yaoundé; form of government: republic; population: 8.8 million (1982); GNP per capita: $880 (1982); ILL rate: 59% (1976); LHO ratio: 1 volume per almost 25 inhabitants.

Library Network
1 national library/22,000 volumes; 11 university libraries/150,000 volumes; 3 school libraries/16,400 volumes; 30 special libraries/125,000 volumes; 5 government agency libraries/16,000 volumes; 2 religious libraries/20,000 volumes. Total: 52 libraries/349,400 volumes.

Publishing Output and Distribution
7 publishers; 2 book titles/n.d. volumes (1979); 2 daily newspapers/35,000 circulation (1982); 17 periodicals/n.d. circulation (1975); 10 booksellers.

Noted Library
Bibliothèque Nationale du Cameroun, B. P. 1053, Yaoundé.

Librarians' Organization
Association des Bibliothécaires, Archivistes, Documentalists et Muséographes du Cameroun, c/o Bibliothèque Universitaire, B.P. 1312 Yaoundé.

CANADA

General Background
Location: North America; capital: Ottawa; form of government; independent state, member of Commonwealth of Nations; population: 24.6 million (1982); GNP per capita: $11,400 (1982); ILL rate: n.d.; LHO ratio: over 6 volumes per inhabitant.

Library Network
1 national library/896,000 volumes (UN, 1981); 2,834 public libraries/45.6 million volumes (UN, 1980); 161 university libraries/43.7 million volumes (UN, 1980); 7,982 school libraries/47.6 million volumes (UN, 1981); 146 special libraries/3.3 million volumes; 38 government agency libraries/6.8 million volumes; 35 religious libraries/1.5 million volumes. Total: 11,197 libraries/149.3 million volumes.

Publishing Output and Distribution
281 major publishers (CAD, 1982); 19,053 book titles/n.d. volumes (1980); 120 daily newspapers/5.5 million circulation (1982); 187 other newspapers/12.6 million circulation (1982); 1,384 periodicals/56.1 million circulation (1982); 2,080 booksellers (no year) (ABTD, 1985).

Noted Libraries
National Library of Canada, 395 Wellington Street, Ottawa; Bibliothèque Nationale du Quebec, 1700 Sain Denis Street, Montreal.

Librarians' Organization
Canadian Library Association, 151 Sparks Street, Ottawa.

CAYMAN ISLANDS

General Background
Location: West Indies; capital: Georgetown; form of government: British dependency; population: 18,000 (1982); GNP per capita: $18,750 (1983); ILL rate: 2.5% (1970); LHO ratio: 2.5 volumes per inhabitant.

Library Network
2 public libraries/6,000 volumes (UN, 1981); 1 university library/20,000 volumes (UN, 1982); 1 school library/10,000 volumes (UN, 1981); 1 nonspecial library/9,000 volumes (UN, 1980). Total: 5 libraries/45,000 volumes.

Publishing Output and Distribution
n.d. publishers; 2 daily newspapers/7,200 circulation (1979); n.d. booksellers.

Noted Library
Georgetown University Library, Georgetown.

CENTRAL AFRICAN REPUBLIC

General Background
Location: Central Africa; capital: Bangui; form of government: republic; population: 2.4 million (1982); GNP per capita: $320 (1981); ILL rate: 67% (1980); LHO ratio: 1 volume per 35 inhabitants.

Library Network
3 university libraries/4,500 volumes; 1 professional school library/8,000 volumes; 6 special libraries/35,000 volumes; 1 government agency library/7,700 volumes; 4 nonspecial libraries/30,000 volumes (UN, 1980). Total: 15 libraries/85,200 volumes.

Publishing Output and Distribution
1 publisher (government owned); 1 daily newspaper/1,000 circulation (1977); 5 booksellers.

Noted Library
Université de Bangui, Bibliothèque, B.P. 1450, Bangui.

CHAD

General Background
Location: Northcentral Africa; capital: N'Djamena; form of government: republic; population: 4.6 million (1982); GNP per capita: $110 (1981); ILL rate: n.d.; LHO ratio: 1 volume per 111 inhabitants.

Library Network
3 university libraries/13,500 volumes; 1 school library/n.d. volumes; 9 special libraries/30,000 volumes; 1 government agency library/700 volumes. Total: 14 libraries/44,200 volumes.

Publishing Output and Distribution
1 publisher (government owned); 4 daily newspapers/1,500 circulation (1982); 5 booksellers.

Noted Library
Université du Tchad, Bibliothèque Universitaire, B.P. 1117 N'Djamena.

CHANNEL ISLANDS (ALDERNEY, GUERNSEY, JERSEY, SARK)

General Background
Location: West Europe; capital: Saint Helier; form of government: separate entity, British administration; population: 134,000 (1981); GNP per capita: $10,830 (1982); ILL rate: n.d.; LHO ratio: 1.5 volumes per inhabitant.

Library Network
2 public libraries/170,000 volumes; 1 special library/35,000 volumes. Total: 3 libraries/205,000 volumes.

Publishing Output and Distribution
4 publishers; n.d. book titles/volumes; n.d. booksellers.

Noted Library
States of Jersey Library Service, Royal Square, St. Helier, Isle of Jersey.

CHILE

General Background
Location: South America; capital: Santiago; form of government: republic; population: 11.4 million (1982); GNP per capita: $1,965 (1983); ILL rate: 11% (1970); LHO ratio: 7 volumes per 10 inhabitants.

Library Network
1 national library/1.2 million volumes; 161 public libraries/581,000 volumes (UN, 1980); 182 university libraries/2.6 million volumes (UN, 1977); 551 school

libraries/1.4 million volumes (UN, 1981); 229 special libraries/1.4 million volumes (ALA, 1976); 10 government agency libraries/800,000 volumes; 2 religious libraries/30,000 volumes. Total: 1,136 libraries/8 million volumes.

Publishing Output and Distribution
15 publishers; 918 book titles/n.d. volumes (1981); 37 daily newspapers/1.3 million circulation (1982); 23 other newspapers/46,300 circulation (1982); 11 booksellers.

Noted Library
Biblioteca Nacional, Direccion de Bibliotecas, Archivos y Museos, Avenida Bernardo O'Higgins 651, Santiago.

Librarians' Organization
Colegio de Bibliotecarios de Chile, Diagonal Paraguay 383, Torre II. Departmento 122, Casilla 3741, Santiago.

CHINA, PEOPLE'S REPUBLIC OF

General Background
Location: Central and South Asia; capital: Beijing (Peking); form of government: republic (socialist state); population: 1,139 million (1990); GNP per capita: $300 (1981); ILL rate: 34.5% (1982); LHO ratio: almost 1 volume per inhabitant.

Library Network (ALA, 1990)
1 national library/15.9 million volumes; 1,162 university libraries/374 million volumes; 2,527 public libraries/290 million volumes; 4,500 special libraries/225 million volumes. Total: 8,190 libraries/904.9 million volumes.

Publishing Output and Distribution
14 publishers; 31,602 book titles/4,958 million volumes (1983); 53 daily newspapers/33.6 million circulation (1982); 224 other newspapers/46 million circulation (1982); 3,100 periodicals/ 138 million circulation (1982); 2 book-sellers (state owned).

Noted Libraries
Zhong-guo Guo Jia Tushugan, 7 Wen Jin Street, Beijing; Shanghai Tushugan, 325 West Nan Jin Lu, Shanghai.

COLOMBIA

General Background
Location: South America; capital: Bogotá; form of government: republic; population: 28.7 million (1982); GNP per capita: $1,380 (1982); ILL rate: 14.8% (1981); LHO ratio: 1 volume per 11 inhabitants.

Library Network
1 national library/540,000 volumes (UN, 1980); 10 public libraries/232,000 volumes; 69 university libraries/1.2 million volumes; 15 school libraries/98,000 volumes; 92 special libraries/1.1 million volumes; 11 government agency libraries/174,000 volumes; 8 religious libraries/80,000 volumes. Total: 206 libraries/3.4 million volumes.

Publishing Output and Distribution
32 publishers; 7,671 book titles/32.7 million volumes (1983); 28 daily newspapers/1.1 million circulation (1982); 8 periodicals/125,000 circulation (1977); 16 booksellers.

Noted Library
Biblioteca Nacional de Colombia, Calle 24, No 5–60, Bogotá.

Librarians' Organization
Associación Colombiana de Bibliotecarios, Calle 10, No 3–16, Bogotá.

CONGO

General Background
Location: Westcentral Africa; capital: Brazaville; form of government: republic; population: 1.6 million (1982); GNP per capita: $1,100 (1981); ILL rate: n.d.; LHO ratio: 1 volume per 6 inhabitants.

Library Network
1 national library/7,000 volumes (UN, 1980); 10 public libraries/55,000 volumes (UN, 1981); 4 university libraries/90,000 volumes; 2 school libraries/41,000 volumes; 12 special libraries/65,000 volumes. Total: 29 libraries/258,000 volumes.

Publishing Output and Distribution
1 publisher (government owned); 5 daily newspapers/23,000 circulation (1982); 2 other newspapers/10,300 circulation (1982); 5 periodicals/25,000 circulation (1977); 4 booksellers.

Noted Library
Bibliothèque Universitaire, B.P. 2025, Brazaville.

Librarians' Organization
Direction Generale des Services de Bibliothèques, Archives et Documentation, B.P. 114, Brazaville.

COOK ISLANDS

General Background
Location: South Pacific Ocean; capital: Avarua; form of government: self-governing dependency of New Zealand; population: 17,000 (1982); GNP per capita: n.d.; ILL rate: n.d.; LHO rate: almost 1 volume per inhabitant.

Library Network
1 public library/15,000 volumes (UN, 1980).

Publishing Output and Distribution
n.d. publishers; 1 daily newspaper/2,000 circulation (1982); 2 other newspapers/ 2,400 circulation (1982); n.d. booksellers.

Noted Library
Cook Islands Library and Museum, Takamoa (source: *Telephone Directory*, 1980).

COSTA RICA

General Background
Location: Central America; capital: San José; form of government: republic; population: 2.3 million (1982); GNP per capita: $1,430 (1981); ILL rate: n.d.; LHO ratio: 7 volumes per inhabitant.

Library Network
1 national library/300,000 volumes (UN, 1977); 195 public libraries/2.7 million volumes (UN, 1980); 56 university libraries/1.4 million volumes (UN, 1982); 2,432 school libraries/11.5 million volumes (UN, 1982); 10 special libraries/ 169,000 volumes; 3 government agency libraries/47,000 volumes. Total: 2,697 libraries/16.1 million volumes.

Publishing Output and Distribution
9 publishers; 71 book titles/110,000 volumes (1981); 4 daily newspapers/ 162,709 circulation (1982); 4 other newspapers/818,400 circulation (1982); 274 periodicals/162,709 circulation (1982); 3 booksellers.

Noted Library
Biblioteca Nacional, Calle 15/17, Avenida 3 and 3 Bis, San José.

Librarians' Organization
Asociación Costarricense de Bibliotecarios, Apartado 3308, San José.

CUBA

General Background
Location: Carribean Sea; capital: Havana; form of government: republic (socialist state); population: 10.6 million (1990); GNP per capita: $2,696 (1981); ILL rate: 4.6% (1979); LHO ratio: 2.5 volumes per inhabitant.

Library Network (ALA, 1990)
1 national library/2.1 million volumes; 82 university libraries/2.3 million volumes; 368 public libraries/4.8 million volumes; 3,636 school libraries/17.3 million volumes. Total: 4,087 libraries/26.5 million volumes.

Publishing Output and Distribution
14 publishers; 1,917 book titles/41 million volumes (1983); 17 daily newspapers/1.1 million circulation (1982); 4 other newspapers/818,400 circulation (1982); 50 periodicals/2.1 million circulation (1982); 1 bookseller (state owned).

Noted Library
Biblioteca Nacional "José Marti," Plaza de la Revolución José Marti, Apartado Oficial 3, La Havana.

CYPRUS

General Background
Location: Middle East; capital: Nicosia; form of government: republic; population: 702,000 (1990); GNP per capita: $3,193 (1981); ILL rate: 9.5% (1976); LHO ratio: 2.2 volumes per inhabitant.

Library Network (ALA, 1990)
1 national library/60,000 volumes; 16 university and college libraries/300,000 volumes; 60 public libraries/500,000 volumes; 144 school libraries/500,000 volumes; 15 special libraries/200,000 volumes. Total: 236 libraries/1.6 million volumes.

Publishing Output and Distribution
1 publisher; 1,137 book titles/2.2 million volumes (1980); 16 daily newspapers/76,000 circulation (1982); 10 other newspapers/61,000 circulation (1979); 105 periodicals/271,700 circulation (1979); 7 booksellers.

Noted Library
Severios Bibliotheki, P.O. Box 34, Nicosia.

Librarians' Organization
Cyprus Library Association, P.O. Box 1039, Nicosia.

CZECHOSLOVAKIA

General Background
Location: Central Europe; capital: Prague, form of government: republic (socialist); population: 15.3 million (1982); GNP per capita: $5,820 (1980); ILL rate: n.d.; LHO ratio: 6.4 volumes per inhabitant.

Library Network
15 national libraries/17.1 million volumes (UN, 1980); 9,776 public libraries/51 million volumes (UN, 1982); 1,684 university libraries/13 million volumes (UN, 1982); 14 special libraries/14.9 million volumes. Total: 11,489 libraries/96 million volumes.

Publishing Output and Distribution
53 publishers; 9,574 book titles/94 million volumes (1983); 30 daily newspapers/4.8 million circulation (1982); 109 other newspapers/942,000 circulation (1982); 932 periodicals/21 million circulation (1982); 3 booksellers (state owned).

Noted Libraries
Státní Knihovna ČSR, Klementinum 190, Prague; Matica Slovenská Knižnica, Mudroňova 13, Martin.

Librarians' Organization
Ústředni Knihovnická Rada ČSSR, Valdštejnká 30, Prague.

DENMARK

General Background
Location: Northwest Europe; capital: Copenhagen; form of government: kingdom; population: 5.1 million (1990); GNP per capita: $13,120 (1981); ILL rate: n.d.; LHO ratio: 15.7 volumes per inhabitant.

Library Network (ALA, 1990)
1 national library/3.4 million volumes; 17 university libraries/7.8 million volumes; 250 public libraries/34.3 million volumes; 275 school libraries/32.2 million volumes; 120 special libraries/3.7 million volumes. Total: 663 libraries/81.4 million volumes.

Publishing Output and Distribution
91 publishers; 9,460 book titles/n.d. volumes (1983); 47 daily newspapers/1.8 million circulation (1982); 11 periodicals/1.2 million circulation (1982); 16 booksellers.

Noted Libraries
Det Kongelige Bibliotek, Christians Brygge 8, Kobenhavn; Statsbiblioteket, Universitets Parken, Arhus.

Librarians' Organization
Danmarks Biblioteksforening, Trekronegrade 15, Copenhaven Valby.

DJIBOUTI

General Background
Location: Northeast Africa; capital: Djibouti; form of government: republic; population: 332,000 (1983); GNP per capita: $480 (1981); ILL rate: n.d.; LHO ratio: 1 volume per 26 inhabitants.

Library Network
1 university library/8,500 volumes.

Publishing Output and Distribution
n.d. publishers; 1 daily newspaper/3,500 circulation (1982).

Noted Library
Arab Maritime Academy Library, Gamal Abdel Nasser Street, Miami, P.O. Box 1029, Alexandria.

DOMINICA

General Background
Location: West Indies; capital: Roseau; form of government: independent state, member of Commonwealth of Nations; population: 86,000 (1982); GNP per capita: $761 (1982); ILL rate: 5.9% (1970); LHO ratio: 1 volume per almost 6 inhabitants.

Library Network
2 public libraries/15,000 volumes (UN, 1981).

Publishing Output and Distribution
n.d. publishers; 20 book titles/n.d. volumes (1981); 4 daily newspapers/8,500 circulation (1979); n.d. booksellers.

Noted Library
Dominica Public Library, Victoria Street, Roseau (source: *Telephone Directory*, 1980).

DOMINICAN REPUBLIC

General Background
Location: West Indies; capital: Santo Domingo; form of government: republic; population: 5.7 million (1982); GNP per capita: $1,260 (1981); ILL rate: 33% (1970); LHO ratio: almost 1 volume per almost 9 inhabitants.

Library Network
1 national library/235,000 volumes (ALA, 1978); 68 public libraries/112,000 volumes (UN, 1980); 8 university libraries/225,000 volumes; 16 special libraries/70,000 volumes. Total: 93 libraries/642,000 volumes.

Publishing Output and Distribution
27 publishers; 2,219 book titles/4.3 million volumes (1980); 9 daily newspapers/ 240,000 circulation (1982); 14 booksellers.

Noted Library
Biblioteca Nacional César Nicolás Penson 91, Plaza de la Cultura, Santo Domingo.

Librarians' Organization
Asociación Dominicana de Bibliotecarios c/o Biblioteca Nacional, Santo Domingo, address above.

ECUADOR

General Background
Location: South America; capital: Quito; form of government: republic; population: 8.9 million (1982); GNP per capita: $1,180 (1981); ILL rate: 25.8% (1974); LHO ratio: about 1 volume per 8 inhabitants.

Library Network
1 national library/60,000 volumes; 9 public libraries/388,000 volumes; 20 university libraries/406,000 volumes; 24 special libraries/200,000 volumes. Total: 54 libraries/1.1 million volumes. (ALA: 97 public, 51 university, 1,576 school (private) and 27 special libraries/n.d. volumes.)

Publishing Output and Distribution
11 publishers; 18 daily newspapers/570,000 circulation (1982); 101 other newspapers/n.d. circulation (1979); 284 periodicals/n.d. circulation (1978); 8 booksellers.

Noted Libraries
Biblioteca Nacional, Garcia Moreno i Sucre, Apartado 163, Quito; Universidad Central de Ecuador, Biblioteca Central, Ciudad Universitaria, Quito.

Librarians' Organization
Asociación Ecuatoriana de Bibliotecarios, Casa de la Cultura Ecuatoriana, Casilla 87, Quito.

EGYPT

General Background
Location: Northwest Africa; capital: Cairo; form of government: republic; population: 44.6 million (1982); GNP per capita: $650 (1981); ILL rate: 61% (1976); LHO ratio: over 1 volume per 3 inhabitants.

Library Network
1 national library/1.5 million volumes; 223 public libraries/1.3 million volumes (UN, 1981); 105 university libraries/3.2 million volumes; 4,565 school libraries/ 8.1 million volumes (UN, 1982); 63 special libraries/1.1 million volumes; 16 government agency libraries/400,000 volumes; 3 religious libraries/83,000 volumes. Total: 4,976 libraries/15.7 million volumes.

Publishing Output and Distribution
20 publishers; 204 book titles/1.8 million volumes (1982); 10 daily newspapers/ 3.4 million circulation; 204 periodicals/1.8 million circulation (1982); 14 booksellers.

Noted Libraries
National Library, Kornish El-Nil Street, Cairo; Ain Shams University Library, Kasr El-Zaafran, Abbasiyah, Cairo.

Librarians' Organization
Egyptian Association for Archives and Librarianship, c/o Library of Fine Arts, 24 El Matbaa Al-Ahlia, Boulac, Cairo.

EL SALVADOR

General Background
Location: Central America; capital: San Salvador; form of government: republic; population: 4.9 million (1982); GNP per capita: $650 (1981); ILL rate: 38% (1975); LHO ratio: 1 volume per 6 inhabitants.

Library Network
1 national library/124,000 volumes (ALA, 1976); 113 public libraries/110,500 volumes (ALA, 1976); 13 university libraries/190,960 volumes (ALA, 1976); 150 school libraries/245,000 volumes (ALA, 1976); 30 special libraries/147,032 volumes (ALA, 1976). Total: 307 libraries/817,492 volumes.

Publishing Output and Distribution
3 publishers; 144 book titles/n.d. volumes (1978); 6 daily newspapers/270,000 circulation (1982); 8 booksellers.

Noted Library
Biblioteca Nacional, 8/A Avenida Norte y Calle Delgado, San Salvador.

Librarians' Organization
Asociación de Bibliotecarios de El Salvador, Urbanización Gerardo Barrios Poligono B, No. 5, San Salvador.

EQUATORIAL GUINEA (SPANISH GUINEA)

General Background
Location: West Africa; capital: Malabo; form of government: republic; population: 381,000 (1982); GNP per capita: $360 (1982); ILL rate: 63% (1980); LHO ratio: 1 volume per 16 inhabitants.

Library Network
1 public library/12,000 volumes (ALA, 1976); 7 university libraries/7,000 volumes (ALA, 1976); 3 special libraries/5,000 volumes (ALA, 1976). Total: 11 libraries/24,000 volumes.

Publishing Output and Distribution
n.d. publishers; 2 daily newspapers/1,000 circulation (1982).

ESTONIA

General Background
Location: Baltic Region; Capital: Tallin; government form: republic; population: 1.5 million (1990); GNP per capita: $2,750 (1992); ILL rate: 0.3% LHO rate: 29 volumes per inhabitant.

Library Network (ALA, 1990)
1 national library/4.3 million volumes; 16 university libraries/4.8 million volumes; 627 public libraries/11 million volumes; 500 school libraries/9 million volumes; 155 special libraries/2.9 million volumes; 124 other libraries/10.1 million volumes. Total: 1;423 libraries/42.1 million volumes.

Publishing Output and Distribution
9 publishing houses/227 titles (ILMP, 1993).

Noted Library
Estonian National (State) Library, Ramatukogu Plats, 1, 200106, Tallin.

Librarians' Organization
n.d.

ETHIOPIA

General Background
Location: East Africa; capital: Addis Ababa; form of government: republic (socialist state); population: 32.7 million (1982); GNP per capita: $140 (1981); ILL rate: 95% (1970); LHO ratio: 1.3 volumes per 100 inhabitants.

Library Network
1 national library/85,000 volumes; 3 public libraries/9,200 volumes; 16 university libraries/90,000 volumes; 22 school libraries/105,000 volumes; 15 special libraries/94,000 volumes; 8 government agency libraries/43,000 volumes; 2 religious libraries/4,500 volumes. Total: 67 libraries/430,700 volumes.

Publishing Output and Distribution
2 publishers; 457 book titles/n.d. volumes (1983); 3 daily newspapers/40,000 circulation (1982); 4 other newspapers/1,600 circulation (1982); 4 periodicals/ 39,000 circulation (1982); 4 booksellers.

Noted Libraries
National Library and Archives of Ethiopia, P.O. Box 717, Addis Ababa; National University Central Library, P.O. Box 1176, Addis Ababa.

Librarians' Organization
Ethiopian Library Association, P.O. Box 30530, Addis Ababa.

FAEROE (FARÖE) ISLANDS

General Background
Location: Atlantic Ocean; capital: Tórshavn; form of government: self-governing part of Denmark; population: 44,000 (1982); GNP per capita: $10,440 (1982); ILL rate: n.d.; LHO ratio: 4.5 volumes per inhabitant.

Library Network
1 national library/91,000 volumes (UN, 1980); 247 public libraries/108,000 volumes (UN, 1981). Total: 248 libraries/199,000 volumes.

Publishing Output and Distribution
n.d.

Noted Library
Faeroe National Library, Tórshavn.

FALKLAND (MALVINAS) ISLANDS

General Background
Location: South America; capital: Port Stanley; form of government: British colony; population: 2,000 (1982); GNP per capita: n.d.; ILL rate: n.d.; LHO ratio: 5 volumes per inhabitant.

Library Network
1 public library/10,000 volumes (UN, 1982).

Publishing Output and Distribution
n.d. publishers; 3 periodicals/2,000 circulation (1979).

Noted Library
Town Council Public Library, Port Stanley.

FIJI (VITI)

General Background
Location: South West Pacific; capital: Suva; form of government: independent state; British monarch is its nominal chief; population: 765,000 (1990); GNP per capita: $2,000 (1981); ILL rate: 21% (1976); LHO ratio: 1.3 volumes per inhabitant.

Library Network (ALA, 1990)
8 university and college libraries/443,000 volumes; 13 public libraries/190,000 volumes; 500 school libraries/300,000 volumes; 120 special libraries/100,000 volumes; 25 other libraries/10,000 volumes. Total: 666 libraries/1,043,000 volumes.

Publishing Output and Distribution
6 publishers; 110 book titles/273,000 volumes (1980); 3 daily newspapers/
67,000 circulation (1982); 4 other newspapers/74,000 circulation (1982); 2
booksellers.

Noted Libraries
University of the South Pacific Library, P.O. Box 1168, Suva; Western Regional
Library Service of Fiji, Tavewa Avenue, Lautora.

Librarians' Organization
Fiji Library Association, P.O. Box 2292, Government Building, Suva.

FINLAND

General Background
Location: North Europe; capital: Helsinki; form of government: republic; population: 4.9 million (1990); GNP per capita: $8,727 (1983); ILL rate: n.d.; LHO
ratio: 10 volumes per inhabitant.

Library Network (ALA, 1990)
1 national library/2 million volumes; 20 university and college libraries/13.3
million volumes; 1,265 public libraries/31.5 million volumes; 26 special librar-
ies/2.2 million volumes. Total: 1,312 libraries/49 million volumes.

Publishing Output and Distribution
24 publishers; 8,594 book titles/n.d. volumes (1983); 64 daily newspapers/2.8
million circulation (1982); 11 other newspapers/1.2 million circulation (1982);
234 periodicals/1.1 million circulation (1979); 9 booksellers.

Noted Libraries
Helsingin Yliopiston Kirjasto, Uniioninkatu 36, Helsinki; Helsingin Kaupun-
ginkinkirjasto, Rikhardinkatu 3, Helsinki.

Librarians' Organization
Suomen Kirjastoseura, Museokatu 18/A 15, Helsinki.

FRANCE

General Background
Location: West Europe; capital: Paris; form of government: republic; population:
54.2 million (1982); GNP per capita: $12,190 (1981); ILL rate: n.d.; LHO ratio:
over 2 volumes per inhabitant.

Library Network
1 national library/10 million volumes (UN, 1980); 7,271 public libraries/50.4
million volumes (UN, 1980); 61 university libraries/17.7 million volumes (UN,
1981); 3,500 school libraries/10 million volumes (ALA, 1976); 500 special li-
braries/16.8 million volumes; 6 nonspecial libraries/3.4 million volumes (UN,

1980); 53 religious libraries/2.9 million volumes. Total: 11,392 libraries/111.2 million volumes.

Publishing Output and Distribution
444 publishers; 35,576 book titles/n.d. volumes (1983); 90 daily newspapers/ 10.3 million circulation (1982); 526 periodicals/16.2 million circulation (1982); 14 booksellers.

Noted Libraries
Bibliothèque Nationale, 58 Rue Richelieu, Paris; Institut de France, Bibliothèque, 23 Quai Conti, Paris.

Librarians' Organization
Association des Bibliothécaires Français, 65 Rue de Richelieu, Paris.

FRENCH GUYANA

General Background
Location: South America; capital: Cayenne; form of government: French overseas department; population: 64,000 (1982); GNP per capita: $3,230 (1982); ILL rate: n.d.; LHO ratio: almost 1 volume per inhabitant.

Library Network
2 public libraries/18,669 volumes (UN, 1980); 1 university library/43,000 volumes (UN, 1981). Total: 3 libraries/61,669 volumes.

Publishing Output and Distribution
1 publisher; 1 book title/2,000 volumes (1981); 1 daily newspaper/1,000 circulation (1982); 14 other newspapers/29,000 circulation (1982); 7 periodicals/ 6,300 circulation (1982); 4 booksellers.

Noted Library
Bibliothèque Franconie, Prefecture de la Guyane, B.P. 303, Cayenne.

FRENCH POLYNESIA (TAHITI)

General Background
Location: South Pacific; capital: Papeete; form of government: local government, French overseas territory; population: 154,000 (1982); GNP per capita: $7,960 (1982); ILL rate: n.d.; LHO ratio: almost 1 volume per 4 inhabitants.

Library Network
2 public libraries/17,000 volumes (UN, 1981); 2 special libraries/4,000 volumes; 1 nonspecial library/16,000 volumes (UN, 1981); 1 government agency library/ 3,000 volumes. Total: 6 libraries/40,000 volumes.

Publishing Output and Distribution
1 publisher; 72 book titles/102,000 volumes (1981); 2 daily newspapers/13,000 circulation (1979); 17 periodicals/25,200 circulation (1979); 4 booksellers.

Noted Library
Bibliothèque Paul Gauguin Museum, B.P. 7029, Taravao.

GABON

General Background
Location: Westcentral Africa; capital: Libreville; form of government: republic; population: 1.7 million; GNP per capita: $4,840 (1982); ILL rate: 85.2% (1982); LHO ratio: over 1 volume per over 8 inhabitants.

Library Network (ALA, 1990)
1 national library/2,500 volumes; 3 university and college libraries/33,000 volumes; 1 public library/60,000 volumes; 61 school libraries/11,500 volumes; 3 special libraries/14,000 volumes; 2 other libraries/15,000 volumes. Total: 71 libraries/136,000 volumes.

Publishing Output and Distribution
1 publisher (government owned); 1 daily newspaper/15,000 circulation (1982); 4 booksellers.

Noted Library
Bibliothèque Centrale de L'Université Omar Bongo, B.P. 13131, Libreville.

GAMBIA

General Background
Location: West Africa; capital: Banjul; form of government: republic; joined Senegal in a confederation called Senegambia; population: 635,000 (1982); GNP per capita: $344 (1983); ILL rate: 49% (1980); LHO ratio: 1 volume per over 3 inhabitants.

Library Network
1 national library/54,720 volumes (ALA, 1976); 5 public libraries/67,000 volumes (UN, 1980); 129 school libraries/35,000 volumes (ALA, 1976); 17 special libraries/24,000 volumes (UN, 1980). Total: 152 libraries/180,720 volumes.

Publishing Output and Distribution
1 publisher (government owned); 101 book titles/7.1 million volumes (1983); 10 periodicals/2,000 circulation (1982); 2 booksellers.

Noted Library
Gambia National Library, Ministry of Education, Youth, Sports, and Culture, P.O. Box 552, Banjul.

GERMANY, EAST (DEMOCRATIC REPUBLIC) (before unification with
West Germany)

General Background
Location: Central Europe; capital: Berlin; form of government: republic (so-
cialist state); population: 16.8 million (1982); GNP per capita: $7,180 (1980);
ILL rate: n.d.; LHO ratio: 5.5 volumes per inhabitant.

Library Network
2 national libraries/9.7 million volumes (UN, 1980); 14,059 public libraries/45.7
million volumes (UN, 1980); 29 university libraries/21.3 million volumes (UN,
1981); 68 professional school libraries/1.1 million volumes; 325 special libraries/
12.6 million volumes; 2 nonspecial libraries/1.6 million volumes (UN, 1980);
26 government agency libraries/1.1 million volumes; 9 religious libraries/
300,000 volumes. Total; 14,520 libraries/93.4 million volumes.

Publishing Output and Distribution
60 publishers; 6,175 book titles/132 million volumes (1983); 39 daily newspa-
pers/8.9 million circulation (1982); 32 other newspapers/9.4 million circulation
(1982); 1,178 periodicals/22 million circulation (1982); 16 booksellers.

Noted Libraries
Deutsche Bücherei, Deutscher Plaz, Leipzig; Deutsche Staatsbibliothek, Unter-
den Linden 8, Berlin.

Librarians' Organization
Bibliotheksverband der Deutschen Demokratischen Republik, Hermann-Matern
Strasse 57, Berlin.

GERMANY, WEST (FEDERAL REPUBLIC) (before unification with East
Germany)

General Background
Location: Northcentral Europe; capital: Bonn; form of government: republic;
population: 61.6 million (1982); GNP per capita: $13,450 (1981); ILL rate: n.d.;
LHO ratio: 4.75 volumes per inhabitant.

Library Network
3 national libraries/9.9 million volumes (UN, 1980); 1,014 public libraries/76.7
million volumes; 145 university libraries/66.7 million volumes (UN, 1981); 58
professional school libraries/704,000 volumes; 737 special libraries/51.4 million
volumes; 76 nonspecial libraries/65.1 million volumes (UN, 1980); 317 government agency libraries/12.2 million volumes; 253 religious libraries/10.4 million
volumes. Total: 2,603 libraries/293.1 million volumes.

Publishing Output and Distribution
882 publishers; 58,489 book titles/n.d. volumes (1983); 359 daily newspapers/
25 million circulation (1982); 49 other newspapers/4.5 million circulation
(1982); 20 booksellers.

Noted Libraries
Deutsche Bibliothek, Zeppelinallee, Frankfurt/Main; Bayerische Staatsbib-
liothek, Ludwigstrasse 16, München; Staatsbibliothek Preussischer Kulturbesitz,
Potsdamerstrasse, Berlin.

Librarians' Organization
Verein Deutscher Bibliothekare c/o Universitätsbibliothek Stuttgart, Holzgarten-
strasse 16, Stuttgart.

GHANA

General Background
Location: West Africa; capital: Accra; form of government: republic; population:
12.2 million (1982); GNP per capita: $400 (1981); ILL rate: 69.8% (1970);
LHO ratio: 1 volume per 25 inhabitants.

Library Network
1 national library/900,000 volumes; 40 public libraries/929,000 volumes (UN,
1977); 35 university libraries/720,000 volumes; 7 school libraries/42,000 volumes; 45 special libraries/300,000 volumes; 18 government agency libraries/
165,000 volumes. Total: 146 libraries/3.1 million volumes.

Publishing Output and Distribution
21 publishers; 145 book titles/n.d. volumes (1982); 5 daily newspapers/345,000
circulation (1979); 13 periodicals/n.d. circulation (1979); 11 booksellers.

Noted Library
Ghana Library Board, Thorpe Road, P.O. Box 663, Accra.

Librarians' Organization
Ghana Library Association, P.O. Box 4105, Accra.

GIBRALTAR

General Background
Location: Mediterranean Sea; capital: Gibraltar; form of government: British
colony; population: 30,000 (1982); GNP per capita: $4,690 (1981); ILL rate:
n.d.; LHO ratio: 1.73 volumes per inhabitant.

Library Network
2 public libraries/19,000 volumes (UN, 1980); 1 university library/5,000 volumes (UN, 1978); 12 school libraries/28,000 volumes (UN, 1978). Total: 15
libraries/52,000 volumes.

Publishing Output and Distribution
n.d. publishers; 1 daily newspaper/2,000 circulation (1982); 5 other newspapers/
2,300 circulation (1982); 5 booksellers.

Noted Libraries
Gibraltar Garrison Library, Library Gardens, Governor's Parade, Gibraltar; John
Mackintosh Hall Library, Gibraltar.

GREECE

General Background
Location: Southeast Europe; capital: Athens; form of government: republic; population: 9.7 million (1981); GNP per capita: $3,540 (1981); ILL rate: 15.6%
(1971); LHO ratio: over 2 volumes per 3 inhabitants.

Library Network
2 national libraries/2.7 million volumes (ALA, 1980); 5 public libraries/174,000
volumes; 9 university libraries/1.2 million volumes; 9 professional school li-
braries/159,000 volumes; 37 special libraries/729,000 volumes; 3 government
agency libraries/1.5 million volumes; 3 religious libraries/42,000 volumes. Total:
68 libraries/6.5 million volumes.

Publishing Output and Distribution
63 publishers; 4,048 book titles/n.d. volumes (1980); 131 daily newspapers/1.1
million circulation (1982); 875 other newspapers/n.d. circulation (1982); 868
periodicals/n.d. circulation (1979); 14 booksellers.

Noted Libraries
Ethnike Bibliotheke Tes Hellados, Odos Venizelou, Athena; Aristoteleion Pa-
nepistimon Thessalonikis Bibliotheke, Odos Panepistimiou, Salonika.

Librarians' Organization
Enossis Ellenon Bibliothekarion, Skouleniou 4, Athena.

GRENADA

General Background
Location: West Indies; capital: Saint George's; form of government: independent
state, British monarch is its nominal chief; population: 113,000 (1982); GNP
per capita: $850 (1981); ILL rate: 2.2% (1970); LHO ratio: almost 1 book per
5 inhabitants.

Library Network
1 public library/15,000 volumes (UN, 1980); 1 university library/5,300 volumes.
Total: 2 libraries/20,300 volumes.

Publishing Output and Distribution
n.d. publishers; 10 book titles/n.d. volumes (1979); 1 daily newspaper/n.d. circulation (1982); 3 periodicals/9,000 circulation (1982); n.d. booksellers.

Noted Library
Saint George's Public Library, Saint George's.

GUADELOUPE

General Background
Location: West Indies; capital; Basse-Terre; form of government; local government, French overseas department; population: 331,000 (1982); GNP per capita: $4,330 (1982); ILL rate: n.d.; LHO ratio: almost 1 volume per 3 inhabitants.

Library Network
2 public libraries/90,000 volumes (UN, 1980); 1 nonspecial library/24,000 volumes (UN, 1980). Total: 3 libraries/114,000 volumes.

Publishing Output and Distribution
n.d. publishers; 1 daily newspaper/33,000 circulation (1982); 26 other newspapers/69,000 circulation (1982); 45 periodicals/142,000 circulation (1982); n.d. booksellers.

Noted Library
Bibliothèque Centrale, Prefecture de la Guadeloupe, Route du Stade "Felix Eboue," B.P. 102, Basse-Terre.

GUAM

General Background
Location: West Pacific Ocean; capital: Agana; form of government: unincorporated United States territory; population: 106,000 (1982); GNP per capita: $5,740 (1982); ILL rate: n.d.; LHO ratio: 6.7 volumes per inhabitant.

Library Network
1 public library/173,000 volumes; 1 university library/255,000 volumes; 46 school libraries/283,000 volumes (UN, 1981). Total: 48 libraries/711,000 volumes.

Publishing Output and Distribution
n.d. publishers; 1 daily newspaper/18,000 circulation (1982); 28 periodicals/n.d. circulation (1979); n.d. booksellers.

Noted Library
Nieves M. Flores Memorial Library, P.O. Box 652, Agana.

GUATEMALA

General Background
Location: Central America; capital: Guatemala City; form of government: republic; population: 7.6 million (1982); GNP per capita: $1,140 (1981); ILL rate: 54% (1973); LHO ratio: 1 volume per almost 3 inhabitants.

Library Network
1 national library/350,000 volumes (ALA, 1978); 93 public libraries/74,000 volumes (ALA, 1978); 169 university libraries/1.7 million volumes (UN, 1981); 19 special libraries/275,000 volumes. Total: 282 libraries/2.4 million volumes.

Publishing Output and Distribution
4 publishers; 574 book titles/n.d. volumes (1981); 9 daily newspapers/179,000 circulation (1981); 18 periodicals/32,000 circulation (1975); 10 booksellers.

Noted Library
Biblioteca Nacional de Guatemala, 5/A Avenida 7–26, Zona 1, Guatemala City.

Librarians' Organization
Asociación Bibliotecologica Guatemalteca c/o The Director of Biblioteca Nacional de Guatemala, address as above.

GUINEA (FRENCH GUINEA)

General Background
Location: West Africa; capital: Conakry; form of government: republic; population: 5.7 million (1990); GNP per capita: $300 (1981); ILL rate: n.d.; ILL ratio: 1 volume per over 3 inhabitants.

Library Network (ALA, 1990)
6 university and college libraries/1.2 million volumes; 6 school libraries/585,000 volumes. Total: 12 libraries/1.8 million volumes.

Publishing Output and Distribution
1 publisher (government owned); 1 daily newspaper/20,000 circulation (1979); 1 other newspaper/13,000 circulation (1982); 1 bookseller.

Noted Library
Bibliothèque Nationale, B.P. 561, Conakry.

GUINEA-BISSAU (PORTUGUESE GUINEA)

General Background
Location: West Africa; capital: Bissau; form of government: republic; population: 594,000 (1982); GNP per capita: $190 (1981); ILL rate: 90% (1979); LHO ratio: 1 volume per 12 inhabitants.

Library Network
1 national library/25,000 volumes; 2 special libraries/24,000 volumes. Total: 3 libraries/49,000 volumes.

Publishing Output and Distribution
n.d. publishers; 1 daily newspaper/6,000 circulation (1982).

Noted Library
Biblioteca Nacional de Guiné-Bissau, Praça do Impero, Bissau.

GUYANA

General Background
Location: South America; capital: Georgetown; form of government: republic; population: 796,000 (1990); GNP per capita: $720 (1981); ILL rate: 8.4% (1970); LHO ratio: 1 volume per 0.9 inhabitant.

Library Network (ALA, 1990)
2 national libraries/235,000 volumes; 2 university libraries/250,000 volumes; 1 public library/30,000 volumes; 18 school libraries/n.d. volumes; 28 special libraries/150,000 volumes. Total: 51 libraries/665,000 volumes.

Publishing Output and Distribution
1 publisher (government owned); 55 book titles/n.d. volumes (1983); 2 daily newspapers/78,000 circulation (1982); 12 other newspapers/26,000 circulation (1979); 65 periodicals/52,600 circulation (1979); 1 bookseller.

Noted Library
National Library, P.O. Box 10240, Georgetown.

Librarians' Organization
Guyana Library Association, 76–77 Main Street, P.O. Box 10240, Georgetown.

HAITI

General Background
Location: West Indies; capital: Port-au-Prince; form of government: republic; population: 5.2 million (1982); GNP per capita: $300 (1981); ILL rate: 78% (1971); LHO ratio: 1 volume per 25 inhabitants.

Library Network
1 national library/19,000 volumes; 13 public libraries/70,438 volumes (ALA, 1976); 11 university libraries/55,000 volumes (ALA, 1976); 7 school libraries/ 49,400 volumes (ALA, 1976); 13 special libraries/64,000 volumes (ALA, 1976). Total: 45 libraries/257,838 volumes.

Publishing Output and Distribution
3 publishers; 4 daily newspapers/20,000 circulation (1982); n.d. booksellers.

Noted Library
Bibliothèque Nationale d'Haiti, Rue Hammerton Killick, Port-au-Prince.

HONDURAS

General Background
Location: Central America; capital: Tegucigalpa; form of government: republic; population: 5.1 million (1990); GNP per capita: $661 (1981); ILL rate: 43.1% (1974); LHO ratio: 1 volume per 5 inhabitants.

Library Network (ALA, 1990)
1 national library/35,000 volumes; 12 university and college libraries/500,000 volumes; 10 public libraries/50,000 volumes; 382 school libraries/300,000 volumes; 2 special libraries/50,000 volumes; 20 other libraries/100,000 volumes. Total: 427 libraries/1 million volumes.

Publishing Output and Distribution
2 publishers; 6 daily newspapers/240,000 circulation (1982); 4 booksellers.

Noted Library
Biblioteca Nacional de Honduras, 6/A Avenida Salvador Mendieta, Tegucigalpa.

Librarians' Organization
Asociación de Bibliotecarios y Archiveros de Honduras, Tres Avenidas, 4 y 5 Calles, no 416 Comayaguela, Tegucigalpa.

HONG KONG

General Background
Location: South Asia; capital: Hong Kong; form of government: British colony; population: 5.2 million (1982); GNP per capita: $5,738 (1981); ILL rate: 22.7% (1971); LHO ratio: almost 1 volume per inhabitant.

Library Network
13 public libraries/1.1 million volumes (UN, 1981); 12 university libraries/1.7 million volumes (UN, 1981); 191 school libraries/1.4 million volumes (UN, 1981); 16 special libraries/246,000 volumes; 9 government agency libraries/ 92,000 volumes; 8 religious libraries/119,000 volumes. Total: 249 libraries/4.7 million volumes.

Publishing Output and Distribution
34 publishers; 5,681 book titles/44.3 million volumes (1983); 7 daily newspapers/ 3 million circulation (1982); 267 other newspapers/n.d. circulation (1982); 173 periodicals/n.d. circulation (1982); 12 booksellers.

Noted Library
Chinese University of Hong Kong Library, Shatin, New Territories, Hong Kong.

Librarians' Organization
Hong Kong Library Association c/o Chinese University of Hong Kong Library, address as above.

HUNGARY

General Background
Location: Central Europe; capital: Budapest; form of government: republic (socialist state); population: 10.5 million (1990); GNP per capita: $2,100 (1981); ILL rate: 1.1% (1980); LHO ratio: 10 volumes per inhabitant.

Library Network (ALA, 1990)
1 national library/7 million volumes; 29 university and college libraries/12.1 million volumes; 2,390 public libraries/53 million volumes; 3,897 school libraries/27.1 million volumes; 91 special libraries/12 million volumes; 35 other libraries/2.9 million volumes. Total 6,443 libraries/114.1 million volumes.

Publishing Output and Distribution
18 publishers; 8,469 book titles/107 million volumes (1983); 27 daily newspapers/2.6 million circulation (1982); 86 other newspapers/6 million circulation (1982); 869 periodicals/12 million circulation (1982); 6 booksellers.

Noted Libraries
Magyar Tudamányos Akadémia Könyvtára, H-1361 Budapest; Országos Széchényi Könyvtár, H-1827 Budapest, at Muzeum Korut 14/16, Budapest.

Librarians' Organization
Magyar Könyvtárosok Egyesülete, H-1368 Budapest, at Molnar 11, Budapest.

ICELAND

General Background
Location: North Atlantic Ocean; capital: Reykjavik; form of government: republic; population: 255,000 (1990); GNP per capita: $12,860 (1981); ILL rate: n.d.; LHO ratio: 32 volumes per inhabitant.

Library Network (ALA, 1990)
1 national library/406,000 volumes; 3 university and college libraries/360,000 volumes; 233 public libraries/7.5 million volumes; 4 special libraries/171,000 volumes. Total: 241 libraries/8.4 million volumes.

Publishing Output and Distribution
35 publishers; 6 daily newspapers/99,000 circulation (1982); 6 periodicals/n.d. circulation (1977); 6 booksellers (1978 book production: 801 titles, KES).

Noted Library
Landsbókasafn Islands, Safnahusinu, Hver Fisgotu, Reykjavik.

Librarians' Organization
Bókavarrdafélag Islands, P.O. Box 7050, Reykjavik.

INDIA

General Background
Location: South Asia; capital: New Delhi; form of government: republic; population: 827 million (1990); GNP per capita: $260 (1981); ILL rate: 65.9% (1971); LHO ratio: 1 volume per 25 inhabitants.

Library Network (ALA, 1990)
4 national libraries/2.6 million volumes; 7,112 university and college libraries/ 188.2 million volumes; 7,180 public libraries/36 million volumes; 62,240 school libraries/64.2 million volumes; 2,000 special libraries/50 million volumes. Total: 78,536 libraries/341 million volumes.

Publishing Output and Distribution
325 publishers; 10,649 book titles/n.d. volumes (1982); 1,334 daily newspapers/ 14 million circulation (1982); 18,603 other newspapers/35 million circulation (1982); 19,937 periodicals/50 million circulation (1982); 27 booksellers.

Noted Libraries
National Library, Belvedere, Calcutta; Gujarat Vidyapith Granthalaya Library, Gandhi Bhavan, Ahmedabad.

Librarians' Organization
Government of India Librarians Association c/o Ministry of Home Affairs Library, Room 26, North Block, New Delhi.

INDONESIA

General Background
Location: Southeast Asia; capital: Jakarta; form of government: republic; population: 153 million (1982); GNP per capita: $520 (1981); ILL rate: 32.7% (1980); LHO ratio: 1 volume per 40 inhabitants.

Library Network
1 national library/525,000 volumes (UN, 1981); 44 public libraries/460,000 volumes (UN, 1979); 42 university libraries/954,000 volumes; 152 special libraries/ 1.3 million volumes (UN, 1977); 14 government agency libraries/550,000 volumes; 1 religious library/74,000 volumes. Total: 254 libraries/3.8 million volumes.

Publishing Output and Distribution
68 publishers; 5,731 book titles/n.d. volumes (1983); 94 daily newspapers/2.2 million circulation (1982); 206 other newspapers/4.3 million circulation (1982); 68 booksellers.

Noted Library
Perpustakan National Library, Jin Imam Bonjog 1, Jakarta.

Librarians' Organization
Ikatan Pustakawan Indonesia c/o Centre for Library Development, Medan Merdeka Selatan II, Belakang, Jakarta.

IRAN

General Background
Location: Southwest Asia; capital: Teheran; form of government: republic; population: 58 million (1990); GNP per capita: $2,160 (1977); ILL rate: 63.5% (1976); LHO ratio: 1 volume per 3 inhabitants.

Library Network (ALA, 1990)
1 national library/500,000 volumes; 270 university and college libraries/5.1 million volumes; 501 public libraries/4.2 million volumes; 2,983 school libraries/216,693 volumes; 254 special libraries/6.9 million volumes; 250 other libraries/2.7 million volumes. Total: 4,259 libraries/19.6 million volumes.

Publishing Output and Distribution
6 publishers; 4,835 book titles/n.d. volumes (1983); 12 daily newspapers/970,000 circulation (1982); 41 other newspapers/n.d. circulation (1982); 180 periodicals/n.d. circulation (1982); 3 booksellers.

Noted Library
National Library, Si-Ye Tir Street, Teheran.

Librarians' Organization
Anjoman-e Ketabdaren-e Iran, P.O. Box 11-1391, Teheran.

IRAQ

General Background
Location: Southwest Asia; capital: Baghdad; form of government: republic; population: 18.9 million (1990); GNP per capita: $3,020 (1980); ILL rate: 85% (ILMP); LHO ratio: 1 volume per 3.5 inhabitants.

Library Network (ALA, 1990)
1 national library/420,000 volumes; 117 university and college libraries/2.2 million volumes; 70 public libraries/1 million volumes; 9,000 school libraries/1.5 million volumes; 3 special libraries/175,000 volumes. Total: 9,191 libraries/5.3 million volumes.

Publishing Output and Distribution
2 publishers; 82 book titles/n.d. volumes (1983); 5 daily newspapers/262,000 circulation (1982); 31 other newspapers/2,000 circulation (1982); 1 bookseller (government owned).

Noted Library
National Library, Al-Jumhuriya Street, Baghdad.

Librarians' Organization
Iraq Library Association, P.O. Box 4081, Adhamya, Baghdad.

IRELAND

General Background
Location: Northwest Europe; capital: Dublin; form of government: republic; population: 3.5 million (1990); GNP per capita: $1,855 (1981); ILL rate: n.d.; LHO ratio: 4.1 volumes per inhabitant.

Library Network (ALA, 1990)
1 national library/550,000 volumes; 7 university and college libraries/4.9 million volumes; 31 public libraries/8.4 million volumes; 62 special libraries/303,000 volumes (1987); 39 other libraries/446,000 volumes. Total: 140 libraries/14.6 million volumes.

Publishing Output and Distribution
48 publishers; 718 book titles/n.d. volumes (1983); 7 daily newspapers/749,000 circulation (1982); 21 other newspaper/1.2 million circulation (1982); 258 periodicals/2.9 million circulation (1979); 12 booksellers.

Noted Library
National Library of Ireland, Kildare Street, Dublin.

Librarians' Organization
Cumann Leabharlann na h-Eireann, Crofton Mansions, 22 Crofton Road, Dun Laoghaire, Dublin.

ISLE OF MAN

General Background
Location: Irish Sea; capital: Douglas; form of government: semi-autonomous island, member of Commonwealth of Nations; population: 60,496 (1971); GNP per capita: n.d.; ILL rate: n.d.; LHO ratio: n.d.

Library Network
3 public libraries/n.d. volumes.

Publishing Output and Distribution
3 publishers; n.d. book or newspaper titles; 3 booksellers.

Noted Library
The Douglas Public Library, Ridgeway Street, Douglas.

ISRAEL

General Background
Location: Middle East; capital: Jerusalem; form of government: republic; population: 5 million (1990); GNP per capita: $5,160 (1981); ILL rate: 12.1% (1971) LHO ratio: 6 volumes per inhabitant.

Library Network (ALA, 1990)
1 national library/3 million volumes; 7 university and college libraries/6.3 million volumes; 983 public libraries/12.4 million volumes; 1,735 school libraries/ 5.6 million volumes; 400 special libraries/2 million volumes (1987). Total: 3,126 libraries/29.3 million volumes.

Publishing Output and Distribution
127 publishers; 1,892 book titles/11.6 million volumes (1982); 36 daily newspapers/825,000 circulation (1981); 52 other newspapers/n.d. circulation (1982); 1,100 periodicals/n.d. circulation (1981); 15 booksellers.

Noted Libraries
Jewish National and University Library, P.O. Box 503, Jerusalem; Tel-Aviv University, E. Sourasky Central Library, Ramat-Aviv Campus, P.O. Box 39038, Tel Aviv.

Librarians' Organization
Israel Library Association, P.O. Box 303, Tel-Aviv.

ITALY

General Background
Location: South Europe; capital: Rome; form of government: republic; population: 56.7 million (1982); GNP per capita: $6,960 (1981); ILL rate: 6.1% (1971); LHO ratio: over 3 volumes per inhabitant.

Library Network
9 national libraries/11.6 million volumes (UN, 1980); 8,686 public libraries/16.9 million volumes (ALA, 1980); 3,060 university libraries/55.1 million volumes (ALA, 1980); 12,042 school libraries/22.4 million volumes (ALA, 1980); 33 general research libraries/12.1 million volumes; 3,876 special libraries/51 million volumes (ALA, 1980); 88 government agency libraries/4.3 million volumes; 553 religious libraries/11.5 million volumes. Total: 28,347 libraries/184.9 million volumes.

Publishing Output and Distribution
371 publishers; 13,718 book titles/147 million volumes (1983); 79 daily newspapers/4.6 million circulation (1982); 8,265 periodicals/n.d. circulation (1982); 18 booksellers.

Noted Libraries
Biblioteca Nazionale Centrale Vittorio Emanuele II, Viale Castro Pretorio 105, Rome; Biblioteca Nazionale Vittorio Emanuele III, Palazzo Reale, Napoli; Biblioteca Nazionale Braidense, Palazzo di Brera, Via Brera 28, Milano.

IVORY COAST

General Background
Location: West Africa; capital: Abidjan; form of government: republic; population: 8.5 million (1982); GNP per capita: $1,200 (1981); ILL rate: 65% (1980); LHO ratio: 1 volume per 35 inhabitants.

Library Network
1 national library/65,000 volumes (UN, 1981); 1 public library/25,000 volumes (UN, 1981); 7 university libraries/97,000 volumes; 3 school libraries/14,000 volumes; 23 special libraries/98,000 volumes. Total: 35 libraries/229,000 volumes.

Publishing Output and Distribution
6 publishers; 46 book titles/3.7 million volumes (1983); 2 daily newspapers/ 85,000 circulation (1982); 6 other newspapers/148,000 circulation (1982); 5 booksellers.

Noted Library
Bibliothèque Nationale, B.P. V/180, Abidjan.

Librarians' Organization
Association pour le Development de la Documentation, des Bibliothèques et Archives de la Cote d'Ivoire c/o Bibliothèque Nationale, address above.

JAMAICA

General Background
Location: West Indies; capital: Kingston; form of government: independent state, British monarch is its nominal chief; population: 2.4 million (1990); GNP per capita: $1,180 (1981); ILL rate: 3.9% (1970); LHO ratio: 1.5 volumes per inhabitant.

Library Network (ALA, 1990)
1 national library/41,615 volumes; 7 university and college libraries/676,688 volumes; 13 public libraries/1.1 million volumes; 948 school libraries/1.7 million volumes; 94 special libraries/245,000 volumes; 14 other libraries/195,000 volumes. Total: 1,077 libraries/4 million volumes.

Publishing Output and Distribution
4 publishers; 143 book titles/n.d. volumes (1978); 3 daily newspapers/104,000 circulation (1982); 11 booksellers.

Noted Library
National Library of Jamaica, The Institute of Jamaica, 12-16 East Street, Kingston.

Librarians' Organization
Jamaica Library Association, P.O. Box 58, Kingston.

JAPAN

General Background
Location: East Asia; capital: Tokyo; form of government: monarchy; population: 123.5 million (1990); GNP per capita: $9,706 (1983); ILL rate: 3.4% (1960); LHO ratio: 7.1 volumes per inhabitant.

Library Network (ALA, 1990)
1 national library/9.6 million volumes; 926 university and college libraries/170.5 million volumes; 1,928 public libraries/162.6 million volumes; 41,591 school libraries/448.3 million volumes; 2,116 special libraries/31 million volumes (UN, 1978). Total: 46,562 libraries/822 million volumes.

Publishing Output and Distribution
132 publishers; 42,977 book titles/655.7 million volumes (1982); 154 daily newspapers/68.1 million circulation (1982); 1,971 periodicals/32 million circulation (1982); 12 booksellers.

Noted Library
Kokuritsu Kokkai Toshokan, 1-10-1 Nagata-cho, Chyioda-ku, Tokyo.

Librarians' Organization
Nihon Toshokan Kyokai, 1-10-1, Taishido, Segatagaya-ku, Tokyo.

JORDAN

General Background
Location: Southwest Asia; capital: Amman; form of government: kingdom; population: 4 million (1990); GNP per capita: $1,620 (1980); ILL rate: 34.9% (1979); LHO ratio: almost 1 volume per 1.2 inhabitants.

Library Network (ALA, 1990)
1 national library/20,000 volumes; 4 university libraries/846,000 volumes; 57 college libraries/80,000 volumes; 39 public libraries/410,000 volumes; 479 school libraries/1.1 million volumes; 104 special libraries/419,000 volumes (1987). Total: 684 libraries/2.9 million volumes.

Publishing Output and Distribution
3 publishers; 5 daily newspapers/71,000 circulation (1982); 4 other newspapers/ 2,200 circulation (1982); 43 periodicals/232,000 circulation (1982); 6 booksellers (1976 book production: 392 titles, KES).

Noted Library
University of Jordan Library, Amman.

Librarians' Organization
Jordan Library Association, P.O. Box 6289, Amman.

KAMPUCHEA (CAMBODIA)

General Background
Location: Southeast Asia; capital: Phnom Penh; form of government: republic (socialist state); population: 6.9 million (1982); GNP per capita: n.d.; ILL rate: 63.9% (1962); LHO ratio: 1 volume per 58 inhabitants.

Library Network
1 national library/33,000 volumes; 5 university libraries/15,000 volumes; 2 school libraries/13,000 volumes; 1 special library/18,000 volumes; 1 religious library/40,000 volumes. Total: 10 libraries/119,000 volumes.

Publishing Output and Distribution
n.d. publishers; 16 daily newspapers/n.d. circulation (1982); n.d. booksellers.

Noted Library
Bibliothèque Nationale, B.P. 4, Phnom Penh.

KENYA

General Background
Location: East Africa; capital: Nairobi; form of government: republic; population: 24.8 million (1990); GNP per capita: $420 (1982); ILL rate: 52% (1980); LHO ratio: 1 volume per 9 inhabitants.

Library Network (ALA, 1990)
1 national library/577,781 volumes; 5 university and college libraries/522,600 volumes; 12 public libraries/700,250 volumes; 26 school libraries/180,300 volumes; 63 special libraries/496,165 volumes; 48 other libraries/52,604 volumes. Total: 155 libraries/2.5 million volumes.

Publishing Output and Distribution
23 publishers; 235 book titles/n.d. volumes (1983); 2 daily newspapers/220,000 circulation (1982); 2 other newspapers/281,000 circulation (1982); 13 booksellers.

Noted Library
Kenya National Library Service, Ngong Road, P.O. Box 30573, Nairobi.

Librarians' Organization
Kenya Library Association, P.O. Box 30197, Nairobi.

KIRIBATI (GILBERT AND ELLIS ISLANDS)

General Background
Location: Pacific Ocean; capital: Tarawa; form of government: republic, member of Commonwealth of Nations; population: 66,000 (1990); GNP per capita: $420 (1981); ILL rate: n.d.; LHO ratio: 0.4 volumes per inhabitant.

Library Network (ALA, 1990)
1 national library/29,877 volumes; 5 university and college libraries/n.d. volumes. 2 public libraries/7,742 volumes. Total: 8 libraries/37,619 volumes.

Publishing Output and Distribution
n.d.

Noted Library
National Library and Archives, Bariki, P.O. Box 6, Tarawa.

KOREA, NORTH (PEOPLE'S DEMOCRATIC REPUBLIC)

General Background
Location: Northeast Asia; capital: Pyongyang; form of government: republic (socialist state); population: 18.7 million (1982); GNP per capita: $736 (1982); ILL rate: n. d.; LHO ratio: over 3 volumes per 2 inhabitants.

Library Network
2 national libraries/6 million volumes (UN, 1970); 228 public libraries/7.1 million volumes (KES, 1964); 4 university libraries/133,000 volumes; n.d. school libraries. Total: 234 libraries/13.2 million volumes.

Publishing Output and Distribution
13 publishers; 19,634 book titles/167 million volumes (1980); 11 daily newspapers/1 million circulation (1982); 1 bookseller (government owned).

Noted Library
State Central Library, Pyongyang.

Librarians' Organization
Library Association of the Democratic People's Republic of Korea, c/o State Central Library, Pyongyang.

KOREA, SOUTH (REPUBLIC OF)

General Background
Location: Southeast Asia; capital: Seoul; form of government: republic; population: 42.7 million (1990); GNP per capita: $1,700 (1981); ILL rate: 12.4% (1972); LHO ratio: over 1.6 volumes per inhabitant.

Library Network (ALA, 1990)
2 national libraries/2.2 million volumes; 305 university and college libraries/
27.5 million volumes; 231 public libraries/5.5 million volumes; 4,468 school
libraries/27.6 million volumes; 358 special libraries/6 million volumes. Total:
5,364 libraries/68.8 million volumes.

Publishing Output and Distribution
48 publishers; 35,512 book titles/112.7 million volumes (1983); 27 daily news-
papers/7.5 million circulation (1982); 117 periodicals/2.2 million circulation
(1977); 6 booksellers.

Noted Library
National Central Library, 100-171 1-ka, Hoehyun-dong, Chung-ku, Seoul.

Librarians' Organization
Korean Library Association, c/o National Central Library, address above.

KUWAIT

General Background
Location: Arabian Peninsula; capital: Kuwait; form of government: sheikdom
(monarchy); 2.1 million (1990); GNP per capita: $20,900 (1981); ILL rate:
32.5% (1980); LHO ratio: almost 2 volumes per inhabitant.

Library Network (ALA, 1990)
1 national library/93,000 volumes; 1 university library/453,000 volumes; 1 public library/737,000 volumes; 570 school libraries/3.1 million volumes; 13 special
libraries/137,000 volumes. Total: 586 libraries/4.5 million volumes.

Publishing Output and Distribution
4 publishers; 45 book titles/981,700 volumes (1982); 7 daily newspapers/
391,000 circulation (1982); 3 other newspapers/475,000 circulation (1982); 1
bookseller.

Noted Library
Kuwait Central Library, P.O. Box 515, Kuwait.

Librarians' Organization
Libraries Department, Kuwait University Library, P.O. Box 17140, Kuwait.

LAOS

General Background
Location: Southeast Asia; capital: Vientiane; form of government: republic (socialist state); population: 4.1 million (1990); GNP per capita: $80 (1981); ILL
rate: 56.4% (1980); LHO ratio: 1 volume per 14 inhabitants.

Library Network (ALA, 1990)
5 university and college libraries/121,000 volumes; 22 school libraries/33,000 volumes; 1 other library/145,000 volumes. Total: 28 libraries/299,000 volumes.

Publishing Output and Distribution
3 publishers; 3 daily newspapers/5,000 circulation (1975); 1 bookseller.

Noted Library
Bibliothèque Nationale, B.P. 704, Vientiane.

Librarians' Organization
Association des Bibliothécaires Laotiens, c/o Bibliothèque Nationale, address above.

LEBANON

General Background
Location: Middle East; capital: Beirut; form of government: republic; population: 2.7 million (1990); GNP per capita: n.d.; ILL rate: 36.5% (1970); LHO ratio: almost 0.75 volume per inhabitant.

Library Network (ALA, 1990)
1 national library/100,000 volumes; 10 university and college libraries/1.5 million volumes; 16 public libraries/100,000 volumes; 10 school libraries/70,000 volumes; 15 special libraries/100,000 volumes. Total: 52 libraries/1.9 million volumes.

Publishing Output and Distribution
15 publishers; 14 daily newspapers/391,000 circulation (1982); 7 booksellers.

Noted Library
Bibliothèque Nationale du Liban, Place de l'Etoile, Beirut.

Librarians' Organization
The Lebanese Library Association, c/o Bibliothèque Nationale, address above.

LESOTHO

General Background
Location: South Africa; capital: Maseru; form of government: kingdom; population: 1.4 million (1982); GNP per capita: $540 (1981); ILL rate: 41.4% (1966); LHO ratio: 1 volume per 12 inhabitants.

Library Network
1 national library/n.d. volumes; 1 university library/100,000 volumes; 1 school library/7,000 volumes; 3 special libraries/18,300 volumes. Total: 6 libraries/ 125,300 volumes.

Publishing Output and Distribution
4 publishers; 4 daily newspapers/47,000 circulation (1982); 1 other newspaper/
10,000 circulation (1982); 3 booksellers.

Noted Library
Lesotho National Library Service, P.O. Box 985, Maseru.

Librarians' Organization
Lesotho Library Association, c/o Lesotho National Library, address above.

LIBERIA

General Background
Location: West Africa; capital: Monrovia; form of government: republic; pop-
ulation: 2.6 million (1990); GNP per capita: $520 (1981); ILL rate: 79% (1974);
LHO ratio: almost 1 volume per almost 5 inhabitants.

Library Network (ALA, 1990)
2 university libraries/200,526 volumes; 3 public libraries/77,700 volumes; 103
school libraries/180,176 volumes; 1 special library/6,000 volumes. Total: 109
libraries/464,402 volumes.

Publishing Output and Distribution
3 publishers; 3 daily newspapers/12,000 circulation (1982); 5 booksellers.

Noted Library
Government Public Library, Ashmun Street, Monrovia.

LIBYA

General Background
Location: North Africa; capital: Tripoli; form of government: republic; popu-
lation: 3.2 million (1982); GNP per capita: $8,450 (1981); ILL rate: 61% (1973);
LHO ratio: 1 volume per over 5 inhabitants.

Library Network
1 national library/35,000 volumes; 3 public libraries/21,000 volumes; 12 university libraries/430,000 volumes; 11 special libraries/53,000 volumes; 7 government agency libraries/63,500 volumes. Total: 34 libraries/602,500 volumes.

Publishing Output and Distribution
4 publishers; 481 book titles/n.d. volumes (1978); 3 daily newspapers/41,000
circulation (1982); 5 periodicals/111,000 circulation (1976); 2 booksellers.

Noted Library
Al-Fateh University, Central Library, P.O. Box 13104, Tripoli.

LIECHTENSTEIN

General Background
Location: West Europe; capital: Vaduz; form of government: principality (monarchy); population: 28,000 (1990); GNP per capita: $16,440 (1980); ILL rate: 0.3% (1981); LHO ratio: 6.5 volumes per inhabitant.

Library Network (ALA, 1990)
1 national library/130,000 volumes; 3 public libraries/24,000 volumes; 7 school libraries/28,000 volumes. Total: 11 libraries/182,000 volumes.

Publishing Output and Distribution
7 publishers; n.d. volumes; 2 newspapers/15,000 circulation (1982); 2 booksellers.

Noted Library
Liechtensteinische Landesbibliothek, Gerbeweg 5, Vaduz.

LITHUANIA

General Background
Location: Baltic Region; capital: Vilnius; government form: republic; population: 3.7 million (1990); GNP per capita: $1,310 (1992); ILL rate: 1.6%; LHO ratio: over 13 volumes per inhabitant.

Library Network (ALA, 1990)
1 national library/1.8 million volumes; 13 university libraries/12 million volumes; 1,700 public libraries/8 million volumes; 2,100 school libraries/22.7 million volumes; 3 special libraries/3.8 million volumes; 43 other libraries/6 million volumes. Total: 3,860 libraries/54.3 million volumes.

Publishing Output and Distribution
20 publishing houses/863 titles (1993).

Noted Library
National Library of Lithuania, Prospect Lenina, 51, Vilnius.

Librarians' Organization
Lithuanian Librarians Association, Didzioji Street 10, 2001 Vilnius.

LUXEMBOURG

General Background
Location: West Europe; capital: Luxembourg; form of government: dukedom (monarchy); population: 380,000 (1990); GNP per capita: $15,910 (1981); ILL rate: n.d.; LHO ratio: 4.5 volumes per inhabitant.

Library Network (ALA, 1990)
1 national library/700,000 volumes; 2 university libraries/150,000 volumes; 4 public libraries/150,000 volumes; 50 school libraries/400,000 volumes; 10 special libraries/320,000 volumes. Total: 67 libraries/1.7 million volumes.

Publishing Output and Distribution
7 publishers; 359 book titles/n.d. volumes (1983); 5 daily newspapers/129,000 circulation (1982); 4 other newspapers/n.d. circulation (1982); 337 periodicals/ n.d. circulation (1982); 11 booksellers.

Noted Library
Bibliothèque Nationale du Grand-Duche de Luxembourg, 37 Boulevard Franklin Delano Roosevelt, Luxembourg.

MACAO (AOMEN)

General Background
Location: Southeast Asia; capital: Macao; form of government: free port, Portuguese overseas province; population: 350,000 (1982); GNP per capita: $2,710 (1982); ILL rate: 20.6% (1970); LHO ratio: 1 volume per almost 5 inhabitants.

Library Network
1 national library/60,000 volumes; 1 public library/18,000 volumes; 3 special libraries/1,000 volumes. Total: 5 libraries/79,000 volumes.

Publishing Output and Distribution
n.d. publishers; 8 daily newspapers/58,000 circulation (1979); 1 bookseller.

Noted Library
Biblioteca Nacional de Macau, Edificio do Leal Senado, Macau.

MADAGASCAR (MALAGASY)

General Background
Location: East Africa; capital: Anananarivo; form of government: republic; population: 11.9 million (1990); GNP per capita: $330 (1981); ILL rate: n.d.; LHO ratio: 1 volume per 18 inhabitants.

Library Network (ALA, 1990)
1 national library/170,000 volumes; 1 university library/180,000 volumes; 300 public libraries/300,000 volumes; 1 special library/33,000 volumes. Total: 303 libraries/683,000 volumes.

Publishing Output and Distribution
9 publishers; 418 book titles/940,000 volumes (1983); 6 daily newspapers/ 55,000 circulation (1982); 11 other newspapers/35,600 circulation (1982); 8 booksellers.

Noted Library
Bibliothèque Nationale, B.P. 257, Anosy, Antananarivo.

MALAWI

General Background
Location: East Africa; capital: Lilongwe; form of government: republic; population: 6.2 million (1982); GNP per capita: $260 (1981); ILL rate: 77.9% (1966); LHO ratio: 1 volume per 7 inhabitants.

Library Network
1 national library/110,000 volumes; 3 public libraries/91,000 volumes (UN, 1977); 7 university libraries/288,000 volumes; 74 school libraries/254,000 volumes (UN, 1977); 19 special libraries/20,000 volumes; 9 government agency libraries/85,000 volumes; 3 religious libraries/23,600 volumes. Total: 116 libraries/871,600 volumes.

Publishing Output and Distribution
3 publishers; 18 book titles/74,000 volumes (1981); 2 daily newspapers/31,000 circulation (1982); 7 periodicals/101,000 circulation (1977); 5 booksellers.

Noted Library
Malawi National Library Service, P.O. Box 30314, Lilongwe.

Librarians' Organization
Malawi Library Association, P.O. Box 298, Zomba.

MALAYSIA

General Background
Location: Southeast Asia; capital: Kuala Lumpur; form of government: independent federated sultanate (monarchy); population: 17.8 million (1990); GNP per capita: $1,840 (1981); ILL rate: 42% (1970); LHO ratio: 2 volumes per 3 inhabitants.

Library Network (ALA, 1990)
1 national library/719,971 volumes; 111 university and college libraries/4.6 million volumes; 70 public libraries/4.2 million volumes; 265 special libraries/2 million volumes. Total: 447 libraries/11.5 million volumes.

Publishing Output and Distribution
34 publishers; 2,801 book titles/n.d. volumes (1982); 47 daily newspapers/2.6 million circulation (1982); 1,917 periodicals/1.2 million circulation (1982); 12 booksellers.

Noted Library
National Library of Malaysia, Jalal Raja Laut, Wisma Thakurdas, Kuala Lumpur.

Librarians' Organization
Persatuan Perpustakan Malaysia, P.O. Box 2545, Kuala Lumpur.

MALDIVES ISLANDS

General Background
Location: Indian Ocean; capital: Malé; form of government: republic; population: 163,000 (1982); GNP per capita: $308 (1980); ILL rate: 17.6% (1977); LHO ratio: n.d.

Library Network
n.d.

Publishing Output and Distribution
n.d. publishers; 2 daily newspapers/1,000 circulation (1982); 3 periodicals/n.d. circulation (1977).

MALI (AFRICAN FRENCH SUDAN)

General Background
Location: West Africa; capital: Bamako; form of government: republic; population: 18.1 million (1990); GNP per capita: $190 (1981); ILL rate: 90% (1976); LHO ratio: 1 volume per 40 inhabitants.

Library Network (ALA, 1990)
1 national library/22,500 volumes; 8 university and college libraries/65,000 volumes; 55 public libraries/115,000 volumes; 36 school libraries/120,000 volumes; 64 special libraries/130,000 volumes. Total: 164 libraries/452,5000 volumes.

Publishing Output and Distribution
2 publishers; 19 book titles/9,000 volumes (1983); 2 daily newspapers/4,000 circulation (1982); 1 periodical/12,500 circulation (1976); 2 booksellers.

Noted Library
Bibliothèque Nationale, Avenue Kasse Keita, B.P. 159, Bamako.

Librarians' Organization
Inspection des Archives, Musées et Bibliothèques de Mali, B.P. 241, Bamako.

MALTA

General Background
Location: Mediterranean Sea; capital: Valletta; form of government: republic; population: 354,000 (1990); GNP per capita: $3,790 (1981); ILL rate: 44% (1948); LHO ratio: 4 volumes per inhabitant.

Library Network (1990, ALA)
2 national libraries/402,000 volumes; 2 university libraries/355,000 volumes; 2 public libraries/426,000 volumes; 1 school library/128,000 volumes; 4 special libraries/90,000 volumes. Total: 11 libraries/1.4 million volumes.

Publishing Output and Distribution
7 publishers; 247 book titles/n.d. volumes (1982); 5 daily newspapers/55,000 circulation (1982); 5 other newspapers/n.d. circulation (1982); 248 periodicals/ n.d. circulation (1982); 6 booksellers.

Noted Library
National Library of Malta, 36 Old Treasury Street, Valleta.

Librarians' Organization
Ghaqda Bibljotekari, 133 Melita Street, Valleta.

MARTINIQUE

General Background
Location: Windward Islands; capital: Fort de France; form of government: local government, French overseas department; population: 326,000 (1982); GNP per capita: $4,670 (1982); ILL rate: 12.2% (1967); LHO ratio: n.d.

Library Network
2 public libraries/n.d. volumes.

Publishing Output and Distribution
n.d. publishers; 21 book titles/43,000 volumes (1981); 1 daily newspaper/32,000 circulation (1982); 7 other newspapers/17,000 circulation (1982); 8 periodicals/ 17,000 circulation (1982); 1 bookseller.

Noted Library
Direction de Services d'Archives de la Martinique, Tartenson, Route de la Clair-ière, B.P. 649, Fort de France.

MAURITANIA

General Background
Location: West Africa; capital: Nouakchott; form of government: republic; pop-ulation: 1.7 million (1982); GNP per capita: $460 (1981); ILL rate: 82.6% (1976); LHO ratio: 1 volume per 40 inhabitants.

Library Network
1 national library/10,000 volumes; 2 public libraries/20,000 volumes; 1 univer-sity library/5,000 volumes; 6 special libraries/4,500 volumes; 6 government agency libraries/2,500 volumes. Total: 16 libraries/42,000 volumes.

Publishing Output and Distribution
2 publishers/n.d. volumes; 1 bookseller.

Noted Library
Bibliothèque Nationale, B.P. 20, Nouakchott.

MAURITIUS

General Background
Location: Southwest Asia; capital: Port Louis; form of government: independent
state, British monarch is its nominal chief; population: 1 million (1990); GNP
per capita: $1,270 (1981); ILL rate: 21% (1980); LHO ratio: 1 volume per
almost 1 inhabitant.

Library Network (ALA, 1990)
1 national library/46,430 volumes; 4 university and college libraries/182,000
volumes; 16 public libraries/362,709 volumes; 26 school libraries/170,000 volumes; 13 special libraries/237,000 volumes. Total: 60 libraries/998,139 volumes.

Publishing Output and Distribution
3 publishers; 80 book titles/175,000 volumes (1982); 7 daily newspapers/67,000
circulation (1982); 7 other newspapers/92,000 circulation (1982); 3 booksellers.

Noted Library
City Library, City Hall, Municipality of Port Louis, P.O. Box 422, Port Louis.

Librarians' Organization
Mauritius Library Association, c/o School of Administration, University of
Mauritius, Reduit.

MEXICO

General Background
Location: Central America; capital: Mexico City; form of government: republic;
population: 86.1 million (1990); GNP per capita: $2,250 (1981); ILL rate: 17.3%
(1980); LHO ratio: 2 volumes per almost 5 inhabitants.

Library Network (ALA, 1990)
1 national library/2.1 million volumes; 853 university and college libraries/8
million volumes; 3,594 public libraries/14 million volumes; 3,261 school li-
braries/9 million volumes; 130 special libraries/2.9 million volumes. Total:
7,839 libraries/36 million volumes.

Publishing Output and Distribution
90 publishers; 2,818 book titles/n.d. volumes (1982); 374 daily newspapers/10.2
million circulation (1982); 483 periodicals/n.d. circulation (1977); 21 booksellers.

Noted Libraries
Biblioteca Nacional de Mexico, Republica de El Salvador 70, Centro, Mexico. DF; Biblioteca Central, Ciudad Universitaria, Villa Obregón, Apartado 70-219, Mexico.

Librarians' Organization
Asociación Mexicana de Bibliotecarios, Apartado 27-102, Mexico.

MONACO

General Background
Location: South Europe; capital: Monaco; form of government: principality (monarchy); population: 26,000 (1982); GNP per capita: n.d.; ILL rate: n.d.; LHO ratio: 7.8 volumes per inhabitant.

Library Network
1 national library/130,000 volumes (UN, 1980); 7 school libraries/12,000 volumes (UN, 1981); 2 special libraries/63,000 volumes. Total: 10 libraries/205,000 volumes.

Publishing Output and Distribution
6 publishers; 105 book titles/n.d. volumes (1982); 2 daily newspapers/11,000 circulation (1982); 105 periodicals/792,000 circulation (1982); 3 booksellers.

Noted Library
Bibliothèque Louis Notari, 8 Rue Louis Notari, Monaco.

MONGOLIA

General Background
Location: Northcentral Asia; capital: Ulan Bator; form of government: republic (socialist state); population: 1.7 million (1982); GNP per capita: $940 (1978); ILL rate: n.d.; LHO ratio: 4.2 volumes per inhabitant.

Library Network
1 national library/2 million volumes (KES, 1979); 1,100 public and school libraries/5 million volumes (KES, 1977); 2 university libraries/350,000 volumes. Total: 1,103 libraries/7.3 million volumes.

Publishing Output and Distribution
1 publisher (state owned); 861 book titles/6 million volumes (1983); 2 daily newspapers/177,000 circulation (1982); 1 bookseller (state owned).

Noted Library
Mongol Ulsiin Ikh Surguli, P.O. Box 377, Ulan Bator.

MONTSERRAT

General Background
Location: West Indies; capital: Plymouth; form of government: internal self-government; British dependency; population: 12,073 (1982); GNP per capita: $2,200 (1981); ILL rate: 3.4% (1970); LHO ratio: 1.2 volumes per inhabitant.

Library Network
1 public library/15,000 volumes.

Publishing Output and Distribution
1 bookseller.

Noted Library
Montserrat Public Library, Plymouth.

MOROCCO

General Background
Location: Northwest Africa; capital: Rabat; form of government: kingdom; population: 21.6 million (1982); GNP per capita: $860 (1981); ILL rate: 78.6% (1971); LHO ratio: 1 volume per 14 inhabitants.

Library Network
1 national library/231,000 volumes; 65 public libraries/674,000 volumes (ALA, 1980); 21 university libraries/205,000 volumes; 5 school libraries/28,000 volumes; 63 special libraries/514,000 volumes; 17 government agency libraries/ 71,000 volumes. Total: 172 libraries/1.7 million volumes.

Publishing Output and Distribution
4 publishers; 80 book titles/n.d. volumes (1982); 10 daily newspapers/255,000 circulation (1982); 7 periodicals/92,000 circulation (1982); 10 booksellers.

Noted Library
Bibliothèque Generale et Archives du Maroc, Avenue Moulay Chérif, Rabat.

MOZAMBIQUE

General Background
Location: East Africa; capital: Maputo; form of government: republic (socialist state); population: 11.1 million (1982); GNP per capita: $270 (1980); ILL rate: 73% (1980); LHO ratio: 1 volume per 33 inhabitants.

Library Network
1 national library/110,000 volumes; 2 public libraries/14,000 volumes; 1 university library/80,000 volumes; 1 school library/4,500 volumes; 10 special libraries/143,000 volumes; 3 government agency libraries/34,000 volumes. Total: 18 libraries/385,500 volumes.

Publishing Output and Distribution
2 publishers; 88 book titles/5.4 million volumes (1983); 3 daily newspapers/
46,000 circulation (1982); 5 booksellers.

Noted Library
Biblioteca Nacional de Moçambique, C.P. 141, Maputo.

NAMIBIA (SOUTH-WEST AFRICA)

General Background
Location: Southwest Africa; capital: Windhoek; form of government: under
mandate of South Africa; population: 1.7 million (1990); GNP per capita: $1,910
(1982); ILL rate: 65% (ILMP); LHO ratio: 1 volume per 2 inhabitants.

Library Network (ALA, 1990)
1 national library/41,300 volumes; 2 university libraries/72,000 volumes; 1 public library/300,623 volumes; 1 science library/420,500 volumes; 12 special li-
braries/73,000 volumes. Total: 17 libraries/907,423 volumes.

Publishing Output and Distribution
2 publishers; 3 daily newspapers/20,000 circulation (1982); 3 periodicals/18,000
circulation (1977); 5 booksellers.

Noted Library
Windhoek Public Library, P.O. Box 3180, Windhoek.

Librarians' Organization
Cultural Promotion, P.O. Box 13186, Windhoek.

NEPAL

General Background
Location: Central Asia; capital: Kathmandu; form of government: kingdom; population: 8.9 million (1990); GNP per capita: $150 (1981); ILL rate: 80.8%
(1975); LHO ratio: 1 volume per 6 inhabitants.

Library Network (ALA, 1990)
1 national library/71,000 volumes; 142 university and college libraries/1 million
volumes; 465 public libraries/n.d. volumes; 71 special libraries/293,944 volumes. Total: 679 libraries/1.4 million volumes.

Publishing Output and Distribution
9 publishers; 43 book titles/70,000 volumes (1980); 29 daily newspapers/
110,000 circulation (1982); 52 periodicals/n.d. volumes (1976); 6 booksellers.

Noted Library
Nepal National Library, Joodha Road, P.O. Box 68, Kathmandu.

NETHERLANDS

General Background
Location: Northwest Europe; capital: The Hague; form of government: kingdom; population: 14.9 million (1990); GNP per capita: $10,790 (1981); ILL rate: n.d.; LHO ratio; over 5.5 volumes per inhabitant.

Library Network (ALA, 1990)
1 national library/2.1 million volumes; 22 university and college libraries/19.3 million volumes; 484 public libraries/42 million volumes; 8,100 school libraries/ n.d. volumes; 691 special libraries/15.5 million volumes; 252 other libraries/2.8 million volumes. Total: 9,550 libraries/81.7 million volumes.

Publishing Output and Distribution
151 publishers; 13,324 book titles/n.d. volumes (1982); 82 daily newspapers/ 4.6 million circulation (1982); 111 other newspapers/1.2 million circulation (1982); 13 booksellers.

Noted Libraries
Koninklijke Bibliotheek, Prins Willem Alexanderhof 5, Gravenhage; Bibliothek der Koninklijke Nederlandse Akademie van Wetenschappen, Kloveniersburg-wal, Amsterdam.

Librarians' Organization
Nederlandse Vereniging van Bibliothecarissen, Documentalisten en Literatu-uronderzoekers, Nolweg 13, Schelluinen.

NETHERLANDS ANTILLES (ARUBA, BONAIRE, CURAÇAO)

General Background
Location: West Indies; capital: Willemstad; form of government: independent state; Dutch monarch is its nominal chief; population: 89,600 (1990); GNP per capita: $5,430 (1982); ILL rate: 7.5% (1971); LHO ratio: over 4.6 volumes per inhabitant.

Library Network (ALA, 1990)
1 university library/100,000 volumes; 5 public libraries/271,414 volumes; 41 school libraries/24,600 volumes; 9 special libraries/35,000 volumes. Total: 56 libraries/431,014 volumes.

Publishing Output and Distribution
6 publishers; 7 daily newspapers/52,000 circulation (1982); 7 booksellers.

Noted Library
Openbare Leeszaal en Bibliotheek, Johan van Walbeeckplein 13, Willemstad, Curaçao.

Librarians' Organization
Asociation di Biblioteka i Archivo di Korsow (Carbido), Stoppelweg 4, Willem-stad, Curaçao.

NEW CALEDONIA

General Background
Location: South Pacific Ocean; capital: Nouméa; form of government: internal self-government; French overseas department; population: 146,000 (1982); GNP per capita: $7,960 (1982); ILL rate: 8.7% (1976); LHO ratio: 1 volume per 3 inhabitants.

Library Network
1 public library/26,000 volumes; 1 special library/6,000 volumes; 1 government agency library/16,000 volumes. Total: 3 libraries/48,000 volumes.

Publishing Output and Distribution
1 publisher; 41 book titles/49,000 volumes (1981); 1 daily newspaper/15,000 circulation (1982); 3 other newspapers/24,000 circulation (1982); 15 periodicals/26,800 circulation (1982); 5 booksellers.

Noted Library
Bibliothèque Bernheim, Bibliothèque Territoriale de la Nouvelle-Caledonie, B.P. G1, Nouméa.

NEW ZEALAND

General Background
Location: South Pacific Ocean; capital: Wellington; form of government: inde-pendent state; British monarch is its nominal chief; population: 3.1 million (1982); GNP per capita: $7,700 (1982); ILL rate: n.d.; LHO ratio: 7.4 volumes per inhabitant.

Library Network
1 national library/4.8 million volumes (UN, 1979); 291 public libraries/6.1 mil-lion volumes (UN, 1979); 40 university libraries/4.3 million volumes; 1,067 school libraries/5.4 million volumes (ALA, 1976); 56 special libraries/1.6 mil-lion volumes; 22 government agency libraries/914,000 volumes. Total: 1,477 libraries/23.1 million volumes.

Publishing Output and Distribution
66 publishers; 2,944 book titles/n.d. volumes (1983); 31 daily newspapers/1 million circulation (1982); 11 periodicals/n.d. circulation (1979); 15 booksellers.

Noted Library
National Library of New Zealand, 44 The Terrace, Wellington.

Librarians' Organization
New Zealand Library Association, 20 Brandon Street, P.O. Box 12212, Wellington.

NICARAGUA

General Background
Location: Central America; capital: Managua; form of government: republic (socialist state); population: 3.8 million (1990); GNP per capita: $860 (1981); ILL rate: 42.5% (1981); LHO ratio: 1 volume per almost 4 inhabitants.

Library Network (ALA, 1990)
13 university and college libraries/281,000 volumes; 412 school libraries/ 595,000 volumes; 6 special libraries/35,000 volumes. Total: 431 libraries/ 911,000 volumes.

Publishing Output and Distribution
7 publishers; n.d. book titles; 3 daily newspapers/147,000 circulation (1982); 9 booksellers.

Noted Library
Biblioteca Nacional, Calle del Triunfo 302, Apartado, 101, Managua.

Librarians' Organization
Asociación Nicaraguense de Bibliotecarios, c/o Biblioteca Nacional, address above.

NIGER

General Background
Location: Westcentral Africa; capital: Niamey; form of government: republic; population: 5.6 million (1982); GNP per capita: $330 (1982); ILL rate: 90% (1980); LHO ratio: 1 volume per over 80 inhabitants.

Library Network
2 university libraries/20,000 volumes; 2 school libraries/21,000 volumes; 5 special libraries/25,000 volumes; 2 government agency libraries/5,000 volumes. Total: 11 libraries/71,000 volumes.

Noted Library
Université de Niamey, Bibliothèque Universitaire, B. P. 237, Niamey.

NIGERIA

General Background
Location: West Africa; capital: Lagos; form of government: republic; population: 108.5 million (1990); GNP per capita: $870 (1981); ILL rate: 66% (1980); LHO ratio: 1 volume per 17 inhabitants.

Library Network (ALA, 1990)
1 national library/558,000 volumes; 110 university and college libraries/4 million volumes; 12 public libraries/1.1 million volumes; 71 special libraries/ 827,762 volumes. Total: 194 libraries/6.5 million volumes.

Publishing Output and Distribution
62 publishers; 1,495 book titles/n.d. volumes (1983); 15 daily newspapers/ 510,000 circulation (1982); 20 booksellers.

Noted Library
National Library of Nigeria, 4 Wesley Street, Lagos.

Librarians' Organization
Nigerian Library Association, Private Mail Bag 12655, Lagos.

NORFOLK ISLAND

General Background
Location: Pacific Ocean; capital: n.d.; form of government: self-rule, Australian dependency; population: 1,800 (SYB); GNP per capita: n.d.; ILL rate: n.d.; LHO ratio: over 8 volumes per inhabitant.

Library Network
1 public library/5,000 volumes (UN, 1980); 1 school library/10,000 volumes (UN, 1982). Total: 2 libraries/15,000 volumes.

Publishing Output and Distribution
n.d. publishers; 2 daily newspapers/2,000 circulation (1982); 2 periodicals/3,100 circulation (1979); n.d. booksellers.

Noted Library
Norfolk Island Public Library.

NORWAY

General Background
Location: North Europe; capital: Oslo; form of government: kingdom; population: 4.2 million (1990); GNP per capita: $12,923 (1983); ILL rate: n.d.; LHO ratio: 9.2 volumes per inhabitant.

Library Network (ALA, 1990)
1 national library/2.2 million volumes; 113 university and college libraries/8.3 million volumes; 465 public libraries/19.1 million volumes; 3,383 school libraries/6.5 million volumes; 172 special libraries/3.8 million volumes. Total: 4,134 libraries/39.9 million volumes.

Publishing Output and Distribution
40 publishers; 5,175 book titles/n.d. volumes (1982); 85 daily newspapers/1.9 million circulation (1982); 80 other newspapers/393,000 circulation (1982); 80 periodicals/393,000 circulation (1982); 14 booksellers.

Noted Library
Universitetsbiblioteket i Oslo, Drammensveien 2, Oslo.

Librarians' Organization
Norsk Bibliotekforening, Malerhausgevein 20, Oslo.

OMAN

General Background
Location: Southeast Asia; capital: Muscat; form of government: sultanate (monarchy); population: 2 million (1990); GNP per capita: $5,920 (1981); ILL rate: n.d.; LHO ratio: 1 volume per 3.8 inhabitants.

Library Network (ALA, 1990)
11 university and college libraries/105,400 volumes; 4 public libraries/41,700 volumes; 134 school libraries/252,900 volumes; 30 special libraries/98,700 volumes. Total: 179 libraries/498,700 volumes.

Publishing Output and Distribution
n.d.

Noted Library
Directorate of the Omani Heritage, Ministry of National Heritage Library, P.O. Box 668, Muscat.

PACIFIC ISLANDS (MARSHALL, BELAU, MICRONESIA)

General Background
Location: West Pacific Ocean; capitals: Majuro, Koror, Kolonga; population: 143,000 (1982); form of government: self-governing entities, freely associated with the United States; GNP per capita: $930 (1982); ILL rate: n.d.; LHO ratio: over 7 volumes per 10 inhabitants.

Library Network
4 university libraries/24,000 volumes (UN, 1982); 40 school libraries/92,000 volumes (UN, 1977). Total: 44 libraries/116,000 volumes.

Publishing Output and Distribution
n.d. publishers; 133 book titles/n.d. volumes (1979), Micronesia; 2 daily newspapers/14,000 circulation (1979), Micronesia; 1 daily newspaper/1,000 circulation (1982), Belau; n.d. booksellers.

Noted Library
University of Kolonga Library, Kolonga, Micronesia.

PAKISTAN

General Background
Location: South Asia; capital: Islamabad; form of government: republic; population: 87.1 million (1982); GNP per capita: $350 (1981); ILL rate: 73.8% (1981); LHO ratio: 1 volume per 14 inhabitants.

Library Network
1 national library/80,000 volumes; 240 public libraries/972,000 volumes (ALA, 1976); 523 university libraries/3.5 million volumes (ALA, 1976); 72 school libraries/479,000 volumes (ALA, 1976); 242 special libraries/1.3 million volumes (ALA, 1976); 32 government agency libraries/377,000 volumes; 1 religious library/20,000 volumes. Total: 1,111 libraries/6.7 million volumes.

Publishing Output and Distribution
57 publishers; 1,600 book titles/n.d. volumes (1981); 106 daily newspapers/1.6 million circulation (1982); 15 booksellers.

Noted Library
National Library of Pakistan, Stadium Road, Islamabad.

Librarians' Organization
Pakistan Library Association, c/o Khyber Medical College, Peshawar.

PANAMA

General Background
Location: between North and South America; capital: Panama City; form of government: republic: population: 2.04 million (1982); GNP per capita: $1,910 (1981); ILL rate: 12.9% (1980); LHO ratio: 1 volume per over 4 inhabitants.

Library Network
1 national library/249,000 volumes (UN, 1977); 18 public libraries/26,000 volumes (UN, 1980); 2 university libraries/14,000 volumes (UN, 1977); 54 school libraries/203,000 volumes (UN, 1977); 1 special library/55,000 volumes (UN, 1983). Total: 76 libraries/547,000 volumes.

Publishing Output and Distribution
7 publishers; 171 book titles/43,000 volumes (1981); 5 daily newspapers/ 124,000 circulation (1982); 10 periodicals/n.d. circulation (1983); 3 booksellers.

Noted Library
Biblioteca Nacional, Calle 22 Este Bis 1265, Apartado 2444, Panama.

Librarians' Organization
Asociación Panameña de Bibliotecarios, c/o Biblioteca Nacional, address above.

PAPUA NEW GUINEA

General Background
Location: Southwest Pacific; capital: Port Moresby; form of government: independent state, British monarch is its nominal chief; population: 3.6 million (1990); GNP per capita: $706 (1983); ILL rate: 67.9% (1971); LHO ratio: 1 volume per 2.4 inhabitants.

Library Network (ALA, 1990)
1 national library/85,000 volumes; 50 university and college libraries/845,000 volumes; 25 public libraries/183,211 volumes; 100 school libraries/456,000 volumes; 70 special libraries/183,000 volumes. Total: 246 libraries/1.8 million volumes.

Publishing Output and Distribution
3 publishers; 1 daily newspaper/29,000 circulation (1982); 7 periodicals/360,000 circulation (1977); 5 booksellers.

Noted Library
University of Papua New Guinea Library, P.O. Box 319, Moresby.

Librarians' Organization
Papua New Guinea Library Association, P.O. Box 5770, Boroko.

PARAGUAY

General Background
Location: South America; capital: Asunción; form of government: republic; population: 4.2 million; GNP per capita: $1,630 (1981); ILL rate: 19.9% (1972); LHO ratio: 1 volume per almost 5 inhabitants.

Library Network (ALA, 1990)
1 national library/40,000 volumes; 26 university and college libraries/178,540 volumes; 20 public libraries/101,944 volumes; 86 school libraries/324,825 volumes; 46 special libraries/156,612 volumes. Total: 179 libraries/801,921 volumes.

Publishing Output and Distribution
4 publishers; 5 daily newspapers/158,000 circulation (1982); 8 booksellers.

Noted Library
Biblioteca y Archivo Nacionales, Mariscal Estigarriba 95, Asunción.

Librarians' Organization
Asociación de Bibliotecarios del Paraguay, Calle Casilla del Correo 1505, Asunción.

PERU

General Background
Location: South America; capital: Lima; form of government: republic; population: 18.2 million (1982); GNP per capita: $1,170 (1981); ILL rate: 27.5% (1972); LHO ratio: 1 volume per less than 2 inhabitants.

Library Network
1 national library/2.5 million volumes (UN, 1981); 520 public libraries/4.1 million volumes (UN, 1980); 3 university libraries/680,000 volumes (ALA, 1980); 81 school libraries/272,000 volumes (UN, 1977); 49 special libraries/683,000 volumes. Total: 654 libraries/8.2 million volumes.

Publishing Output and Distribution
17 publishers; 704 book titles/n.d. volumes (1983); 68 daily newspapers/1.4 million circulation (1982); 37 other newspapers/2.7 million circulation (1982); 507 periodicals/n.d. circulation (1982); 13 booksellers.

Noted Library
Biblioteca Nacional de Peru, Avenida Abancay, Apartado 2335, Lima.

Librarians' Organization
Asociación Peruana de Bibliotecarios, General La Fuente 592, Lima.

PHILIPPINES

General Background
Location: East Asia; capital: Manila; form of government: republic; population: 50.7 million (1982); GNP per capita: $790 (1981); ILL rate: 17.4% (1970); LHO ratio: 1 volume per almost 6 inhabitants.

Library Network
1 national library/686,000 volumes; 498 public libraries/1.4 million volumes (UN, 1977); 689 university libraries/5.8 million volumes (ALA, 1976); 22 school libraries/432,000 volumes; 47 special libraries/379,000 volumes; 17 government agency libraries/176,000 volumes; 4 religious libraries/145,000 volumes. Total: 1,278 libraries/9.01 million volumes.

Publishing Output and Distribution
32 publishers; 839 book titles/n.d. volumes (1982); 22 daily newspapers/1.9 million circulation (1982); 10 booksellers.

Noted Library
National Library of the Philippines, Teodoro Kalaw Street, P.O. Box 2926, Ermita, Manila.

Librarians' Organization
Philippine Library Association, c/o National Library of the Philippines, address above.

POLAND

General Background
Location: East Europe; capital: Warsaw; form of government: republic (socialist state); population: 36.2 million (1982); GNP per capita: $3,900 (1980); ILL rate: 1.2% (1978); LHO ratio: 7.5 volumes per inhabitant.

Library Network
1 national library/1.8 million volumes (UN, 1980); 26,587 public libraries/94.5 million volumes (UN, 1980); 1,064 university libraries/34.3 million volumes (UN, 1980); 25,000 school libraries/100 million volumes (ALA, 1976); 4,632 special libraries/31.4 million volumes (UN, 1983); 126 nonspecial libraries/11.8 million volumes (UN, 1980). Total: 57,410 libraries/273.8 million volumes.

Publishing Output and Distribution
48 publishers; 8,789 book titles/194 million volumes (1983); 42 daily newspapers/7.9 million circulation (1982); 48 other newspapers/2.2 million circulation (1982); 2,045 periodicals/28 million circulation (1982); 7 booksellers.

Noted Library
Biblioteka Narodowa, Uliça Hamkiewicza 1, Warsaw.

Librarians' Organization
Stowarzyszenie Bibliotekarzy Polskich, Uliça Konopczyńskiego 5-7, Warsaw.

PORTUGAL

General Background
Location: West Europe; capital: Lisbon; form of government: republic; population: 10.5 million (1990); GNP per capita: $2,237 (1981); ILL rate: 29% (1970); LHO ratio: 2 volumes per inhabitant.

Library Network (ALA, 1990)
1 national library/2.2 million volumes; 229 university and college libraries/4 million volumes; 173 public libraries/4.8 million volumes; 768 school libraries/ 3.3 million volumes; 275 special libraries/4.2 million volumes; 81 other libraries/ 2.9 million volumes. Total: 1,527 libraries/21.4 million volumes.

Publishing Output and Distribution
62 publishers; 8,647 book titles/57 million volumes (1983); 21 daily newspapers/482,000 circulation (1982); 915 periodicals/n.d. circulation (1982); 12 booksellers.

Noted Library
Biblioteca Nacional, Rua Ocidental do Campo Grande 83, Lisbon.

Librarians' Organization
Associação Portuguesa de Bibliotecarios Arquivistas e Documentalistas, c/o Biblioteca Nacional, address above.

PUERTO RICO

General Background
Location: West Indies; capital: San Juan; form of government: self-governing commonwealth, associated with the United States; population: 3.6 million (1990); GNP per capita: $3,720 (1982); ILL rate: 12.2% (1980); LHO ratio: 2.5 volumes per inhabitant.

Library Network (ALA, 1990)
35 university and college libraries/6 million volumes; 132 public libraries/ 800,000 volumes; 825 school libraries/3.1 million volumes. Total: 992 libraries/ 9.9 million volumes.

Publishing Output and Distribution
9 publishers; n.d. book titles; 5 daily newspapers/598,000 circulation (1982); 10 booksellers.

Noted Library
Biblioteca General de Puerto Rico, Instituto de Cultura Puertorriqueña, Apartado 4184, San Juan.

Librarians' Organization
Sociedad de Bibliotecarios de Puerto Rico, c/o Universidad de Puerto Rico, Rio Piedras.

QATAR

General Background
Location: Southwest Asia; capital: Doha; form of government: sheikdom (monarchy); population: 368,000 (1990); GNP per capita: $27,720 (1981); ILL rate: 48.9% (1981); LHO ratio: 2.9 volumes per inhabitant.

Library Network (ALA, 1990)
1 national library/173,810 volumes; 2 university libraries/259,000 volumes; 6 public libraries/158,415 volumes; 173 school libraries/427,672 volumes; 6 special libraries/32,677 volumes; 2 other libraries/36,000 volumes. Total: 190 libraries/1.1 million volumes.

Publishing Output and Distribution
n.d. publishers; 337 book titles/2.2 million volumes (1980); 3 daily newspapers/ 30,000 circulation (1982); 1 other newspaper/3,500 circulation (1982); n.d. periodicals/191,000 circulation (1982); 3 booksellers.

Noted Library
National Library, P.O. Box 205, Doha.

REUNION

General Background
Location: Indian Ocean; capital: St. Denis; form of government: local government, French overseas department; population: 517,000 (1982); GNP per capita:
$4,000 (1982); ILL rate; 37% (1967); LHO ratio: 1 volume per 17 inhabitants.

Library Network
3 public libraries/n.d.; 1 university library/30,000 volumes (UN, 1981). Total:
4 libraries/30,000 volumes.

Publishing Output and Distribution
n.d. publishers; 79 book titles/n.d. volumes (1983); 2 daily newspapers/59,000
circulation (1982); 53 periodicals/109,000 circulation (1979); 3 booksellers.

Noted Library
Bibliothèque de Centre Universitaire de la Reunion, Campus du Chaudron,
Sainte-Clotilde.

ROMANIA

General Background
Location: Southeast Europe; capital: Bucharest; form of government: republic
(socialist state); 23.2 million (1990); GNP per capita: $2,540 (1981); ILL rate:
n.d.; LHO ratio: over 8 volumes per inhabitant.

Library Network (ALA, 1990)
2 national libraries/15.8 million volumes; 44 university and college libraries/
23.1 million volumes; 6,900 public libraries/72.2 million volumes; 10,987
school libraries/61 million volumes; 2,908 special libraries/21.9 million volumes. Total: 20,841 libraries/194 million volumes.

Publishing Output and Distribution
23 publishers; 6,702 book titles/79.7 million volumes (1982); 36 daily news-
papers/4.2 million circulation (1982); 24 other newspapers/685,000 circulation
(1982); 1 bookseller (government owned).

Noted Libraries
Biblioteca Academiei Republicii Socialiste România, Calea Victoriei 125, Bucharest; Biblioteca Centrală de Stat, Strada Ion Ghica 4, Bucharest.

Librarians' Organization
Asociaţia Bibliotecarilor din RSR, c/o Biblioteca Centrală de Stat, address
above.

RWANDA

General Background
Location: Central Africa; capital: Kigali; form of government: republic; population: 7.1 million (1990); GNP per capita: $250 (1981); ILL rate: 50% (1980); LHO ratio: 1 volume per over 22 inhabitants.

Library Network (ALA, 1990)
1 national library/6,000 volumes; 9 university and college libraries/157,000 volumes; 5 special libraries/30,000 volumes; 1 public library/30,000 volumes; 5 school libraries/50,000 volumes; 5 other libraries/50,000 volumes. Total: 26 libraries/323,000 volumes.

Publishing Output and Distribution
2 publishers; 1 daily newspaper/30,000 circulation (1982), 13 periodicals/13,000 circulation (1982); 3 booksellers.

Noted Library
Bibliothèque de l'Université Nationale du Rwanda, B.P. 54, Butare.

SAINT CHRISTOPHER (ST. KITTS)-NEVIS

General Background
Location: West Indies; capital: Basseterre; form of government: independent state, British monarch is nominal chief; population: 44,000 (1980); GNP per capita: $1,040 (1981); ILL rate: 2.4% (1970); LHO ratio: n.d.

Library Network
1 public library/n.d. volumes.

Publishing Output and Distribution
n.d. publishers; 5 book titles/1,000 volumes (1982); 2 daily newspapers/9,000 circulation (1982); 1 other newspaper/3,500 circulation (1982); n.d. booksellers.

Noted Library
Saint Christopher Public Library, Basseterre.

SAINT HELENA

General Background
Location: Atlantic Ocean, near Africa; capital: Jamestown; form of government: British dependency; population: 5,000 (1982); GNP per capita: n.d.; ILL rate: 2.9% (1970); LHO ratio: n.d.

Library Network
1 public library/n.d. volumes.

Publishing Output and Distribution
n.d. publishers; 1 daily newspaper/1,200 circulation (1982); 2 periodicals/500 circulation (1979); n.d. booksellers.

Noted Library
Saint Helena Public Library, Jamestown.

SAINT LUCIA

General Background
Location: West Indies; capital: Castries; form of government: independent state, British monarch is nominal chief; population: 122,000 (1982); GNP per capita: $970 (1981); ILL rate: 18.3% (1970); LHO ratio: 1 volume per almost 2 inhabitants.

Library Network
1 public library/38,000 volumes; 1 university library/24,000 volumes (UN, 1981). Total: 2 libraries/62,000 volumes.

Publishing Output and Distribution
n.d. publishers; 16 book titles/33,000 volumes (1981); 1 daily newspaper/4,000 circulation (1982); 1 other newspaper/4,500 circulation (1982); n.d. booksellers.

Noted Library
Central Library of Saint Lucia, P.O. Box 103, Castries.

SAINT VINCENT AND THE GRENADINES

General Background
Location: West Indies; capital: Kingstown; form of government: independent state, British monarch is its nominal chief; population: 99,000 (1982); GNP per capita: $630 (1981); ILL rate: 4.4% (1970); LHO ratio: over 1 volume per inhabitant.

Library Network
1 public library/100,000 volumes; 1 university library/8,000 volumes; 1 government agency library/5,000 volumes. Total: 3 libraries/113,000 volumes.

Publishing Output and Distribution
n.d. publishers; 7 daily newspapers/10,000 circulation (1977); n.d. booksellers.

SAMOA, AMERICAN

General Background
Location: Pacific Ocean, South Asia; capital: Pago Pago; form of government: unincorporated territory of the United States; population: 34,000 (1982); GNP per capita: n.d.; ILL rate: n.d.; LHO ratio: 2.6 volumes per inhabitant.

Library Network
1 university library/14,000 volumes (UN, 1982); 26 school libraries/76,000 volumes (UN, 1982). Total: 27 libraries/90,000 volumes.

Publishing Output and Distribution
n.d. publishers; 2 daily newspapers/7,000 circulation (1982); n.d. booksellers.

Noted Library
Library of the American Samoa, Utulci (source: *Telephone Directory*, 1976–77).

SAMOA, WESTERN

General Background
Location: Southwest Pacific Ocean; capital: Apia; form of government: independent commonwealth state; population: 142,000 (1982); GNP per capita: $350 (1976); ILL rate: 22% (1971); LHO ratio: 1 volume per almost 3 inhabitants.

Library Network
1 public library/36,000 volumes; 1 university library/15,000 volumes; 1 school library/5,000 volumes. Total: 3 libraries/56,000 volumes.

Publishing Output and Distribution
n.d. publishers; 8 daily newspapers/n.d. circulation (1979); n.d. booksellers.

Noted Library
Nelson Memorial Public Library, P.O. Box 598, Apia.

SAN MARINO

General Background
Location: Northeast Italy; capital: San Marino; form of government: republic; population: 21,000 (1982); GNP per capita: n.d.; ILL rate: n.d.; LHO ratio: over 12 volumes per inhabitant.

Library Network
1 public library/250,000 volumes (GLE); 5 school libraries/22,000 volumes (UN, 1983); 1 special library/2,000 volumes (UN, 1983). Total: 7 libraries/274,000 volumes.

Publishing Output and Distribution
n.d. publishers; 7 daily newspapers/1,300 circulation (1982); 8 other newspapers/11,000 circulation (1982); 11 periodicals/n.d. circulation (1982); n.d. booksellers.

Noted Library
Biblioteca di Stato e l'Archivio Statale, c/o Palazzo Valoni, Contada delle Mura, San Marino.

SAUDI ARABIA

General Background
Location: Southwest Asia; capital: Riyadh; form of government: kingdom; population: 14.8 million (1990); GNP per capita: $12,600 (1981); ILL rate: 75.4% (1980); LHO ratio: 1 volume per over 7 inhabitants.

Library Network (ALA, 1990)
1 national library/225,000 volumes; 7 university and college libraries/1.5 million volumes; 60 public libraries/150,000 volumes; 8 special libraries/200,000 volumes. Total: 76 libraries/2.1 million volumes.

Publishing Output and Distribution
2 publishers; 218 book titles/n.d. volumes (1980); 12 daily newspapers/60,000 circulation (1970); 80 periodicals/n.d. circulation (1982); 7 booksellers.

Noted Library
National Library, King Faisal Street, Riyadh.

SENEGAL

General Background
Location: West Africa; capital: Dakar; form of government: republic; joined Gambia in a confederation called Senegambia; population: 7.3 million (1990); GNP per capita: $430 (1981); ILL rate: 94.8% (1961); LHO ratio: 1 volume per over 7 inhabitants.

Library Network (ALA, 1990)
1 national library/26,000 volumes; 2 university libraries/588,724 volumes; 8 public libraries/121,050 volumes; 6 school libraries/69,845 volumes; 58 special libraries/189,304 volumes. Total: 75 libraries/994,923 volumes.

Publishing Output and Distribution
10 publishers; 42 book titles/169,000 volumes (1983); 1 daily newspaper/45,000 circulation (1982); 10 booksellers.

Noted Library
Archives du Senegal, Immeuble Administratif, Avenue Roume, Dakar.

Librarians' Organization
Association Nationale des Bibliothécaires, Archivistes et Documentalistes Senegalais, c/o Ecole de Bibliothécaires, Archivistes et Documentalistes, P.O. Box 3252, Dakar.

SEYCHELLES

General Background
Location: South Asia; capital: Victoria; form of government: republic; popula-
tion: 67,378 (1990); GNP per capita: $1,800 (1982); ILL rate: 42.3% (1971);
LHO ratio: 2.8 volumes per inhabitant.

Library Network (ALA, 1990)
1 national library/35,000 volumes; 1 public library/42,000 volumes; 22 school
libraries/93,859 volumes; 1 special library/21,000 volumes. Total: 25 libraries/
191,859 volumes.

Publishing Output and Distribution
n.d. publishers; 33 book titles/n.d. volumes (1980); 2 daily newspapers/4,000
circulation (1982); 2 other newspapers/3,000 circulation (1982); 4 periodicals/
n.d. circulation (1982); 2 booksellers.

Noted Library
Public Library of Seychelles, Victoria.

SIERRA LEONE

General Background
Location: West Africa; capital: Freetown; form of government: republic; population: 3.6 million (1982); GNP per capita: $320 (1981); ILL rate: 93.3%
(1963); LHO ratio: 1 volume per 5 inhabitants.

Library Network
1 national library/157,000 volumes; 11 public libraries/347,932 volumes (ALA,
1976); 7 university libraries/185,000 volumes (ALA, 1976); 13 school libraries/
4,000 volumes (ALA, 1976); 12 special libraries/34,440 volumes (ALA, 1976);
17 government agency libraries/21,000 volumes. Total: 61 libraries/749,372
volumes.

Publishing Output and Distribution
3 publishers; 1 daily newspaper/10,000 circulation (1982); 6 other newspapers/
52,000 circulation (1979); 3 booksellers.

Noted Library
Sierra Leone Library Board, P.O. Box 326, Freetown.

Librarians' Organization
Sierra Leone Library Association, c/o Sierra Leone Library Board, address
above.

SINGAPORE

General Background
Location: Southeast Asia; capital: Singapore; form of government: republic; population: 3 million (1990); GNP per capita: $6,521 (1983); ILL rate: 17.1% (1980); LHO ratio: over 7 volumes per inhabitant.

Library Network (ALA, 1990)
1 national library/2.3 million volumes; 6 university libraries/2.1 million volumes; 373 school libraries/4.7 million volumes; 84 special libraries/13.1 million volumes. Total: 464 libraries/22.2 million volumes.

Publishing Output and Distribution
30 publishers; 1,927 book titles/8.3 million volumes (1983); 12 daily newspapers/706,000 circulation (1982); 5 other newspapers/327,000 circulation (1982); 1,506 periodicals/n.d. circulation (1982); 20 booksellers.

Noted Library
National Library, Stamford Road, Singapore.

Librarians' Organization
Library Association of Singapore, c/o National Library, address above.

SOLOMON ISLANDS

General Background
Location: Southeast Pacific Ocean; capital: Honiara; form of government: independent state, British monarch is nominal chief; population: 321,000 (1990); GNP per capita: $640 (1981); ILL rate: n.d.; LHO ratio: 1 volume per 3.8 inhabitants.

Library Network (ALA, 1990)
1 national library/20,000 volumes; 3 university and college libraries/43,500 volumes; 8 public libraries/n.d. volumes; 22 school libraries/n.d. volumes; 2 special libraries/22,000 volumes. Total: 36 libraries/85,500 volumes.

Publishing Output and Distribution
n.d. publishers; 2 daily newspapers/5,000 circulation (1981).

Noted Library
Solomon Island National Library, Honiara.

SOMALIA

General Background
Location: East Africa; capital: Mogadishu; form of government: republic; population: 5.1 million (1981); GNP per capita: $280 (1981); ILL rate: 93.8% (1980); LHO ratio: 1 volume per over 77 inhabitants.

Library Network
2 university libraries/55,000 volumes (ALA, 1980); 6 special libraries/10,800 volumes; 2 government agency libraries/3,000 volumes. Total: 10 libraries/ 68,800 volumes.

Publishing Output and Distribution
2 publishers; 2 daily newspapers/5,000 circulation (1970); 2 booksellers.

Noted Library
National Library of Higher Education and Culture, Mogadishu.

SOUTH AFRICA

General Background
Location: South Africa: capital: Pretoria; form of government: republic; population: 35 million (1990); GNP per capita: $2,770 (1981); ILL rate: 43% (1960); LHO ratio: 1.3 volumes per inhabitant.

Library Network (ALA, 1990)
2 national libraries/1.4 million volumes; 84 university and college libraries/7.5 million volumes; 675 public libraries/32 million volumes; 381 special libraries/ 3.6 million volumes; 112 other libraries/1.5 million volumes. Total: 1,254 libraries/46 million volumes.

Publishing Output and Distribution
78 publishers; over 2,000 book titles/n.d. volumes (partial computation based on ILMP, dozens of publishers did not mention number of book titles); 30 daily and other newspapers/3.1 million circulation (source: *Official Yearbook of South Africa*, 1982); n.d. periodicals; 21 booksellers.

Noted Libraries
South African Library, Queen Victoria Street, Cape Town; State Library, Vermeulen Street, P.O. Box 397, Pretoria.

Librarians' Organization
African Library Association of South Africa, c/o Library, University of the North, Private Bag X5090, Pietersburg.

SOVIET UNION (after the fall of Communism in 1990, 15 independent states emerged)

General Background
Location: East Europe and North Asia; capital: Moscow; form of government: socialist state (federation); population: 269 million (1982); GNP per capita: n.d.; ILL rate: 0.3% (1970); LHO ratio: 18 volumes per inhabitant.

Library Network
3 national libraries/56 million volumes (KES, 1980); 133,000 public libraries/
1,935 million volumes (UN, 1982); 860 university libraries/400 million volumes
(KES, 1980); 154,000 school libraries/862 million volumes (UN, 1980); 650,000
special libraries/2,026 million volumes (KES, 1980). Total: 937,863 libraries/
5,279 million volumes.

Publishing Output and Distribution
60 publishers (ILMP), 200 (KES); 82,581 book titles/1,969 million volumes
(1982); 772 daily newspapers/109 million circulation (1982); 7,563 other news-
papers/66 million circulation (1982); n.d. periodicals; 1 bookseller (government
owned).

Noted Libraries
Gosudarstvennaîa Ordena Lenina Biblioteka SSSR Imeni V.I. Lenina, Prospekt
Kalinina 3, Moscow; Gosudarstvennaîa Publichnaîa Biblioteka Imeni M.E. Sal-
tykova-Shchedrina, Sadovaîa Ulitsâ 18, Leningrad; Biblioteka Akademii Nauk
SSSR, Birzhevaîa Liniîa 1, Leningrad.

Librarians' Organization
Bibliotechnyĭ Sovet, Ministerstvo Kul'tury SSSR, c/o Gosudarstvennaîa Ordena
Lenina Biblioteka SSSR Imeni V.I. Lenina, address above.

Note: In this edition, data for Russia and other republics (except Estonia, Lithuania, and
Ukraine) are not yet available.

SPAIN

General Background
Location: West Europe; capital: Madrid; form of government: kingdom; popu-
lation: 39 million (1990); GNP per capita: $4,173 (1983); ILL rate: 7.4% (1981);
LHO ratio: 1.2 volumes per inhabitant.

Library Network (ALA, 1990)
1 national library/3 million volumes; 567 university and college libraries/15.1
million volumes; 3,285 libraries/26.3 million volumes; 13 other libraries/634,337
volumes. Total: 3,866 libraries/45 million volumes.

Publishing Output and Distribution
193 publishers; 32,138 book titles/273 million volumes (1982); 104 daily news-
papers/2.9 million circulation (1982); 24 periodicals/1 million circulation (1982);
23 booksellers.

Noted Libraries
Biblioteca Nacional, Paseo de Recoletos 20, Madrid; Biblioteca Universitaria de
Barcelona, Gran Via de las Cortes Catalanas 585, Barcelona.

Librarians' Organization
Asociación Española de Archiveros, Bibliotecarios, Museólogos y Documental-istas, Paseo de Recoletos 20, Madrid.

SRI LANKA (CEYLON)

General Background
Location: Indian Ocean; capital: Colombo; form of government: republic (socialist); population: 16.9 million (1990); GNP per capita: $300 (1981); ILL rate: 13.9% (1981); LHO ratio: 1 volume per 3.3 inhabitants.

Library Network (ALA, 1990)
1 national library/44,000 volumes; 52 university and college libraries/1.5 million volumes; 580 public libraries/n.d. volumes; 3,700 school libraries/2.8 million volumes; 150 special libraries/627,483 volumes; 300 other libraries/n.d. volumes. Total: 4,783 libraries/5 million volumes.

Publishing Output and Distribution
15 publishers; 1,951 book titles/17.6 million volumes (1983); 24 daily newspapers/1.6 million circulation (1982); 108 other newspapers/n.d. circulation (1979); 405 periodicals/1.5 million circulation (1979); 2 booksellers (state owned).

Noted Library
National Museum Library, P.O. Box 854, Sir Marcus Fernando Mawatha, Colombo.

Librarians' Organization
Sri Lanka Library Association, c/o University of Sri Lanka, Colombo Campus, P.O. Box 1698, Colombo

SUDAN

General Background
Location: Northwest Africa; capital: Khartoum; form of government: republic; population: 19.4 million (1982); GNP per capita: $380 (1981); ILL rate: 90.4% (1956); LHO ratio: 1 volume per 20 inhabitants.

Library Network
83 public libraries/114,000 volumes (ALA, 1976); 14 university libraries/ 423,000 volumes; 4,676 school libraries/89,000 volumes (ALA, 1976); 110 special libraries/286,000 volumes (ALA, 1976); 6 government agency libraries/ 14,000 volumes. Total: 4,889 libraries/926,000 volumes.

Publishing Output and Distribution
3 publishers; 138 book titles/n.d. volumes (1979); 6 daily newspapers/105,000 circulation (1982); 9 other newspapers/206,000 circulation (1982); 25 periodicals/200,400 circulation (1982); 6 booksellers.

Noted Library
University of Khartoum, Main Library, P.O. Box 321, Khartoum.

Librarians' Organization
Sudan Library Association, P.O. Box 1361, Khartoum.

SURINAME

General Background
Location: South America; capital: Paramaribo; form of government: republic; population: 407,000 (1982); GNP per capita: $3,030 (1981); ILL rate: 35% (1978); LHO ratio: 1.25 volumes per inhabitant.

Library Network
68 public libraries/268,000 volumes (UN, 1978); 2 university libraries/29,000 volumes (UN, 1978); 49 school libraries/60,000 volumes (UN, 1978); 27 special libraries/27,000 volumes (UN, 1978); 7 nonspecial libraries/129,000 volumes (UN, 1977). Total: 153 libraries/513,000 volumes.

Publishing Output and Distribution
16 publishers; 925 book titles/n.d. volumes (1976); 5 daily newspapers/30,000 circulation (1982); 24 periodicals/39,000 circulation (1979); 1 bookseller.

Noted Library
Universiteit van Suriname, Bibliothek, Sophie Redmondstraat 118, Paramaribo.

SWAZILAND

General Background
Location: South Africa; capital: Mbabane; form of government: kingdom; population: 585,000 (1982); GNP per capita: $760 (1981); ILL rate: 44.8% (1976); LHO ratio: almost 1 volume per inhabitant.

Library Network
1 national library/66,000 volumes; 10 public libraries/337,274 volumes (ALA, 1976); 5 university libraries/91,000 volumes; 28 school libraries/43,538 volumes (ALA, 1976); 7 special libraries/17,865 volumes (ALA, 1976); 3 government agency libraries/3,200 volumes. Total: 54 libraries/558,877 volumes.

Publishing Output and Distribution
1 publisher; 1 daily newspaper/9,000 circulation (1982); 1 periodical/2,600 circulation (1982); 2 booksellers.

Noted Library
-Swaziland National Library Service, P.O. Box 1461, Mbabane.

SWEDEN

General Background
Location: North Europe; capital: Stockholm; form of government: kingdom; population: 8.3 million (1982); GNP per capita: $10,890 (1983); ILL rate: n.d.; LHO ratio: over 11.4 volumes per inhabitant.

Library Network
1 national library/2 million volumes (UN, 1980); 2,204 public libraries/40.2 million volumes (UN, 1980); 40 university libraries/11.7 million volumes; 553 school libraries/35.7 million volumes (UN, 1983); 20 special libraries/3.7 million volumes; 44 government agency libraries/1.6 million volumes. Total: 2,862 libraries/94.9 million volumes.

Publishing Output and Distribution
124 publishers; 8,036 book titles/n.d. volumes (1983); 114 daily newspapers/ 4.3 million circulation (1982); 72 other newspapers/469,000 circulation (1982); 13 booksellers.

Noted Library
Kungliga Biblioteket, Humlegarden. P.O. Box 5039, Stockholm.

Librarians' Organization
Sveriges Allmänna Biblioteksförening, Winstrupsgatan 10, P.O. Box 1706, Lund.

SWITZERLAND

General Background
Location: Central Europe; capital: Berne; form of government: republic; population: 6.4 million (1982); GNP per capita: $17,450 (1981); ILL rate: n.d.; LHO ratio: 6.40 volumes per inhabitant.

Library Network
1 national library/1.1 million volumes (UN, 1980); 31 public libraries/4.2 million volumes; 211 university libraries/20.1 million volumes; 2,764 school libraries/ 2.4 million volumes (ALA, 1976); 1,276 special libraries/10.2 million volumes (ALA, 1976); 15 government agency libraries/1.9 million volumes; 30 religious libraries/1.4 million volumes. Total: 4,328 libraries/41.3 million volumes.

Publishing Output and Distribution
351 publishers; 11,405 book titles/n.d. volumes (1982); 90 daily newspapers/ 2.4 million circulation (1982); 167 other newspapers/883,000 circulation (1982); 1,533 periodicals/31 million circulation (1979); 17 booksellers.

Noted Library
Schweizerische Landesbibliothek/Bibliothèque Nationale Suisse, Hallwylstrasse 15, Berne.

Librarians' Organization
Association des Bibliothécaires Suisses/Vereinigung Schweizerische Bibliothekare, c/o Schweizerische Landesbibliothek, address above.

SYRIA

General Background
Location: Southwest Asia; capital: Damascus; form of government: republic;
population: 12.1 million (1990); GNP per capita: $1,570 (1981); ILL rate: 60%
(1970); LHO ratio: 1 volume per over 4.5 inhabitants.

Library Network (ALA, 1990)
1 national library/151,600 volumes; 5 university libraries/596,000 volumes; 92
public libraries/1 million volumes; 903 school libraries/800,000 volumes; 10
special libraries/50,000 volumes. Total: 1,011 libraries/2.6 million volumes.

Publishing Output and Distribution
6 publishers; 119 book titles/553,000 volumes (1983); 6 daily newspapers/
65,000 circulation (1982); 8 other newspapers/71,000 circulation (1979); 48 pe-
riodicals/453,000 circulation (1979); 5 booksellers.

Noted Library
Al Zahiriah National Library, Bab el Barid, Damascus.

TAIWAN (REPUBLIC OF CHINA)

General Background
Location: South Pacific; capital: Taipei; form of government: republic; population: 20.5 million (1990); GNP per capita: $2,682 (1983); ILL rate: 54.5%
(1956); LHO ratio: 2.5 volumes per inhabitant.

Library Network (ALA, 1990)
1 national library/1.8 million volumes; 122 university and college libraries/14.6
million volumes; 256 public libraries/6.6 million volumes; 2,444 school librar-
ies/20.4 million volumes; 491 special libraries/5.5 million volumes. Total: 3,314
libraries/8.9 million volumes.

Publishing Output and Distribution
12 publishers; 6,819 book titles/n.d. volumes (1983); 31 daily newspapers/n.d.
circulation (1979); 990 periodicals/n.d. circulation (1982); 8 booksellers.

Noted Libraries
National Central Library, 43 Nan Hai Road, Taipei; National Taiwan Normal
University Library, 162 Ho Ping Road, Taipei.

Librarians' Organization
Library Association of China, c/o National Central Library, address above.

TANZANIA

General Background
Location: East Africa; capital: Dar es Salaam; form of government: republic; population: 19.1 million (1982); GNP per capita: $280 (1981); ILL rate: 53.7% (1978); LHO ratio: 1 volume per 16 inhabitants.

Library Network
1 national library/100,000 volumes (ALA, 1976); 20 public libraries/404,000 volumes (UN, 1980); 65 university libraries/380,000 volumes (ALA, 1976); 130 school libraries/325,000 volumes (ALA, 1976); 63 special libraries/175,000 volumes (UN, 1976). Total: 279 libraries/1.3 million volumes.

Publishing Output and Distribution
13 publishers; 246 book titles/n.d. volumes (1982); 3 daily newspapers/208,000 circulation (1982); 7 other newspapers/177,000 circulation (1979); 69 periodicals/646,000 circulation (1979); 9 booksellers.

Noted Library
Tanzania Library Service, P.O. Box 9283, Dar es Salaam.

Librarians' Organization
Tanzania Library Association, P.O.Box 2645, Dar es Salaam.

THAILAND

General Background
Location: Southeast Asia; capital: Bangkok; form of government: kingdom; population: 48.4 million (1982); GNP per capita: $770 (1981); ILL rate: 12% (1980); LHO ratio: 1 volume per almost 9 inhabitants.

Library Network
1 national library/1.2 million volumes (UN, 1981); 375 public libraries/1.6 million volumes; 34 university libraries/1.5 million volumes; 4 school libraries/19,000 volumes; 28 special libraries/460,000 volumes; 26 nonspecial libraries/764,000 volumes (UN, 1981); 28 government agency libraries/375,000 volumes. Total: 496 libraries/5.9 million volumes.

Publishing Output and Distribution
52 publishers; 5,645 book titles/n.d. volumes (1982); 69 daily newspapers/2.5 million circulation (1982); 275 other newspapers/n.d. circulation (1982); 16 booksellers.

Noted Library
Ho Samut Haeng Chat National Library, Samsen Road, Bangkok.

Librarians' Organization
Thai Library Association, 273-275 Viphavadee Rangsit Road, Phayathai, Bangkok.

TOGO

General Background
Location: West Africa; capital: Lomé; form of government: republic; population: 2.7 million (1982); GNP per capita: $380 (1981); ILL rate: 84% (1970); LHO ratio: 1 volume per 25 inhabitants.

Library Network
.1 national library/15,000 volumes; 1 university library/50,000 volumes (UN, 1982); 2 school libraries/4,500 volumes; 10 special libraries/43,000 volumes; 4 government agency libraries/12,000 volumes. Total: 18 libraries/124,500 volumes.

Publishing Output and Distribution
3 publishers; 3 daily newspapers/15,000 circulation (1982); 4 booksellers.

Noted Library
Bibliothèque Nationale, Avenue de la Victoire, B.P. 1002, Lomé.

Librarians' Organization
Association Togolaise de la Documentation, des Bibliothèques, Archives et Musées, c/o Bibliothèque de l'Université du Benin, B.P. 1515, Lomé.

TONGA

General Background
Location: Southwest Asia; capital: Nukualofa; form of government: kingdom; population: 101,000 (1982); GNP per capita: $530 (1981); ILL rate: 0.4% (1976); LHO ratio: 1 volume per over 3 inhabitants.

Library Network
1 university library/6,000 volumes (UN, 1981); 10 school libraries/28,000 volumes (UN, 1978); 2 special libraries/4,000 volumes (UN, 1978). Total: 13 libraries/38,000 volumes.

Publishing Output and Distribution
n.d. publishers; 2 nondaily newspapers/8,000 circulation (1982); n.d. booksellers.

Noted Library
Teachers Training College Library, Nukualofa.

TRINIDAD AND TOBAGO

General Background
Location: West Indies; capital: Port of Spain; form of government: republic; population: 1.2 million (1982); GNP per capita: $5,670 (1981); ILL rate: 7.8% (1970); LHO ratio: over 1 volume per inhabitant.

Library Network
1 national library/429,000 volumes; 3 public libraries/607,000 volumes (ALA, 1976); 1 university library/222,000 volumes (UN, 1981); 24 special libraries/ 138,400 volumes (ALA, 1976). Total: 29 libraries/1.4 million volumes.

Publishing Output and Distribution
4 publishers; 186 book titles/n.d. volumes (1978); 4 daily newspapers/168,000 circulation (1982); 14 booksellers.

Noted Library
Central Library of Trinidad and Tobago, 20 Queens Park East, P.O. Box 547, Port of Spain.

Librarians' Organization
Library Association of Trinidad and Tobago, P.O. Box 1177, Port of Spain.

TUNISIA

General Background
Location: North Africa; capital: Tunis; form of government: republic; population: 6.7 million (1982); GNP per capita: $1,420 (1981); ILL rate: 53% (1980); LHO ratio: almost 1 volume per 2 inhabitants.

Library Network
1 national library/1 million volumes (UN, 1977); 221 public libraries/875,000 volumes (UN, 1980); 6 university libraries/240,000 volumes; n.d. school libraries/935,000 volumes (ALA, 1980); 37 special libraries/276,000 volumes; 3 government agency libraries/11,000 volumes. Total: 268 libraries/3.3 million volumes.

Publishing Output and Distribution
11 publishers; 172 book titles/6 million volumes (1981); 5 daily newspapers/ 272,000 circulation (1982); 13 other newspapers/4,000 circulation (1979); 5 booksellers.

Noted Library
Dar al Kutub al Wataniyya Bibliothèque Nationale, 20 Souk El Attarini, Tunis.

Librarians' Organization
Association Tunisienne de Documentalistes, Bibliothécaires et Archivistes, 43 Rue de la Liberté, Le Bardo.

TURKEY

General Background
Location: South Europe and Asia Minor; capital: Ankara; form of government: republic; population: 58.6 million (1990); GNP per capita: $1,540 (1981); ILL rate: 31.2% (1980); LHO ratio: 1 volume per 2.2 inhabitants.

Library Network (ALA, 1990)
1 national library/1.5 million volumes; 29 university and college libraries/5.3 million volumes; 938 public libraries/7.8 million volumes; 4,915 school libraries/9.3 million volumes; 375 special libraries/1.8 million volumes; 11 other libraries/578,000 volumes. Total: 6,269 libraries/26.3 million volumes.

Publishing Output and Distribution
15 publishers; 6,869 book titles/n.d. volumes (1983); 1,115 daily newspapers/ 3.8 million circulation (1979); 618 periodicals/n.d. circulation (1977); 9 booksellers.

Noted Library
Millî Kütüphane, Kumrular Sokak 3, Yenisehir, Ankara.

Librarians' Organization
Türk Kütüphaneciler Dernegi, Elgün Sokağ 8/12, Yenisehir, Ankara.

TURKS AND CAICOS ISLANDS

General Background
Location: West Indies; capital: Grand Turk; form of government: British colony; population: 6,000 (1982); GNP per capita: n.d.; ILL rate: 1.9% (1970); LHO ratio: over 2 volumes per inhabitant.

Library Network
1 public library/7,000 volumes (UN, 1980); 1 school library/6,000 volumes (UN, 1982). Total: 2 libraries/13,000 volumes.

Publishing Output and Distribution
n.d.

Noted Library
Public Library of Turks and Caicos Islands, Grand Turk.

UGANDA

General Background
Location: East Africa; capital: Kampala; form of government: republic; population: 18.8 million (1990); GNP per capita: $220 (1981); ILL rate: 47.7% (1980); LHO ratio: 1 volume per 2.6 inhabitants.

Library Network (ALA, 1990)
3 university libraries/600,000 volumes; 1 public library/150,000 volumes; 350 school libraries/6.2 million volumes; 30 special libraries/100,000 volumes. Total: 384 libraries/7.1 million volumes.

Publishing Output and Distribution
4 publishers; n.d. volumes; 1 daily newspaper/25,000 circulation (1982); 4 booksellers.

Noted Library
Public Libraries Board, Buganda Road, P.O. Box 4262, Kampala.

Librarians' Organization
Uganda Library Association, P.O. Box 5894, Kampala.

UKRAINE

General Background
Location: Eastern Europe; capital: Kiev; form of government: republic; population: 52 million (1990); GNP per capita: $1,670 (1992); ILL rate: n.d.; LHO ratio: 1 volume per inhabitant.

Library Network (ALA, 1990)
1 national library/12.5 million volumes; 153 university libraries/23.5 million volumes; 22,300 public libraries/4 million volumes; school libraries/n.d. volumes; 1,035 special libraries/12.5 million volumes. Total: 23,489 libraries/52.5 million volumes.

Publishing Output and Distribution
217 publishing houses/217 titles (1993).

Main Library
Derzhavna Biblioteka Ukrainy (State Library of Ukraine), M. Grushevsky 1, 252001, Kiev 1.

UNITED ARAB EMIRATES

General Background
Location: Southwest Asia; capital: Dubai; form of government: federated sheikdom (monarchy); population: 790,000 (1982); GNP per capita: $24,660 (1981); ILL rate: 46.5% (1975); LHO ratio: almost 1 volume per 4 inhabitants.

Library Network
1 national library/70,000 volumes (UN, 1977); 4 public libraries/17,000 volumes (UN, 1977); 1 university library/95,000 volumes (UN, 1982); 2 special libraries/13,000 volumes. Total: 8 libraries/195,000 volumes.

Publishing Output and Distribution
1 publisher; 84 book titles/1.5 million volumes (1983); 9 daily newspapers/67,000 circulation (1982); 3 periodicals/2,000 circulation (1977); 1 bookseller.

Noted Library
Dubai Public Library, P.O. Box 67, Dubai.

UNITED KINGDOM

General Background
Location: Northwest Europe; capital: London; form of government: kingdom; population: 55.7 million (1982); GNP per capita: $9,110 (1981); ILL rate: n.d.; LHO ratio: almost 4 volumes per inhabitant.

Library Network
3 national libraries/20.5 million volumes (UN, 1980); 16,244 public libraries/ 131.3 million volumes (UN, 1980); 554 university libraries/24 million volumes (UN, 1980); n.d. school libraries/31 million volumes (UN, 1979); 320 special libraries/13.5 million volumes. Total: 17,121 libraries/220.3 million volumes.

Publishing Output and Distribution
711 publishers; 50,981 book titles/n.d. volumes (1983); 113 daily newspapers/ 23.4 million circulation (1982); 1,032 other newspapers/32.7 million circulation (1982); 20 booksellers.

Noted Libraries
The British Library, Great Russell Street, London; National Library of Scotland, George IV Bridge, Edinburgh; National Library of Wales, Aberystwyth, Dyfed.

Librarians' Organization
The Library Association, 7 Ridgmount Street, London.

UNITED STATES

General Background
Location: North America; capital: Washington, D.C.; form of government: republic; population: 248.7 million (1990); GNP per capita: $12,820 (1981); ILL rate: 0.5% (1979); LHO ratio: almost 9 volumes per inhabitant.

Library Network (ALA, 1990)
3 national libraries/29.2 million volumes; 1,607 university and college libraries/ 633.8 million volumes; 9,068 public libraries/600 million volumes; 102,538 school libraries/923 million volumes; 11,146 special libraries/19.8 million volumes (UN, 1977). Total: 124,362 libraries/2.2 billion volumes.

Publishing Output and Distribution
13,900 publishers (1982)-BPA; 76,976 book titles/n.d. volumes (1981); 1,710 daily newspapers/62.4 million circulation (1982); 7,471 other newspapers/44 million circulation (1982); 735 weekend periodicals/54 million circulation (1980); 762 weekly periodicals/40 million circulation (1980); 19,049 booksellers (1982)-BPA.

Noted Libraries
Library of Congress, 10 First Street, South East, Washington, D.C.; New York Public Library, 42nd Street and 5th Avenue, New York; Harvard University Library, Cambridge, Massachusetts.

Librarians' Organization
American Library Association, 50 East Huron Street, Chicago, Illinois.

URUGUAY

General Background
Location: South America; capital: Montevideo; form of government: republic; population: 3 million (1990); GNP per capita: $2,820 (1981); ILL rate: 6.1% (1975); LHO ratio: over 1.2 volume per inhabitant.

Library Network (ALA, 1990)
1 national library/890,000 volumes; 118 university and college libraries/1.1 million volumes; 87 public libraries/237,969 volumes; 69 school libraries/187,835 volumes; 138 special libraries/1.2 million volumes. Total: 413 libraries/3.6 million volumes.

Publishing Output and Distribution
12 publishers; 837 book titles/n.d. volumes (1981); 24 daily newspapers/558,000 circulation (1982); 58 other newspapers/n.d. circulation (1979); 545 periodicals/ n.d. circulation (1983); 12 booksellers.

Noted Library
Biblioteca Nacional de Uruguay, 18 de Julio 1790, Casilla de Correo 452, Montevideo.

Librarians' Organization
Agrupación Bibliotecologica del Uruguay, Cerro Largo 1666, Montevideo.

VANUATU (NEW HEBRIDES)

General Background
Location: Pacific Ocean; capital: Vila; form of government: republic; population: 126,000 (1982); GNP per capita: $350 (1981); ILL rate: n.d.; LHO ratio: 1 volume per 9 inhabitants.

Library Network
1 public library/13,900 volumes.

Publishing Output and Distribution
n.d. publishers; 2 daily newspapers/2,500 circulation (1982).

Noted Library
Cultural Center Library, Vila.

VATICAN (HOLY SEE)

General Background
Location: South Europe; capital: Vatican City; form of government: papal state; population: 1,000 (1982); GNP per capita: n.d.; ILL rate: n.d.; LHO ratio: 5,500 volumes per inhabitant.

Library Network
1 national library/900,000 volumes; 1 public library/37,000 volumes (UN, 1980); 17 university libraries/2.6 million volumes (UN, 1981); 2 special libraries/700,000 volumes (UN, 1979); 3 nonspecial libraries/597,000 volumes (UN, 1980); 20 religious libraries/648,000 volumes. Total: 44 libraries/5.5 million volumes.

Publishing Output and Distribution
3 publishers; 191 book titles/183,000 volumes (1983); 1 daily newspaper/70,000 circulation (1982); 42 periodicals/38,000 circulation (1982); 1 bookseller.

Noted Library
Biblioteca Apostolica Vaticana, Citta del Vatican.

VENEZUELA

General Background
Location: South America; capital: Caracas; form of government: republic; population: 14.7 million (1982); GNP per capita: $4,644 (1982); ILL rate: 17.6% (1971); LHO ratio: 1 volume per over 4 inhabitants.

Library Network
1 national library/765,000 volumes (UN, 1980); 373 public libraries/977,000 volumes (UN, 1980); 131 university libraries/1.3 million volumes (UN, 1977); 46 school libraries/105,000 volumes (UN, 1978); 35 special libraries/224,000 volumes (UN, 1977). Total: 586 libraries/3.4 million volumes.

Publishing Output and Distribution
24 publishers; 4,200 book titles/n.d. volumes (1981); 61 daily newspapers/2.7 million circulation (1982); 45 other newspapers/467,800 circulation (1982); 160 periodicals/4.6 million circulation (1982); 16 booksellers.

Noted Library
Biblioteca Nacional, Avenida Universidad y Congreso Nacional, Caracas.

Librarians' Organization
Colegio de Bibliotecologos y Archivologos de Venezuela, Apartado 6282, Caracas.

VIETNAM

General Background
Location: Southeast Asia; capital: Hanoi; form of government: republic (socialist); population: 66.2 million (1990); GNP per capita: $100 (1982); ILL rate: 16% (1979); LHO ratio: 1 volume per 4.4 inhabitants.

Library Network (ALA, 1990)
1 national library/1.8 million volumes; 230 university libraries/4.2 million volumes; 20,044 public libraries/8 million volumes; 6,637 school libraries/n.d. volumes; 276 special libraries/1.4 million volumes. Total: 27,188 libraries/15.4 million volumes.

Publishing Output and Distribution
14 publishers; 1,495 book titles/37 million volumes (1981); 4 daily newspapers/ 500,000 circulation (1982); 15 periodicals/257,000 circulation (1977); 1 bookseller (state owned).

Noted Libraries
Thu Vien Quoc Gia Viet Nam, 31 Trang Thi, Hanoi; Bibliothèque de Science Generales, 69 Ly tu Trong, Ho Chi Minh.

Librarians' Organization
Hoi Thu-Vien Viet Nam, 8 Le Qui Don, Ho Chi Minh.

VIRGIN ISLANDS, AMERICAN

General Background
Location: West Indies; capital: Charlotte Amalie; form of government: American territory, with a local government, administered by U.S. Department of the Interior; population: 116,000 (1982); GNP per capita: $8,090 (1982); ILL rate: n.d.; LHO ratio: over 2 volumes per inhabitant.

Library Network
4 public libraries/52,000 volumes; 1 university library/65,000 volumes; 2 special libraries/129,000 volumes. Total: 7 libraries/246,000 volumes.

Publishing Output and Distribution
n.d. publishers; 3 daily newspapers/17,000 circulation (1982); 2 other newspapers/9,000 circulation (1982); n.d. booksellers.

Noted Library
College of the Virgin Islands, Ralph M. Paiewonsky Library, Charlotte Amalie, St. Thomas.

VIRGIN ISLANDS, BRITISH

General Background
Location: West Indies; capital: Road Town; form of government: British colony; population: 12,000 (1982); GNP per capita: n.d.; ILL rate: 1.7% (1970); LHO ratio: 3 volumes per inhabitant.

Library Network
4 public libraries/29,000 volumes (UN, 1980); 2 school libraries/7,000 volumes (UN, 1982). Total: 6 libraries/36,000 volumes.

Publishing Output and Distribution
n.d. publishers; 20 book titles/3,000 volumes (1982); 1 daily newspaper/1,700 circulation (1982); n.d. booksellers.

Noted Library
Public Library of Virgin Islands, Road Town.

YEMEN (after the unification of North and South Yemen; both mentioned in the first edition as separate countries)

General Background
Location: Southwest Asia; capital: San'a; form of government: republic; population: 11.6 million (1990); GNP per capita: $460 (1981); ILL rate: 80% (1990); LHO ratio: 1 volume per 109 inhabitants.

Library Network (ALA, 1990)
1 national library/2,000 volumes; 6 university libraries/60,000 volumes; 3 public libraries/40,000 volumes. Total: 10 libraries/102,000 volumes.

Publishing Output and Distribution
n.d. publishers; 6 daily newspapers/56,000 circulation (1970); 1 bookseller.

Noted Library
Great Mosque Library, Al Jamla al Kebir, San'a.

YUGOSLAVIA (before the secession of Bosnia-Hercegovina, Croatia, Slovenia, Macedonia)

General Background
Location: Southeast Europe; capital: Belgrade; form of government: republic (socialist); population: 22.6 million (1982); GNP per capita: $2,790 (1981); ILL rate: 16.5% (1971); LHO ratio: 3.8 volumes per inhabitant.

Library Network
8 national libraries/8.1 million volumes (UN, 1980); 2,101 public libraries/24.1 million volumes (UN, 1980); 398 university libraries/10.6 million volumes (UN, 1980); 8,458 school libraries/29.8 million volumes (UN, 1980); 1,072 special

libraries/10.8 million volumes (UN, 1977); 11 nonspecial libraries/3.4 million volumes (UN, 1980). Total: 12,048 libraries/86.8 million volumes.

Publishing Output and Distribution
94 publishers; 10,931 book titles/65 million volumes (1983); 27 daily newspapers/2.2 million circulation (1982); 2,991 other newspapers/12.5 million circulation (1979); 1,408 periodicals/9 million circulation (1979); 15 booksellers.

Noted Libraries
Nacionalna i Sveučilišna Biblioteka, Marulićev Trg 21, Zagreb; Narodna Biblioteka SR Srbje, Skerlićeva 1, Belgrad.

Librarians' Organization
Savez Društava Bibliotekara Jugoslavije, Postanski Fah 136, Priština.

Note: Date for the new states of former Yugoslavia not yet available.

ZAIRE

General Background
Location: Southcentral Africa; capital: Kinshasa; form of government: republic; population: 28.3 million (1980); GNP per capita: $210 (1981); ILL rate: 45.5% (1980); LHO ratio: 1 volume per 11 inhabitants.

Library Network
1 national library/1.2 million volumes; 15 public libraries/200,000 volumes (UN, 1977); 15 university libraries/585,000 volumes; 9 school libraries/102,000 volumes; 40 special libraries/458,000 volumes; 12 government agency libraries/ 50,000 volumes. Total: 92 libraries/2.6 million volumes.

Publishing Output and Distribution
13 publishers; 231 book titles/n.d. volumes (1979); 5 daily newspapers/45,000 circulation (1982); 15 booksellers.

Noted Library
Bibliothèque Nationale, 10 Boulevard Colonel Rshatshi, B.P. 3090, Kinshasa-Gombe.

Librarians' Organization
Association Zairoise des Archivistes, Bibliothécaires et Documentalistes, B.P. 805, Kinshasa.

ZAMBIA

General Background
Location: Southcentral Africa; capital: Lusaka; form of government: republic; population: 8 million (1990); GNP per capita: $600 (1981); ILL rate: 52.7% (1969); LHO ratio: 1 volume per 5 inhabitants.

Library Network (ALA, 1990)
2 national libraries/350,000 volumes; 12 university libraries/400,000 volumes; 7 public libraries/420,000 volumes; 2 special libraries/40,000 volumes; 78 school libraries/100,000 volumes; 65 special libraries/250,000 volumes. Total: 166 libraries/1.6 million volumes.

Publishing Output and Distribution
8 publishers; 454 book titles/235,000 volumes (1983); 2 daily newspapers/113,000 circulation (1982); 3 other newspapers/116,000 circulation (1979); 8 booksellers.

Noted Library
Zambia Library Service, Educational Services Centre, P.O. Box 30802, Lusaka.

Librarians' Organization
Zambia Library Association, P.O. Box 32839, Lusaka.

ZIMBABWE (RHODESIA)

General Background
Location: Southcentral Africa; capital: Harare; form of government: republic; population: 7.5 million (1982); GNP per capita: $780 (1984); ILL rate: 31.2% (1980); LHO ratio: 1 volume per almost 6 inhabitants.

Library Network
2 national libraries/165,000 volumes; 14 public libraries/443,000 volumes; 12 university libraries/274,000 volumes; 100 school libraries/261,000 volumes (UN, 1980); 12 special libraries/113,000 volumes; 10 government agency libraries/136,000 volumes; 1 religious library/6,000 volumes. Total: 151 libraries/1.4 million volumes.

Publishing Output and Distribution
15 publishers; 533 titles/263,000 volumes (1982); 2 daily newspapers/155,000 circulation (1982); 14 booksellers.

Noted Libraries
National Free Library of Zimbabwe, Twelfth Avenue, P.O. Box 1773, Bulawayo; National Archives, Private Bag 7729, Causeway, Harare.

Librarians' Organization
Zimbabwe Library Association, P.O. Box 3133, Harare.

II
THE LIBRARIAN'S
SPECIAL INTERESTS

____ 2 ____
Noted Librarians,
Past and Present

This section has 192 entries, encompassing a wide range of individuals from over 30 countries who built extensive private or public collections, established new libraries or were, or still are, associated with specific libraries. The perusal of entries will reveal facts that are little known or unknown to the librarians at large.

Each entry provides the person's name, dates of birth and death, main areas of activity, a description of the person's involvement in the field of librarianship and a relevant source (in parentheses) confirming the person's library work or contributions. It is understood that the cited reference source is just one out of several existent for each.

Bibliography

Ash, Lee, ed. *A Biographical Dictionary of Librarians in the United States and Canada.* Chicago: American Library Association, 1970.
Bobinski, George et al., eds. *Dictionary of American Library Biography.* Littleton, CO: Libraries Unlimited, 1978.
Boorstin, Daniel J. *The Discoverers.* New York: Vintage Books, 1983.
Chernow, Barbara A., and George A. Vallasi, eds. *The Columbia Encyclopedia.* 5th ed. New York: Columbia University Press, 1993.
Der Grosse Brockhaus in Zwölf Bänden. Westbaden: F.A. Brockhaus, 1977–1981.
Diccionario Enciclopedico Salvat Universal. Barcelona: Salvat Editores, 1981.
Enciclopedia Universal Ilustrada. Madrid: Espasa-Calpe, 1982.
Gran Enciclopedia Rialp. Madrid: Ediciones, Rialp, 1981.
Gran Larousse Encyclopedique en Dix Volumes. Paris: Librairie Larousse, 1964.
Knigovedenie: Ėnt͡siklopedicheskiĭ Solvar'. Moskva: Sovetskai͡a Ėnt͡siklopedii͡a, 1985.
New Catholic Encyclopedia. New York: McGraw-Hill, 1967–1979 (17 volumes).

New Century Cyclopedia of Names. New York: Appleton-Century-Crofts, 1954.

Richter, John Henry, and John Boynton. "Librarians and Archivists on Stamps." In *Topical Time*, vols. 29–40, reprint, 1955–1956.

Wallerstein, Immanuel, and John F. Stephens. *Libraries and Our Civilizations: A Report Prepared for the Governor of the State of New York.* Binghamton, N.Y., 1978.

Webster's Biographical Dictionary. Springfield, Mass.: G. & C. Merriam, 1943.

Wedgeworth, Robert, ed. *World Encyclopedia of Library Information Services.* 3d ed. Chicago: American Library Association, 1993.

Wiegand, Wayne A. *Supplement of Dictionary of American Biography.* Littleton, CO: Libraries Unlimited, 1978.

ALESSANDRI PALMA, ARTURO (1868–1950) Chilean lawyer and politician, served as president of his country twice (1920, 1935), member of several cabinets; in 1893, before starting his political career, he worked as a librarian at the National Library in Santiago (GER, v.1, 625).

ANDERSON, EDWIN HATFIELD (1861–1947) American librarian, lawyer, and author. Served as director of the New York State Library, the Library School in Albany, and of the New York Public Library. Developed the circulation and reference divisions, municipal reference services, photostating, and traveling book wagons. Was American Library Association president (1913–14). Wrote about training library staff (Harry L. Lydenberg, "Edwin Hatfield Anderson, 1861–1947," in *ALA Bulletin*, 41, August 1947, 258–259).

ANDREWS, CLEMENT WALKER (1858–1930) American librarian and author. Developed the John Crerar Library, Chicago as a first-class public and scholarly library specializing in pure and applied sciences. Introduced printed library catalog card exchanges with other libraries, also printed lists of current periodicals. Was American Library Association president (1906–1907). Wrote about the university library (Jens Christian Bay, "Dr. Clement Walker Andrews, 1858-1930," in *Libraries*, 36, 1931, 1–5).

ARISTOTLE (384–322 B.C.) Greek philosopher, a forefather of university and public libraries; he collected books, notes, scientific records, and laboratory specimens, described them, and presented them as illustrations to his lectures (G. Downey, *Aristotle: Dean of Science*, New York: Watts, 1962, 126–27).

ASSURBANIPAL (668–627 B.C.) Assyrian king, great lover of books and arts ordered re-editing and cataloging the entire literature of his land and founded the greatest library of his time (30,000 tablets in cuneiformic script) at Nineveh (NCCN, v.1, 245).

AVICENNA (IBN SINA), **ABU ALI-AL-HUSSEIN** (980–1037) Arabian physician and scholar, author of numerous books; after receiving a large library as a gift from a prince, he personally organized, classified, and described the books on various subjects and in many languages (GLE, v.7, n.p.)

BAQUERIZO MORENO, ALFREDO (1859–1951) Ecuadorian author and statesman, served as president of his country two times (1916, 1931); in 1890 he was director of the Public Library of Guayaquil, his native city (TT, 20).

BAY, JENS CHRISTIAN (1871–1962) American, Danish-born librarian, scholar, and author. As chief of the John Crerar Library, Chicago, he assembled a great collection of autographs and developed a large collection of Danish literature, folklore, and civilization. He extensively wrote and contributed to the fields of literature, science, and bibliography (Lawrence S. Thompson, "Jens Christian Bay, Bibliologist," in *Libri*, 12, no. 4, 1963, 320–330).

BENEDICT OF NURSIA, SAINT (480?–543?) Italian monk, patron saint of the medieval manuscript and godfather of the Catholic monastic libraries: started his achievements with the library of the Abbey of Montecasino (D, 491).

BERLIOZ, LOUIS HECTOR (1803–1869) French romantic composer, worked as assistant librarian (1838–1852) and later as librarian (1852–1869) at the Paris Conservatory (W.J. Turner, *Berloiz: The Man and His Time*, New York: Vienna House, 1934, 214).

BIANU, ION (1888–1935) Romanian professor, specialized in philology, organized the library of the Romanian Academy, and later served as its director for over thirty years; he also was the only librarian ever to become member of the academy (*Dicţionar Enciclopedic Român*, Bucureşti, Editura Politícă, 1966, v.1, 351).

BILLINGS, JOHN SHAW (1838–1913) American librarian, physician, teacher, and author. Developed the Medical Library of the U.S. Surgeon General, compiled an index to medical literature (over 400,000 titles), and later served as first director of the New York Public Library. Was American Library Association president (1902–1903), wrote on medical subjects, and published a dictionary of catalogs and indexes (Harry Lydenberg, *John Shaw Billings, Creator of the National Medical Library and its Catalogs, First Director of the New York Public Library*, Chicago: American Library Association, 1924).

BISHOP, WILLIAM WARNER (1871–1955) American librarian, teacher, and author. Worked for the Library of Congress (reading room, book selection, interlibrary loans), and later as library chief at the University of Michigan, Ann Arbor, for over 25 years. Used his language skills for international library connections, and wrote on several topics: practical librarianship, cataloging, library specialization, Carnegie libraries. Was American Library Association president (1918–1919) (Rudolph H. Gjelsmess, "William Warner Bishop, 1871–1955," in *Libri*, 6 (1955), 3–5).

BODLEY, SIR THOMAS (1545–1613) British librarian, traveler, philanthropist, and author. He developed the Bodleyan Library at Oxford University, endowing it with rare books and manuscripts. Took interest in all aspects of library work, including shelving and furniture, and personally directed the librarian's daily activities (even prohibited the librarian from being married). Published an autobiography and statutes of the Oxford Public Library (L.F. Richardson, "Illustrious Librarian," in *Librarian and Book World*, 34 (March 1945), 100–101).

BOGLE, SARAH C.N. (1870–1932) American librarian, teacher, and author. Worked as a librarian for the Queens Borough Public Library (New York City), for the Carnegie Library in Pittsburgh for over 10 years, and as Assistant Secretary of the American Library Association for another 10 years. She wrote on library work with children, on education for school librarians, and on recruiting and training black librarians (Harrison W. Craver, "Sarah C.N. Bogle: An Appreciation," in *ALA Bulletin* (August 1932), 488–490).

BOORSTIN, DANIEL (b. 1914) American historian, scholar, lawyer, author, editor of numerous publications, holder of several prizes, was appointed Librarian of Congress by President Gerald Ford in 1975 and retired in the summer of 1987 (WWA, 1984–1985, v.1, 335).

BORGES, JORGE LUIS (1899–1986) Argentinian author, Nobel prize winner in literature, in 1938 worked as a public librarian in Buenos Aires, was fired under Juan Perón's regime, and later was appointed director of the Biblioteca Nacional (1955) of his native country (DES, v.4, 255).

BOSTWICK, ARTHUR ELMORE (1860–1942) American multilingual librarian, scholar, and author. Started as director of circulation at the New York Public Library, later became library chief and developed several branches and programs for apprentices, pioneered children's collections, as well as operating traveling libraries. Was American Library Association president (1907–1908), wrote on love of books, and published *The American Public Library*, a standard volume reissued in several editions, as well as other books related to librarianship (Joseph A. Boromé, "Arthur A. Bostwick," in *Dictionary of American Biography*, Supplement 3, 1941, 90–91).

BOWKER, RICHARD ROGERS (1848–1933) American library administrator, journalist, businessman, publisher, and author. Was one of the American Library Association cofounders (1876), manager of *Library Journal*, and editor of *Publishers Weekly* for over 50 years. Helped organizing and improving American and foreign libraries (Vatican, League of Nations), and wrote numerous articles on librarianship for library journals ("Richard R. Bowker, 1848–1933," in Publishers Weekly, vol. 124, November 18, 1933, 1764–1768)

BRAINE, JOHN GERARD (b. 1922) English author, worked as an assistant librarian (1940–1951) at the Bingley Public Library, branch librarian (1954–1956) at the Northumberland County Library, and branch librarian (1956–1957) at the West Riding Branch of the Yorks County Library (WW 1984–1985, 257).

BRAY, THOMAS (1656–1730) British librarian, clergyman, and author. Established parochial libraries in England, Wales, and America (Maryland, Boston, New York, Pennsylvania, and New Jersey). Published several books regarding the nature and set-up of parochial libraries, lending libraries to clergy and lay subscribers, as well as library classification (William D. Houlette, "Parish Libraries and the Work of Reverend Thomas Bray," in *Library Quarterly*, 4, 1934, 588–609).

BRETT, WILLIAM HOWARD (1846–1918) American librarian, teacher, and author. As director of the Cleveland Public Library he reorganized it, cataloged it according to Dewey classification, issued a cumulative index to articles (later taken over by the *Reader's Guide* of the Wilson Company), served as one of the first children's librarians, and advocated free access to library shelves. He was American Library president (1896–1897), Dean of Library School at Western Reserve University, and published in library journals (P.J. Conmy, "William Howard Brett: Apostle of Good Faith in Public Librarianship," in *American Libraries* 6, September 1975, 465).

BRITTON, THOMAS (1654–1714) English musical impresario for 36 years, charcoal seller, and great book collector and bibliographer: was one of the organizers of the Harleian Library (F. Muir, *Irreverent and Thoroughly Incomplete Social History of Almost Everything*, New York: Stein and Day, 1967, 23).

BROWN, JAMES DUFF (1862–1914) British librarian and author. He developed the Mitchell Library in Glasgow, where he worked as a librarian for over 10 years. Later worked in several branches in London, advocated free access to library shelves, published his own professional journal, *The Library World*, as well as a manual of library economy and books on library classification, shelving, and music library (Ernest A. Savage, "James Duff Brown after Fifty Years," in *Library Review*, 135, 1960, 489–495).

BUDÉ GUILLAUME (1467–1540) French linguist, historian, lawyer and humanist, in 1532 was in charge of the Royal Library at Fontainbleau, near Paris (GLE, v.2, n.p.).

CAIN, JULIEN (1887–1974) French librarian and author. Was general manager of the Bibliotheque Nationale (Paris) for over 30 years, and director of all French libraries after World War II. He contributed to the organization of French libraries on modern principles, and extensively published on various subjects: French literature, history of the French National Library, book publishing, and others (J. Le Thève, "Julien Cain, 1887–1974," in *Libri*, 25, September 1975, 165–167).

CALCAGNINUS (CALCAGNINI), COELIUS (CELIO) (1479–1541) Italian scholar and humanist, collected a large library and spent all his life reading in the library of Ferrara; he donated his books to the library and asked to be buried in the library of his native city; his wish was fulfilled and a plaque witnesses this event to our day (*Buch über Buch*, Bern: Benteli Verlag, 1972, n.p.).

CAREY, MIRIAM ELIZA (1858–1937) American librarian, teacher, and author. Developed prison libraries, libraries in mental wards, in sanatoria, in schools for delinquents, in hospitals for the insane, in schools for the blind, the deaf and feeble-minded, in schools for crippled children. She served as supervisor of institutional librarianship at Minnesota Board of Control, and published on library service in state institutions (Perrie Jones, "Pioneer in Institution Libraries," in *Library Journal*, 62, February 1, 1937, 116–117).

CARNEGIE, ANDREW (1835–1919) American industrialist and great philanthropist, honorary member of the American Library Association, known as "patron saint of libraries," gave $56,162,662 for the establishment of 2,509 public libraries named after the benefactor, in English-speaking countries; 1,679 of these libraries are in the United States (AL, April 1981, 184).

CASANOVA-DE SEINGALT, GIOVANNI GIACOMO (1725–1798) Italian adventurer, author, gambler and spy, served as librarian, starting 1785, for 13 years at the castle of Count Waldstein in Bohemia, where he wrote his famous memoirs to prevent him "from going mad or dying of grief" (NCCN, v.1, 843).

CELAKOVSKY, FRANTISEK L. (1799–1852) Czech professor, specialized in Slavic literature and folklore, poet and scholar, worked as a librarian (1802–1836) at the private library of Count Ferdinand Kinsky in Prague (TT, 23).

CELTES (PICKEL), **CONRADUS** (KONRAD) **PROTUCIUS** (1459–1508) German humanist, teacher and author, lectured at various universities, worked as court librarian (1497–1508) under Emperor Maximilian I and organized the court library in Vienna (CE, 369).

CHARLES I (CHARLEMAGNE) **THE GREAT** (742–814) French king and emperor, established a rich library at his palace at Aachen, developing it into a cultural center for scholars from various countries; he was also the founder of many schools for children and required that each school have its scriptorium, a room for copying books (D, 495).

CHAZANOWITZ, JOSEPH (1844–1919) Jewish physician from Lithuania who died in poverty, but spent all his money on books, donated his personal, very large, and valuable collection of books (1895) to the Jerusalem University; it became the nucleus of the Hebrew University Library (SJE, 1203).

COLBERT, JEAN-BAPTISTE (1619–1683) French statesman, chief of government under Louis XIV of France, architect, and holder of various ministerial portfolios, also the supervisor of the Royal Library and substantially increased the developments of its collections (GLE, v.3, n.p.)

COLLIJN, ISAC GUSTAV ALFRED (1875–1949) Swedish scholar, member of the Swedish Academy of Antiquities and History; starting 1896 he worked as a librarian at the University of Upsala and later became director (1916–1940) of the Royal Library in Stockholm (KES, 280).

CONSTANTINE THE AFRICAN (1020–1087) Catholic traveler and translator, collected works from Egypt, Persia, Chaldea, and India for over forty years and translated them into Latin; he assembled a collection of over 6,500 books and donated them to the Monastery of Montecasino, Italy (D, 492).

CORTES CASTRO, LEON (1882–1946) Guatemalan politician, member of several cabinets, president of his country (1936–1940), and author of several reforms, worked as director of the National Archives between 1911 and 1914 (TT, 23).

COSTER, CHARLES THEODORE HENRI DE (1827–1879) Belgian author and folklore collector, publisher, worked for a short period (about 1850) at the National Archives in Brussels (TT, 23).

COTTON DE HOUSSAYES, JEAN-BAPTISTE (1727–1783) French librarian and author. Was head librarian at the Sorbonne University, and wrote about the qualities and duties of librarians. In his opinion, the librarian should be knowledgeable in arts, literature, and sciences; know bibliography and each book and its place in the library, welcome and receive visitors with politeness, and express himself gracefully ("Jean Baptiste Cotton de Houssayes," in *Dictionnaire de Biographie Francaise*. Paris: Letouzet et Ane, 1961, vol. 9, 854–855).

CRUNDEN, FREDERICK MORGAN (1847–1911) American, English-born librarian and author. Was director of the St. Louis Public Library, and strived to make it a model for the country. Developed good relations between schools and libraries; was first president of the Missouri Library Association and American Library Association president (1889–1890). Wrote on the value of the public library to the community and the functions of public library trustees (Bertha Doane, "Frederick Morgan Crunden, Library Statesman," in *Wilson Library Bulletin*, 29, February 1955, 446–449).

CUTTER, CHARLES AMMI (1837–1907) American librarian and author. Worked for the Harvard University Library, Boston Atheneum, and Forbes Library (Northhampton, MA) in the capacity of cataloger and head librarian. He recataloged library collections with tens of thousands of entries, expanding classification rules of cataloging, and wrote on this subject. Was American Library president (1887–1888) and a supporter of Melvil Dewey (William Parker Cutter, *Charles Ammi Cutter*, Chicago: American Library Association, 1931).

DAHL, SVEND (1887–1963) Danish author on book history and library development, served as librarian (1925–1943) at the University of Copenhagen and later director (1943–1952) of Royal Library in the same city (KES, 165).

DANA, JOHN COTTON (1856–1929) American librarian, lawyer, and author. Served as head of the Denver Public School and its library, also worked as librarian in Springfield, MA and Newark, NJ for 30 years. He was an excellent speaker, advocated open shelves in the library, popularized library holdings through local publications, and published books on various subjects: ancient classics, literature of libraries, library primers, and others. Was American Library Association president (1895–1896) (Chalmers Hadley, *John Cotton Dana: A Sketch*, Chicago: American Library Association, 1943).

DE LOS SANTOS, CRISTOBAL EPIFANIO (1871–1928) Philippino journalist, historian, lawyer and statesman, worked as librarian (1925–1928) at the Philippine Library and Museum in Manila (TT, 22).

DELISLE, LÉOPOLD VICTOR (1824–1910) French librarian and author. Was director of the Bibliothèque Nationale for over 30 years, developed collections of new books, set up new rules for cataloging, classification of manuscripts, and started printing catalogs of books. He edited and published many volumes of manuscripts, as well as works on Latin literature and the Middle Ages (Eugène Gabriel Ledos, ''M. Léopold Delisle et la Bibliothèque Nationale,'' in *Revue des Bibliotheques*, 34, 1927, 116–151).

DEWEY, MELVIL (1851–1931) American librarian, teacher, and author. Compiled the world-famous Dewey Decimal Classification System, worked as librarian for Amherst (MA), at the library of Columbia College of New York; served as secretary of the Board of Regents of the University of the State of New York, conducted the Library Bureau at Lake Placid, New York for over 25 years, and started the Library School at Columbia University. He was twice American Library Association president (1890–1891; 1892–1893), and founded the *American Library Journal* (Grosvenor Dawe, *Melvil Dewey: Seer, Inspirer, Doer, 1851–1931*, New York: Lake Placid Club, 1931).

DOES (DOUSA), **JAN** (JANUS) **VAN DER** (1545–1604) Dutch statesman, was the curator of Leyden University and later (1575–1604) served as its first librarian (NCCN, v.1, 1326).

DOWNS, ROBERT BINGHAM (1903–1991) American librarian, teacher, and author. Was director of the university library at Illinois, Urbana, and dean of the Graduate School of Library Science at the same university. He also worked as library consultant for foreign governments, and published several books and articles on famous ancient, modern, and American books, books that changed the world, American library resources, and others. Was American Library Association president (1952–1953) ("Robert Bingham Downs," in *Who's Who in America, 1974–75.* Chicago: Marquis Who's Who, 1975).

DZIATKO, CARL (1842–1903) German librarian, scholar, and author. Served as chief librarian at the universities of Freiburg, Breslau, and Göttingen, taught library science, and established rules of cataloging. Was an expert on incunabula, on the Gutenberg Bible, and wrote on the status of German research libraries. He founded the Association of German Library Workers (1887) and published commentaries on ancient classics (Paul Shenke, "Karl Dziatko," in *Zentralblatt für Bibliothekswesen*, 20, 1903, 133–137).

EAMES, WILBERFORCE (1855–1937) American self-educated librarian, scholar, and bibliophile. Worked for the New York Public Library, had a facility with foreign languages (including Sanskrit, Sumerian, Chinese, Japanese), wrote extensively on books related to America, on the Alonguin language, early New England catechisms, and others (Harry M. Lydenberg, "Wilberforce Eames," in *Library Journal*, vol. 63 (January 1, 1938), pp. 22–23).

EBERT, FRIEDRICH ADOLPH (1791–1834) German librarian and author. Worked in the library of the King of Saxony (Dresden), and in the library of the Duke of Brunswick. Wrote extensively on education for the library profession and library service, and compiled important bibliographies. He advocated librarians' independence and considered that any library item, including manuscripts, should be available to patrons (E. M. Goldschmidt, "Pioneer Professional: F. A. Ebert," in *Library Quarterly*, 40, April 1970, 223–35).

EDWARDS, EDWARD (1812–1886) British self-educated librarian and author. Worked for the British Museum, the Manchester Public Library, and Oxford University. Was an ardent supporter of municipal library development, taught library staff, and published several books and articles on public libraries, lives of the founders of the British Museum, works on library classification, libraries and their founders from ancient times until the 1950s (W. A. Munford, *Edward Edwards, 1812–1886, Portrait of a Librarian*, London: Library Association, 1963).

EHRLE, FRANCISCO (FRANZ), **CARDINAL** (1845–1934) German librarian, Jesuit priest, historian, and author. Worked as chief administrator of the Vatican Library for over 20 years, and archivist for the Roman Catholic Church.

He studied the operations of large libraries in Germany and Austria, wrote extensively on library subjects in Italian, German, and Latin languages, as well as on manuscript cataloging. (E. Heyse Dummer, ''Cardinal Franz Ehrle: In Commemoration of a Double Anniversary,'' in *Library Quarterly*, 16, 1946, 335–340).

ELMENDORF, THERESA HUBBELL [WEST] (1855–1932) American librarian and author. Worked as deputy assistant of the Milwaukee Public Library, and later as the first woman City Librarian of Denver, and in the same capacity in Buffalo, New York, for over 20 years. She also was the first woman president of the American Library Association (1911–1912), and of the New York Library Association; she wrote articles for library journals and produced a valuable readers' list on poetry and poets (F. W. Faxon, ''Theresa West Elmendorf,'' in *Bulletin of Bibliography*, 14, May/August 1931, 93–94).

EMINESCU, MIHAIL (1850–1889) Romanian prominent poet, his works were translated in 31 foreign languages; he worked as a librarian (1874–1876) at the University of Iaşi (Yassy) Library and later (1884–1886) as its director (A. Pop, *Contribuţii Documentare la Biografia lui Mihai Eminescu*, Bucureşti: Editura Academiei R.S.R., 1969, 137–63).

ENGELS, FRIEDRICH (1820–1895) German socialist, closest friend and associate of Karl Marx, industrialist and author, worked for a short time as librarian at the Schiller-Anstalt Library in his native country (TT, 20).

ERATOSTHENUS (276–195 B.C.) Greek geographer, developed a technique of measuring the earth, which is still in use; he served as head librarian of the Library of Alexandria, one of the greatest libraries in the world. (D, 95).

ESDALE, ARUNDEL JAMES KENNEDY (1880–1956) British librarian, teacher, and author. Worked for the British Museum for about 15 years, taught bibliography at the School of Librarianship at University College, London, at Cambridge University, and at Birmingham University. Was president of the British Library Association during World War II years, published profusely on libraries and English literature subjects, a students' manual of bibliography, sources of English literature, famous libraries of England, and history of the British Museum (H. M. Cashmore et al. ''Arundell Esdale, 1880–1956,'' in *Library Association Record*, 58, 1956, 321–325).

ESPEJO, FRANCIS JAVIER EUGENIO DE SANTA CRUZ (1747–1795) Ecuadorian physician and author, fighter for his country's independence; he was director of the Quito Library and organized it as a public library (DES, v.9, 116).

EVANS, LUTHER HARRIS (1902–1981) American librarian, teacher, and author. Was Librarian of Congress after World War II, and director of the United States National Commission to UNESCO. He wrote extensively on federal libraries, copyright, automation, international library cooperation, library education, and several other subjects (Jens C. Bay, "Charles Evans, 1850–1935," in *ALA Bulletin*, 29, March 1935, 163–164).

FAIRCHILD, MARY SALOME CUTLER (1855–1921) American librarian, teacher, and author. Served as Melvil Dewey's vice director at the New York State Library School (Albany) and as librarian of the New York State Library for the Blind. Selected for the library profession only intellectually strong and highly promising young people, and required a college degree for admission to library school. She compiled a bibliography of cataloging rules, wrote on modern library movement in America, and pioneered Sunday opening of libraries (Joseph A. Borome, "Mary Salome (Cutler) Fairchild," in *Notable American Women, 1607–1950*, vol. 1, Cambridge, Mass: Belknap Press, 1971, 593–594.

FIGUEROA, FRANCISCO ACUÑA DE (1790–1862) Uruguayan poet, author of his country's national anthem and of the Paraguayan anthem, director (1840) of the Library and Museum of Montevideo (NCCN, v. 2, 1554).

FLETCHER, WILLIAM ISAAC (1844–1917) American librarian, teacher, and author. Worked for the Boston Atheneum, and Amherst College Library, where he conducted a summer school for librarianship. He modernized his library, and was one of the founders of the American Library Association (1876), and its president (1891–1892). He cooperated with W.F. Poole on the indexing of periodical articles, later known as *Reader's Guide to Periodical Literature*, and edited the *Literary Index* (George S. Bobinski, "William Isaac Fletcher, an Early American Library Leader," in *Journal of Library History*, 5, April 1970, 101–118).

FLEXNER, JENNIE MAAS (1882–1944) American librarian, teacher, and author. Worked as head of circulation for the Louisville Public Library and later for the New York Public Library. Wrote extensively on book circulation functions, charging systems, publicity, importance of interview between librarian and reader, role and functions of readers' advisory service, assistance to immigrant refugee readers, and adult education (Sidney Ditzion, "Jennie M. Flexner," in *Dictionary of American Biography*, Supplement 1941–1945, 280–281).

FOSS, SAM WALTER (1858–1911) American poet and fiction author, served as librarian at Somerville, Massachusetts Branch starting 1898 until the end of his life, and constantly listed himself as librarian and author (WWA, 1910–1911, 671).

FOSTER, WILLIAM EATON (1851–1930) American librarian and author. Worked at the Boston Public Library and later as director of the Providence (Rhode Island) Public Library for over 50 years. He developed a children's department of the library, a visible information desk, specialized collections of art, music, architecture, and foreign books. Also collections on slavery, jewelry, printing, business. He was a founding member of the American Library Association (1876), published monthly reference lists, wrote on history and library topics (H.L. Koopman, "William Eaton Foster: An Appreciation," in *Library Journal*, 55, 1930, 282–283).

FRANKLIN, BENJAMIN (1706–1790) American statesman, author, publisher, inventor and scholar, in 1731 founded the Philadelphia Library Company, the first subscription library in America; he also possessed a very valuable personal library, considered the largest in America in his time (C. Van Doren, *Benjamin Franklin*, New York: Viking, 1938, 104–5, 750, 761).

GARNETT, RICHARD (1835–1906) British multilingual librarian, and author. He worked for the British Museum for several decades, printed the catalogs of the British Museum, wrote on library classification, librarianship, bibliography, and contributed to *Encyclopedia Britannica* and British National Bibliography. Also published poetry, translations of Greek classics, lists of noted British literary figures (Carolyn G. Heilbrun, "Richard Garnett," in his *Garnett Family*. London: Allen & Unwin, 1961, 202–205).

GIRARD (PÈRE GREGOIRE), **JEAN-BAPTISTE** (1765–1850) Swiss Franciscan priest and educator, served as archivist (1799–1803) of the Ministry of Church and Science in Bern (TT, 21).

GOETHE, JOHANN WOLFGANG VON (1749–1832) German poet, dramatist, statesman and scientist, supervisor (1797–1832) of the duke Karl August's library in Weimar and also supervisor (1817–1832) of the Jena University Library (TT, 21).

GREEN, SAMUEL SWEET (1837–1918) American librarian, preacher and author. Worked as director of the Worcester, MA, Public Library, pioneered library opening on Sundays, stressed the importance of courtesy to library patrons, and that no inquirer should be left without an answer in the library. Was American Library Association president (1891–1892), and president of the World Congress of Librarians in Chicago (1893). Wrote on public libraries and history topics, antiquities, sensational fiction in libraries, and other subjects (Frederick W. Ashley, "Samuel S. Green," in *Dictionary of American Biography*, vol. 4, 557–558).

GREENWOOD, THOMAS (1851–1908) British librarian and author, considered by some "the apostle on English library movement." Worked as branch librarian at the Sheffield Public Library, later became a publisher, journalist, and businessman. Wrote on the importance of public libraries, advocated the need of a public library in each town, published library yearbooks, and was active in the British Library Association (Sidney Horrocks, "Thomas Greenwood and His Library," in *Manchester Review*, 8, Spring 1959, 269–277).

GRILLPARZER, FRANZ (1791–1872) Austrian poet and dramatist; after completion of law studies he worked as an archival clerk (1813) at the Ministry of Finance in Vienna and later became director (1832–1856) of the same archives (GB, v.5, 24).

GRIMM, JACOB LUDWIG KARL (1785–1863) German author, linguist and professor, librarian (1808) of Jerome Bonaparte, king of Westfalia; he later served as librarian (1816–1829) of the Electoral Library in Kassel and after that worked as librarian (1830–1837) at the Göttingen University (NCCN, v.2, 1840).

GRIMM, WILHELM KARL (1786–1859) German author, linguist, and professor, brother of Jacob Grimm, co-author and close associate of the former, served as librarian at the Göttingen University (NCCN, v. 2, 1840).

HAINES, HELEN ELIZABETH (1872–1961) American librarian, teacher, and author. She started on the staff of *Library Journal*, and later edited the *Annual Library Index;* taught acquisition in library schools, led training classes in public libraries, wrote articles for library journals, and published book reviews. She was thoroughly acquainted with books in several fields (biography, history, travel, nature, sociology, religion, fiction) and published a valuable reference title called *Living with Books*. She advocated intellectual freedom (Everett T. Moore, "The Intellectual Freedom Saga in California: The Experience of Four Decades," in *California Librarian*, 35, 1974, 49–57).

HALLER, ALBRECHT VON (1708–1777) Swiss physician, anatomist, botanist, poet and professor; he worked as city physician and chief librarian (1735) of the Municipal Library of Zurich (NCCN, v.2, 1892).

HANDLIN, OSCAR (b. 1915) American historian and educator, specialized in immigration dynamics, holder of several prizes for his books; he served as trustee (1973) of the New York Public Library and starting 1979 is director of the Harvard University Library (WWA, 1984–1985, v.1, 1369).

HANSON, JAMES CHRISTIAN (1860–1945) American, Norwegian-born multilingual librarian, teacher, and author. Served as cataloger at the Newberry Library in Chicago, chief cataloger at the Library of Congress, and taught at the Graduate Schools of Librarianship at Chicago, Columbia, and Michigan universities. He compiled his own lists of classification and cataloging, rejecting Dewey's decimal system. He produced a dictionary catalog on cards (3" x 5"), offering some cards for sale or exchange, and contributed to several library journals (Jens Christian Bay, "James Christian Meinich Hanson," in *Library Quarterly*, 14, January 1944, 57–59).

HARNACK, ADOLF VON (1851–1930) German theologian and church historian, prolific author, director (1905–1921) of the Prussian State Library (GB, v.5, 188).

HARVARD, JOHN (1607–1638) American teacher and assistant pastor; he donated half of his estate and over 300 books from his own collection to establish a college and college library, later named after the benefactor (CE, 915).

HERRICK, MARGARET BUCK (n.d.) American executive director of the Academy of Motion Picture Arts and Sciences; she started her career as a children's librarian (1928) in Spokane, Illinois, later was director of the city library (1929–1931), and then librarian (1931–1943) of the Academy; served as executive director (1943–1970) and since 1971 as director emeritus (WWA, 1977–1981, v.7, 269).

HEWINS, CAROLINE MARIA (1846–1926) American librarian and author. Served as head librarian of the Hartford (CT) Public Library for over 50 years; she opened a children's library, coached children actors, participated in children's parades and festivals. She advocated cooperation between libraries and schools, served on the ALA Council, and was American Library Association vice president (1891–1892). She contributed to library journals and published guiding books for children, young readers, and parents (Jennie D. Lindquist, "Caroline M. Hewins and Books for Children," in *Horn Book*, 29, February 1953, 13–27).

HOELDERLIN, JOHANN CHRISTIAN FRIEDRICH (1770–1843) German poet, court librarian (1804–1806) for the count of Hessen-Homburg (TT, 21).

HOOKWAY, HARRY THURSTON (b. 1921) English scientist, held various positions in industry and government institutions and since 1973 serves as deputy chairman and chief executive of the British Library (formerly British Museum) Board (WW, 1984–1985, 1102).

HOOVER, J. EDGAR (1895–1972) lawyer, FBI director for almost five decades, worked as an indexer (1913–1917) in the cataloging division of the Library of Congress while completing his law studies taking evening courses (O.

Demaris, *Oral Biography of J. Edgar Hoover*, New York: Harper and Row, 1975, 4).

HUME, DAVID (1711–1776) English philosopher, historian, and economist, librarian (1752–1757) at the library of the Faculty of Advocates in Edinburgh (NCCN, v.2, 2079).

HUNYADI (CORVIN), **MATYAS** (1443–1490) Hungarian king, great philanthropist and protector of arts, established the first Hungarian printing house (1473), collected over 2,000 rare books and manuscripts, presently part of the world famous Corviniana collection at the National Library in Budapest (KES, 340).

JAST, LOUIS STANLEY (1868–1944) British librarian, teacher, and author. Worked for the Peterborough and Croyden libraries, and as chief librarian of the Manchester Public Library. Taught librarianship at several schools, founded the periodical *Library World*, was a prolific writer, and contributed articles to several periodicals; also published books on library topics, community, Indian history, poetry and plays, as well as books for children (W.G. Fry and W.A. Munford, *Louis Stanley Just: A Biographical Sketch*, London: Library Association, 1966).

JEFFERSON, THOMAS (1743–1826) American president, cataloged and classified materials for the University of Virginia; his own collection, consisting of more than 10,000 books assembled during fifty years, was sold to the U.S. Congress and became the nucleus of the Library of Congress (S. Padover, *Jefferson Profile*, New York: John Day, 1956, 244–45).

JENNINGS, JUDSON TOLL (1872–1948) American librarian and author. Worked as director of the Seattle Public Library for over 35 years. Developed the library into a large metropolitan library, inspired enthusiasm in library staff, wrote that librarianship is not exclusively a woman's job; published articles and books on library's role in education, on children and adult education; and served as the American Library Association president (1924–1925) ("Judson Toll Jennings," in *Library Journal*, 73, May 1, 1948, 729).

JEWETT, CHARLES COFFIN (1816–1868) American librarian and author. Worked as librarian for Brown University and the Smithsonian Institution, and later as the superintendent of the Boston Public Library. He advocated nationwide centralized cataloging, established the dictionary arrangement of catalogs, cataloging rules, and helped in improving U.S. copyright procedures. Also introduced easy access to library books, and published on the history of Brown University, various aspects of cataloging rules, and public libraries in the United

States (Joseph A. Borome, *Charles Coffin Jewett*, Chicago: American Library Association, 1951).

JÖCHER, CHRISTIAN GOTTLIEB (1694–1758) German scholar, taught philosophy and history at the Leipzig University, became librarian (1742) of his university, and compiled a dictionary with bibliographic information on 60,000 scientists from various countries (KES, 226).

JOHANAN BEN ZAKKAI (?–80 A.D.), Jewish rabbi, leader of the Pharisees, contributor to Jewish religious rules, founded in 70 A.D. the Jabneh Academy and special library, gathering a group of teachers and scholars committed to the collection, preservation, publication, and dissemination of Jewish heritage (LOC, 15).

KALLAW, TEODORO M. (1884–1940) Philippino lawyer and professor, worked as a librarian (1916–1917) at the Philippine Library and Museum in Manila and once again (1929–1940) until the end of his life (TT, 21).

KANT, IMMANUEL (1724–1804) German philosopher, author of numerous books, worked as assistant librarian (1766–1772) at the Königsberg Castle library (NCCN, v.2, 2245).

KOPCZYŃSKI, ONUFRY (1735–1817) Polish teacher, scholar, author, linguist, member of a commission of education and its librarian; starting in 1773 he cataloged over 200,000 books (*Encyklopedia Wiedzy o Książce*, Wraclaw: Zaklad Me Ossolińskich, 1971, 1202).

KOPITAR, BARTOLOMEJ (JERNEY) (1780–1844) Slovenian linguist, teacher, specialized in Slavic literatures, author of the first Slovenian grammar; after moving to Vienna (1810) he served as censor of Slovenian books and as librarian at the emperor's court (*Ėnfsiklopedicheskiĭ Slovar' Granat*, Moskva: A. & I. Granat, 1913, v.25, 159).

KÖRÖSI, CSOMA SÁNDOR (1784–1842) Hungarian traveler, linguist, traveled to Asia, resided in Tibet, worked as assistant librarian (1831–1841) for the Asiatis Society of Bengal in Calcutta (E. Baktay, *Körösi Csoma Sándor*, Budapest: Gondolat, 1963, 225).

KROEGER, ALICE BERTHA (1864–1909) American librarian, teacher, and author. Served as director of the Drexel Institute of Technology (Philadelphia), and also as director of the institute's library school. She lectured on bibliography in the state of Pennsylvania, selected titles, and produced the first *Guide to the Study and Use of Reference Books*, a volume which became a standard reference tool for library students, teachers, and librarians. The guide was later updated by Constance Winchell, Isadore Mudge, Eugene Sheehy, and Robert Baley (10th edition) (Harriet D. MacPherson, "Alice B. Kroeger," in *Notable American Women*, vol. 2, Cambridge, Mass.: Belknap Press, 1975, 348–349).

KRUPSKAĨA (UL'ĨANOVA), **NADEZHDA KONSTANTINOVNA** (1869–1939) Russian revolutionary, wife of V.I. Lenin, cultural activist and doctor in pedagogical sciences, occupied various government positions related to education, founded the Soviet system of library organization, wrote and lectured extensively on the role of libraries and readers in the socialist society, with special stress on book selection and budget utilization (KES, 294).

KRYLOV, IVAN ANDREEVICH (1769–1844) Russian author, journalist, playwright and poet, noted for his fables, worked as assistant librarian (1812–1841) at the Imperial Library in Saint Petersburg (NCCN, v.2, 2337).

LANE, WILLIAM COOLIDGE (1859–1931) American librarian and author. Was in charge of cataloging at Harvard College, and director of the Boston Atheneum. Served as American Library Association president (1898–1899) and wrote on Harvard's library collections, on special collections in American libraries, and historical and theological topics. He also compiled specialized catalogs (W.S. Merrill, "William Coolidge Lane, 1859–1931," in *Libraries*, 36, 1931, 155–157).

LARNED, JOSEPHUS NELSON (1836–1913) American self-educated librarian, journalist, poet, essayist, and historian. Was director of the Buffalo, New York, Young Men's Association library for over a decade, reorganizing and modernizing its collection. He wrote on reference books, American literary history; published text-books for high school students, biographies, and others. Was American Library Association president (1893–1894), and also published poems (B. Young, "Josephus Larned and the Public Movement," in *Journal of Library History*, 10, October 1975, 323–340).

LARRAÑAGA, DAMASO ANTONIO (1771–1849) Uruguayan scholar, fighter for independence of Argentina, public librarian (1814) in Buenos Aires; he donated many personal books to the library, influenced the government to establish the Buenos Aires Public Library, and gave the inaugural speech (EUI, v.29, 879).

LEGLER, HENRY EDWARD (1861–1917) American, Swiss-born librarian, journalist, and author. Worked as secretary of the Wisconsin Free Library Commission, on American Library Association's Publication Board, and as director of the Chicago Public Library. He increased traveling library collections, developed a music department with sections for operas, musical instruments, as well as classroom libraries in city schools. He wrote on various subjects (American literature, history, biography, education, library topics), served as American Library Association president (1912–1913), and also published poems (Carl B. Roden, "Henry Edward Legler," in *Bulletin of Bibliography*, 14, 1932, 21–22).

LEIBNITZ (LEIBNIZ), **GOTTFRIED WILHELM** (1646–1716) German philosopher, mathematician, physicist, lawyer, and author, worked as librarian (1676–1690) at the Ducal Library in Hannover and later as librarian (1690–1716) at the Herzog August Library in Wolfenbüttel, where he cataloged 30,000 books (GB, v.7. 74).

LESSING, GOTTHOLD EPHRAIM (1729–1781) German dramatist and theater critic, worked as librarian (1770–1781) at the Herzog August Library in Wolfenbüttel (CE, 1206).

LI, DAZHAO (LI TA-CHAO) (1889–1927) Chinese professor of economics, essayist, and founder of the Chinese Communist Party, was director of the Peking University Library and helped Mao Zedong acquire a position as library assistant in that library (R. Payne, *Mao Tse-Tung*, Shanhai: Ci Shu Chu Ban She, 1969, 71).

LOBACHEVSKIĬ, NIKOLAĬ IVANOVICH (1793–1856) Russian mathematician and university professor, reorganized the Kazan University Library, bought new books, and later (1825–1835) served as library director (*Bol'shai̇a Sovetskai̇a Ėnt͡siklopedii̇a*, Moskva: Sovetskai̇a Ėnt͡siklopedii̇a 1973, v.14, 586).

LOCKE, GEORGE HERBERT (1870–1937) Canadian librarian, teacher, and author. Worked as director of the Toronto Public Library for three decades, lectured on the history of education at Harvard and Chicago universities, surveyed the condition of Canadian libraries, visiting all provinces, and made recommendations for upgrading the level of these libraries. Served as American Library Association president (1926–1927), and wrote on library and English history topics (M.W. Wallace, "George Herbert Locke, 1870–1937," in *Ontario Library Review*, 21, May 1937, 59–60).

LOMONOSOV, MIKHAIL VASIL'EVICH (1711–1765) Russian encyclopedist, scholar, linguist, poet, and author, university professor, starting 1735 collected and organized a huge personal library on various subjects and in many languages: it passed through several private hands and ultimately was acquired by the Helsinki University Library (KES, 326).

LONGFELLOW, HENRY WADSWORTH (1807–1882) American poet and professor of modern languages, worked as a librarian (1829–1835) at the Bowdoin College, Brunswick, Maine (*Oxford Companion to American Literature*, New York: Oxford University Press, 1956, 423).

LOPES, FERNAÕ (1380–1460) Portuguese historian and father of the Portuguese official historiography, served as the keeper of the Royal Archives (1418–1451) at Torre de Tombo in Lisbon (TT, 23).

LUGONES, LEOPOLDO (1874–1938) Argentinian poet and fiction author, scholar, served as director of the National Library of Teachers in Buenos Aires starting 1930 until the end of his life (GER, v.14, 578).

MAC INNES, HELEN CLARK (1907–1985) American author whose books are almost all best-sellers and some have been made into motion pictures; she served as cataloger (1928) at the Glasgow University Library, England, before coming to the United States (R. McHenry, *Liberty's Women*, Springfield, Mass.: G.C. Merriam, 1980, 263).

MAC LEISH, ARCHIBALD (1892–1982) American poet, lawyer, playwright, holder of Pulitzer prizes, cofounder of UNESCO, worked as Librarian of Congress (1939–1944) as an appointee of President Franklin D. Roosevelt (CE, 1274).

MAI, ANGELO (1782–1851) Italian cardinal, started his career (1813) as secretary of the Ambrosiana Library, Milan, and discovered lost works of Cicero, Homer, and other ancient authors. He served as Vatican Librarian (1819–1838) and later attained the rank of cardinal (NCE, v.9, 79).

MAMUN, ABU-L-ABBAS ABD-ALLAH (786–833) Arab caliph belonging to the Abbasid family, great protector of culture and science, lover of books, founded the House of Wisdom in Baghdad and ordered the translation of Greek books into Arabic; he established a library as the main feature of the cultural institution (LOC, 6).

MAO ZEDONG (TSE-TUNG) (1893–1976) Chinese Communist leader and president of his country, library assistant (1918) at the Beijin (Peking) University Library in the periodicals section; his function was to carry the periodicals to readers' tables, his salary was the same as that of a coolie (AL, November 1976, 628–31).

MARCELLUS II (born MARCELLO CERVINI), **POPE** (1501–1555) Italian cardinal, diplomat, served as Librarian of the Vatican starting 1548 until 1554, when he was elected pope (NCE, v.9, 191).

MARTEL, CHARLES (1860–1945) American, Swiss-born librarian and author. He worked at the Newberry Library in Chicago, and later as chief of the cataloging department at the Library of Congress for over 20 years. He compiled a modern book classification permitting infinite expansion, solved difficult problems in cataloging, continued to print Library of Congress catalog cards, and published studies dealing with cataloging and classification encountered in practice (Harriet Wheeler Pierson, "Charles Martel," in *ALA Cataloging and Classification Yearbook*, 9, 1940, 11–17).

MARX, ALEXANDER (1879–1954) American Jewish historian and professor, immigrated from Germany, taught at the Jewish Theological Seminary in New York and also became librarian; he built up its library to a leading position in America (SJE, 1275).

MAXIMILIAN I (1459–1519) German emperor, great lover of book collections and sponsor of book publishing; at his own expense, he hired the best artists of his time, such as Albrecht Dürer, as book illustrators (KES, 330).

MAZARIN, JULES (1602–1661) French government official, organized one of the greatest libraries of his time (1634), sent agents to various European countries to purchase valuable books; his library with over 45,000 books was opened to the public and later became part of the Bibliothèque Nationale in Paris (KES, 329).

MEDINA, JOSÉ TORIBIO (1852–1930) Chilean publisher and diplomat, scholar, author of numerous books, collected a personal library of over 40,000 valuable books and offered them to his country's Biblioteca Nacional in Santiago; he also published a special bibliography on Spanish American books and book publishing (NCCN, v.2, 2696).

MENENDEZ PELAYO, MARCELINO (1856–1912) Spanish author and historian, member of the Spanish Academy, served as director (1898–1912) of the Biblioteca Nacional in Madrid, reorganized the library on modern principles, visited several European libraries, and even after retirement reorganized his personal library and donated it to the city of Santander (GER, v.15, 541).

METCALF, KEYES DEWIT (1889–1983) American librarian, international consultant, and author. Worked as chief of reference department at the New York Public Library, librarian at Harvard University and later director of this university's libraries for 20 years. Developed Harvard's library staff and collections (from 4 to 6 million volumes), and wrote on planning academic and research library buildings, administrative aspects of libraries, library training. He served as American Library Association president (1941–1942), and traveled on all continents as adviser to various libraries and government agencies (D.C.

Weber, "Keyes D. Metcalf," in *College and Research Libraries*, 37, July 1976, 346).

MICHELET, JULES (1798–1874) French historian and author, state official and professor, was chief (1831–1852) of the history section of the National Archives of France (GLE, v.7, n.p.).

MICKIEWICZ, ADAM (1798–1855) Polish poet and patriot, professor, forced into exile after conflicts with Russian Tsarist authorities, settled in France, served as librarian (1845–1848) at the Bibliotheque d'Arsenal after his suspension as university professor in Paris (GLE, v.4, n.p.).

MILAM, CARL HASTINGS (1908–1963) American library administrator and author. Served as secretary of the Indiana Public Library Commission, director of the Birmingham (AL) Library, secretary of the American Library Association for almost three decades, and director of the United Nations Library after World War II. Was instrumental in the founding of IFLA (International Federation of Library Associations), and developed ties with various foreign libraries. Wrote multiple articles on Latin American cooperation, libraries and adult education, hospital libraries, college library standards, and others (Ralph Munn, "Carl Milam, the Administrator," in *ALA Bulletin*, 4, September 15, 1948, 3–4).

MITCHELL, SYDNEY BANCROFT (1878–1951) American, Canadian-born librarian, teacher, and author. He was director of the School of Library Science at the University of California, and became a creative leader despite several physical handicaps. Was considered one of the most influential advisers on librarianship in the West, wrote extensively on both library topics and horticulture, his favored hobby, and published the history of education for librarianship in California (Lawrence Clark Powell, "Mitchell of California," in *Wilson Library Bulletin*, May 1954, 778–790).

MOORE, ANNE CARROLL (1871–1961) American librarian, teacher, and author. Worked as children's librarian for the New York Public Library for over 35 years, taught librarianship at the Iowa State Library Commission School and the Graduate School of Librarianship at Berkeley, CA, and wrote several children's books. She tended to create a mood for children's reading, publishing numerous book reviews and books on children's books. Her books appeared in several editions (Frances L. Spain, "Tribute to Miss Moore," in *Library Journal*, 86, February 15, 1961, 846–847).

MORENO, MARIANO (1778–1811) Argentinian statesman and fighter for his country's independence, established a school of mathematics, a leading newspaper, and a public library in Buenos Aires (*Gran Dicccionario Enciclopedico Durvan*, Bilbao: Durvan, 1977, v.8, 375).

MUBARAK, SUZANNE (b. 193?) educator and wife of Hosni Mubarak, president of Egypt, reorganized 20 schools on modern principles, each time starting with the school library, and established several public libraries (*New York Times*, 1 October 1985, C9).

MURATORI, LODOVICO ANTONIO (1672–1750) Italian historian and author, founder of the Italian modern historiography, worked as librarian (1694–1700) at the Ambrosiana Library in Milan, and for the rest of his life (1700–1750) he served in the same capacity for the Duke of Modena (NCE, v.10, 81).

NAUDÉ, GABRIEL (1600–1653) French physician, author, and great librarian, organized Cardinal Mazarini's library with over 40,000 volumes and wrote a pioneer treatise on librarianship, insisting on public access to private libraries; he also worked as librarian for Cardinal Barberini of Rome (KES, 376).

NICHOLAS V (born TOMMASO PARENTUCELLI), **POPE** (1398–1455) Italian cardinal, great lover of books, built up a large personal library, including 807 Latin and 353 Greek manuscripts, planned and organized the Medici Library of the Monastery of San Marco in Florence, and the Vatican Library (NCE, v. 10, 443).

NICHOLSON, EDWARD WILLIAMS BYRON (1849–1912) British librarian, scholar, and author. Was librarian at the London Institution, and later worked for the Oxford University library for over 30 years. He founded the British Library Association (1877), published books on British music, Biblical criticism, and book binding. He also wrote on folklore, keltic topics, numismatics, and published a catalog on Malay manuscripts (W.A. Munford, "Nicholson of the Bodleian," in *Library Review*, 143, 1962, 507–512).

OPPENHEIM(ER), DAVID (1664–1736) Czech Jewish book collector and rabbi, moved to Germany, spent all his financial resources on purchasing manuscripts and rare Hebrew books, built up a large personal library with about 800 manuscripts and over 5,000 printed books, which later (1829) were acquired by the Bodleian Library of Oxford University (SJE, 1451).

OWENS, MAJOR (b. 1936) American black politician, presently U.S. Congressman, worked as a librarian (1958–1968) in the Language and Literature Division of the Brooklyn Public Library and later as branch librarian of the same library system, was elected New York State senator, and since 1983 member of the U.S. Congress; he is the first librarian ever to become congressman (AL, Dec. 1982, 671).

PALMA Y LASSO, JOSÉ JOAQUIN (1844–1911) Guatemalan journalist, served as director (1887–1892) of the National Library of his country (TT, 23).

PANIZZI, ANTHONY (1797–1879) Italian politician; exiled to England he worked as assistant librarian (1837), keeper of printed books (1837–1856), and subsequently became chief librarian (1856–1867) of the British Museum Library; he was knighted for his library services, but later returned to Italy and became a senator (CE, 1594).

PARDO DE TAVERA, TRINIDAD H. (1857–1925) Philippino physician, public official, author, and anthropologist, served as director (1923–1925) of the Philippine Library and Museum in Manila (TT, 22).

PAUL V (born CAMILLO BORGHESE), **POPE** (1552–1621) Italian cardinal, an outstanding scholar, directed religious orders to teach Latin, Greek, Hebrew, and Arabic in the universities, assembled a large personal library, and donated many books to the Vatican Library; he also was the founder of the Vatican Archives (NCE, v. 11, 16).

PEARSON, EDMUND LESTER (1880–1937) American librarian, journalist, and author. Worked for the New York Public Library, wrote and published his own books on various topics (biographies, librarianship, crime), and also contributed a column on librarianship to the *Boston Transcript.* Attracted attention through his *Old Librarian Almanac*, a spoof on librarianship and librarians (Earle F. Wallbridge, "Edmund Lester Pearson," in *Dictionary of American Biography*, New York: Scribner, 1944, vol. 22, 522).

PHILIP II (1527–1598) Spanish king, also king of Naples and Sicily, built the Escorial Library, encouraged the acquisition and preservation of materials of historic value, including thousands of Arabic manuscripts, materials related to the history of Spain, Spanish church, and rare books (LOC, 8).

PHOTIUS (820–892) Greek theologian, controversial patriarch of Constantinople, one of the most learned men of his time, assembled a large personal library, described and cataloged hundreds of books by Greek and Roman historians, orators, and grammarians (LOC, 5).

PIUS II (born ENEA SILVIO PICCOLOMINI), **POPE** (1405–1464) Italian cardinal, distinguished representative of papal humanism, fine orator, writer, diplomat, in 1440 organized the manuscripts at the Court Library of Emperor Frederick III in Vienna (NCE, v. 11, 393).

PIUS VII (born BARNABA CHIARAMONTI), **POPE** (1742–1823) Italian cardinal of aristocratic descent; while teaching at the Abbey of Saint John in Parma, he learned new bibliographical techniques (1766–1775) and later became librarian at the Monastery St. Paul near Rome (NCE, v. 11, 400).

PIUS XI (born ACHILLE AMBROGIO DAMIANO RATTI) **POPE** (1857–1939) Italian cardinal, before becoming pope, served as a professor at a major seminary in Milan, and librarian (1888–1911) at the Ambrosiana Library, becoming its director in 1907; he worked also as librarian (1911–1918) at the Vatican Library and became its director starting 1914 (NCE, v. 11, 411).

PLATINA, BARTOLOMEO (1421–1481) Italian historian, author, humanist, served as Vatican librarian under Pope Sixtus IV, even though a previous Pope—Paul II—arrested him; painter Melozzo da Forli devoted a painting to the installation of Platina as librarian. (NCE, v. 11, 430).

PLUMMER, MARY WRIGHT (1856–1916) American librarian, linguist, teacher, and author. Worked as cataloger at the St. Louis Public Library, director of Pratt Institute Free Library, and later as head of the New York Public Library's Library School. She promoted high standards for admission in library schools, and published valuable books on small libraries, joys of reading, librarian training, library economy, and others. She served as American Library Association president (1915–1916), and made translations from several foreign languages (B. M. Holbrook, "Mary Wright Plummer," in *Wilson Library Bulletin*, 13, February 1939, 409).

POOLE, WILLIAM FREDERICK (1821–1894) American librarian, historian, and author. He worked as librarian for the Boston Mercantile Library Association, Boston Public Library, Cincinnati Public Library, and later as head of the Chicago Public Library and Newberry Library for over 20 years. He was one of the organizers of the American Library Association (1876), served as its president (1888–1889), as associated editor of the *Library Journal*, and published both books and articles dealing with history topics, library architecture, the university library, and others (S.H. Kessler, "William Frederick Poole, Librarian-Historian," in *Wilson Library Bulletin*, 28, May 1954, 788–790).

PORTAN, HENRICK GABRIEL (1739–1804) Finnish historian and professor, author of treatise on the history of the Finnish literature, served as assistant librarian (1764–1772) at the Turku University, and later as its director until 1777 (TT, 22).

PTOLEMY I, SOTER (323–283 B.C.) Greek general, later king of Egypt, a great lover of books, founded the Alexandria Library with about 700,00 volumes, the greatest in the ancient world, and made a heaven for scholars (WBD, 1219).

PUTNAM, HERBERT (1861–1955) American librarian, lawyer, and author. Worked as librarian for the Minneapolis Public Library, Brown University and Boston Public Libraries, and later Library of Congress for over 40 years. Under his leadership the Library of Congress developed into the best collection of books in the world. He established a national Union Catalog on cards, acquired valuable incunabula, history, Hispanic, Slavic, music scores, pictorial, and other collections. Served as American Library Association president twice (1898–1899; 1903–1904), and published materials on the importance of the Library of Congress (*Herbert Putnam, 1861–1955: A Memorial Tribute*, Washington, D.C.: Library of Congress, 1956).

RANGANATHAN, SHIYALI RAMARITA (1892–1972) Indian librarian, mathematician, and author. Considered the father of modern Indian librarianship, he encouraged young people to become librarians, created the Colon classification, which is used in computer-assisted document finding systems, and formulated five laws of library science focusing on the importance of the book. He was a very prolific author, writing on library classification, reference materials, education for librarians, and other related topics (B. I. Palmer, "Shiyali Ramarita Ranganathan," in *Library Association Record*, 74, November 1972, 228–229).

RATHBONE, JOSEPHINE ADAMS (1864–1941) American librarian, teacher, and author. Worked as assistant cataloger at the Pratt Institute Free Library, teaching almost every course in the curriculum, including current events. Her curriculum combined theory with practice in medium and small libraries. She wrote extensively in the library press about women librarians and other noted librarians, and served as American Library Association president (1931–1932) (Harry M. Lydenberg, "Josephine Adams Rathbone, 1864–1931," in *ALA Bulletin* 35, (June 1941), 367–368).

RICHARDSON, ERNEST CUSHING (1860–1939) American multilingual librarian, teacher, and author. He worked as librarian for the Hartford Theological Seminary (CT), teacher of bibliology, and later as director of the Princeton University Library and professor of bibliography for over 35 years. He was a very prolific author, publishing 25 books and over 150 articles, book reviews, and reports on various subjects: history, paleography, librarianship, importance of the national Union Catalog, library cooperation, philosophy of librarianship, library history. Served as American Library Association president (1905–1906). (D.Y. Hadadian, "Ernest Cushing Richardson, 1860–1939," in *College and Research Libraries*, 33, March 1972, 122–126).

RIDER, FREMONT (1885–1962) American librarian and author, poet, dramatist, editor, and publisher. Worked as director of the Wesleyan University Library (CT) for over 20 years, and increased the library collection and its usefulness. Was editor of the *Business Digest* and the *Library Journal*, wrote books on library research, advocated the importance of microcards and micropublications. Also published poems and plays (Fremont Rider, *A Master of*

None: Autobiography in the Third Person, Middletown, Conn.: Godfrey Memorial Library, 1955).

ROCHA, DARDO (1838–1921) Argentinian politician, educator, and statesman, after the completion of law studies, became the chief (1863) of the Buenos Aires Public Library (EUI, v. 51, 1122).

RODO, JOSÉ ENRIQUE (1871–1917) Uruguayan author, professor of literature, philosopher, statesman, was named director (1900) of the National Library in Montevideo and served in this capacity for two years (DES, v. 17, 454).

RUMÎANTŜEV, NICKOLAÏ PETROVICH (1754–1826) Russian count, occupied high government positions, encouraged book publishing at his expenses, collected over 28,000 manuscripts on Russian history and literature, presently part of the V.I. Lenin Library in Moscow (KES, 475).

SHAMURIN, EVGENII IVANOVICH (1889–1962) Russian librarian, lawyer, journalist, and author. He served on the Russian Book Chamber in Moscow for over 40 years, being involved in editorial work, cataloging, bibliographic activities, interlibrary cooperation, and other related aspects. He published books on the history of libraries, library terminology, preparation of annotations, and other subjects (Y.I. Masanov and I.B. Gracheva, *E.I. Shamurin, 1889–1962*, Moscow: Kniga, 1970).

SHARP, KATHARINE LUCINDA (1865–1914) American multilingual librarian, teacher, and author. She founded the Library School at the Armour Institute, Chicago, and later served as director of the Library School and as director of the library at the University of Illinois at Urbana. She upgraded Dewey standards for admission in library schools, was a founder of the Illinois Library Association, served on the American Library Association Council for over a decade, and wrote on Illinois libraries (Laurel Grotzinger, "The Pro-Feminist Librarian at the Turn of the Century: Two Studies," in *Journal of Library History*, 10, July 1975, 195–213).

SHERA, JESSE HAUK (1903–1989) American librarian, teacher, and author. Served as professor at the Graduate Library School of Chicago University, and later as Dean of the School of Library Science at Western Reserve University (Cleveland) for two decades. His prolific and influential writings focused on automation, library school, bibliographic organization, computer knowledge, library history, public libraries, history of information science, sociological foundations of librarianship, and several other subjects (B.C. Brooks, "Jesse Shera and the Theory of Bibliography," in *Journal of Librarianship*, 5, October 1973, 233–235).

SIGURDSSON, JON (1811–1879) Icelandic linguist, historian, and statesman, poet and playwright, studied and cataloged Icelandic manuscripts, assembled a large personal library of books and manuscripts on his native country, served as archivist and librarian (1845–1865) of the Norse Archaeological Society (*Webster's Dictionary of Names*, Springfield, Mass., 1943, 1364).

SLAVEIKOV, PENCHO PETROV (1868–1912) Bulgarian poet, publisher and journalist, served as director (1898–1908) of the Sofia Library (*Kratke Blgarska Ėnfsiklopediîa*, Sofia: Blgarska Akademiîa na Naukite, 1967, v.4, 549).

SOLZHENITSYN, ALEKSANDR ISAEVICH (b. 1918) Russian author, Nobel Prize winner in literature, prominent dissident, exiled from his native country, was prison librarian (1947) while serving a seven-year prison sentence for criticizing Stalin (*Gulag Arkhipelago: 1918–1956*, New York: Harper and Row, 1975, pp. III–IV, 479).

SORBON, ROBERT DE (1201–1274) French theologian, author, a benefactor, gave his personal library to the University of Paris in 1250, which later became the nucleus of the university's library (LOC, 7).

SPOFFORD, AINSWORTH RAND (1825–1908) American self-educated librarian, bookseller, publisher, and author. Served as chief aide to the Librarian of Congress for over 30 years. He had an outstanding memory as a source of factual knowledge, advocated for the Library of Congress to be the U.S. national library, and developed its collection from 60,000 to over 1 million volumes in over 30 years. He also was a prolific author, publishing books on various topics: the formation of public and private libraries, literature of foreign authors, humor, and others (John Y. Cole, "Ainsworth Rand Spofford: the Valliant and Persistent Librarian of Congress," in *Library of Congress Quarterly Journal*, 33, April 1976, 92–115).

STEARNS, LUTIE EUGENIA (1866–1943) American librarian, author, and teacher. Worked as circulation librarian at the Milwaukee Public Library and as a member of the Wisconsin Free Library Commission for 20 years. She lectured to library classes, placed over 1,500 traveling collections in rural communities, advocated women's rights, contributed to newspapers and library journals, and published a basic book on library administration (Earl Tannenbaum, "The Library Career of Lutie Eugenia Stearns," in *Wisconsin Magazine of History*, Spring 1950, 159–165).

STRINDBERG, JOHAN AUGUST (1848–1912) Swedish novelist and dramatist, poet and painter, worked as assistant librarian (1874-1882) at the Royal Library in Stockholm and cataloged oriental books (WBD, 1423).

SWIETEN, GERARD FREIHERR VON (1700–1772) Austrian physician and counselor during the reign of Maria Theresa, worked as court librarian (1745–1772), served as chief of the book revision commission, and was founder of a medical school (GB, v. 11, 214).

SZABO, ERWIN (1877–1918) Hungarian socialist, writer, and anarchist theoretician, translated works of Karl Marx into Hungarian, starting 1911 served as head of the Budapest Public Library until the end of his life (GB, v. 11, 234).

TCHELEBI (MUSTAFA BEN ABDALLAH, also known as HAJI KALFA), **KATIB** (1599–1658) Turkish historian, assistant to the chief of the Imperial College in Istanbul, compiled a bibliographic lexicon annotating 18,550 Arabic, Turkish, and Persian books (NCCN, v.2, 1884).

TEGNER, ESAIAS (1782–1846) Swedish poet, professor, and bishop, served as assistant librarian (1801–1805) and later (1805–1812) as Vice Librarian of the Lund University (GB, v. 11, 299).

THWAITES, REUBEN GOLD (1853–1913) American librarian, journalist, editor, and author. He served as Superintendent-Secretary of the Wisconsin State Historical Society for over 25 years, and constantly developed and diversified the society's collection of books. He proved to be one of the most prolific librarian-authors, publishing 15 titles (history, literature) and editing over 100 books. He was American Library Association president (1899–1900), and also wrote extensively on library subjects (Frederick Jackson Turner, *Reuben Gold Thwaites, a Memorial Address*, Madison: State Historical Society of Wisconsin, 1914).

TISSÉRANT, EUGÈNE CARDINAL (1884–1972) French clergyman, librarian, teacher, and author. Was Director of the Vatican Library and archivist of the Holy Roman Catholic Church, and introduced a new cataloging system for printed books. Published various scholarly books on church history, codices of oriental manuscripts kept in the library, as well as papers on the Vatican library. He also was professor of oriental studies ("Eugène Cardinal Tissérant)," in *New Catholic Encyclopedia*, vol. 16, Supplement 1967–1974, Washington, D.C.: Catholic University of America, 1974).

TOBOLKA, ZDENEK (1874–1951) Czech historian, politician, professor, served as librarian (1897–1938) of Prague University and organized the first courses in library science; he published extensively on library subjects (KES, 533).

TOLSTOY, LEV NIKOLAEVICH (1828–1910) Russian classical author, assembled a large library in his house at Iasnaia Poliana with over 22,000 books and journals in 35 languages; also organized a circle of readers in the same place (KES, 534).

TRAJAN, MARCUS ULPIUS (53–117) Roman emperor, conqueror of many lands, including Dacia (presently Romania), built the Trajan Forum in Rome, and shortly before his death (114) founded the Ulpian Library, the largest in the Roman Empire (LOC, 3).

TYLER, ALICE SARAH (1859–1944) American librarian, teacher, and author. Worked as cataloger for the Cleveland Public Library, for the Iowa State Library Commission, and later as director of the Library School at Case Western Reserve University for two decades. She added new courses to the curriculum (school libraries, library and community welfare, library work with children, hospital library service), and served as American Library Association president (1920–1921). Lectured and wrote on education for librarianship, recruitment for library schools (Cora Richardson Scott, *Alice Sarah Tyler: A Biographical Study*, Cleveland: Case Western Reserve University, 1951).

UTLEY, GEORGE BURWELL (1876–1946) American librarian, scholar, and author. He was director of the Newberry Library, Chicago, for over 20 years, and substantially increased its collection by acquiring valuable incunabula to visualize the development of printing. He was American Library Association president (1922–1923), and also worked as ALA's secretary and editor of ALA publications. He wrote numerous articles dealing with ALA history, biographies, library activities (Chalmers Hadley, "George Burwell Utley," in *ALA Bulletin*, 40, November 1946, 429–430).

VARRO, MARCUS TERENTIUS (116–27 B.C.) Roman scholar, the most learned man of his time, author of about 600 books, philosopher; he was proscribed by Emperor Anthony, but managed to survive, became librarian under Emperor Augustus, and director of a public library under Emperor Caesar (NCCN, v.3, 3992).

WARREN, ALTHEA (1886–1958) American librarian, teacher, and author. She worked for the Chicago Public Library, and later as head of San Diego and Los Angeles public libraries, and also taught at the library schools of Michigan, Wisconsin, and Southern California universities. She started subject specializations of book collections, was American Library Association president (1943–1944), and wrote on public library administration (Martha Boaz, *Fervent and Full of Gifts: the Life of Althea Warren*, New York: Scarecrow Press, 1961).

WERGELAND, HENRICK ARNOLD (1808–1845) Norwegian poet, editor, dramatist, fighter for his country's independence, statesman, member of the Norwegian Parliament, was keeper (1840–1845) of the Royal Archives (TT, 23).

WILSON, HALSEY WILLIAM (1868–1954) American librarian, book publisher, and author. Started as a book dealer, then published *Cummulative Index of Books* and *United States Catalog*, followed by the standard library reference tools: *Reader's Guide to Periodical Literature* and *Book Review Digest* at the beginning of the twentieth century. Gradually, the Wilson Company became the largest publishing firm of reference books in the world. He was active in the American Library Association, and also published articles on early periodicals in Pennsylvania, and the necessity of cooperative librarianship (Rudolf Engelbarts, *Librarian Authors: A Bibliography*, Jefferson, N.C.: Farland, 1981).

WILSON, LOUIS ROUND (1876–1976) American librarian, philologist, and author. He served as librarian at Chapel Hill University (NC), taught librarianship, and later became Dean of the Graduate School of Librarianship at the University of Chicago. Was a cofounder of the North Carolina Library Association, advocated Ph.D. programs in library schools, and became a talented surveyer of libraries. He published several books on the library and college instruction, the role of the university library, library planning, and other subjects. Was American Library Association president (1935–1936) (E.G. Holley, "Louis Round Wilson Centennial Day," in *Journal of Library History*, 12, (Spring 1977), 170–176).

WINSOR, JUSTIN (1831–1897) American multilingual librarian, historian, and author. He served as superintendent of the Boston Public Library, and as head librarian of the Harvard College Library, was one of the founders of *Library Journal*, and twice American Library Association president (1876–1877; 1895–1896). He published a valuable book on the history of Boston, and a critical history of America, as well as other publications on manuscripts, maps, Shakespeare, bibliographies, and others (F.G. Kilgour, "Justin Winsor," in *College and Research Libraries*, 3, December 1941, 64–66).

3

Who Said What on Books, Libraries, and Librarians

This section has 125 entries, consisting of a selection of noted people's views on books and libraries, or sayings on the same subject, covering various historical periods from ancient times to the present. The quotations reproduced in this section represent 24 countries, even though the majority of them are of American and British origin. A sizable number of these quotations are little known to researchers, or were rendered into English for the first time.

Each name entry provides the author's name, dates of birth and death, main areas of activity, followed by a relevant quotation and its source in parentheses. It is understood that whenever a reference source is mentioned it is only one out of several existent for each. The entry for sayings provides its national origin, followed by the text and its source in parentheses.

Bibliography

Barron, Joseph L. *A Treasury of Jewish Quotations.* South Brunswick, N.Y.: A.S. Barnes, 1965.

Champion, Selwyn. *Racial Proverbs: A Selection of the World's Proverbs Arranged Linguistically.* New York: Barnes & Noble, 1950.

Cowan, Lore, and Maurice Cowan. *The Wit of the Jews.* Nashville, Tenn.: Aurora Publishers, 1970.

Dupré, P. *Encyclopedie des Citations.* Paris: Éditions de Trévise, 1959.

Edwards, Tryon, and Jonathan Edwards. *The New Dictionary of Thoughts. A Cyclopedia of Quotations.* New York: Standard Book Company, 1954.

Goicochea, Cesáreo. *Diccionario de Citas.* 2nd ed. Barcelona: Editorial Labor, 1962.

Helwig, Gerhard. *Buch der Zitate.* Munchen: Mosaic, 1981.

Hurd, Charles. *A Treasury of Great American Quotations.* New York: Hawthorn Books, 1964.

Library News (published by Urban Libraries Council) 5 (Winter 1982).

Likthenshtein, Efim Semenovich. *Slovo o Knige.* Moskva: Kniga, 1974.

Murphy, Edward F. *The Crown Treasury of Relevant Quotations.* New York: Crown, 1978.

Seldes, George. *Great Quotations.* New York: Lyle-Stuart, 1960.

Telepin, M. IA. *Pokhvala Knige.* Moskva: Kniga, 1978.

Tesoros de España: Ten Centuries of Spanish Books. Madrid: Ministerio de Cultura, 1985.

ALCOTT, AMOS BRONSON (1799–1888), American educator and philosopher.

"That is a good book which is opened with expectation, and closed with delight and profit" ("Learning Books" in *Table Talk*, cited in B. Boyle, *Home Book of American Quotations*, New York: Dodd, Mead, 1967, 63).

ANDREEV, LEONID NIKOLAEVICH (1871–1919), Russian author.

"If man were destined to become God, then the book would have to be his throne" (cited in SOK, 34).

ARABIC SAYING

"A book is a garden carried in the pocket" (cited in RP, 330).

ASHE, ARTHUR (1943–1993), American tennis player, national and international champion.

"Throughout my formal education I spent many, many hours in public and school libraries. Libraries became courts of last resort, as it were. The current definitive answer to almost any question can be found within the four walls of most libraries" (cited in LN, 1).

ASIMOV, ISAAC (1920–   ), American author.

"I have written 240 books on a wide variety of topics. . . . Some of it I based on education I received in my school, but most of it was backed by other ways of learning—chiefly in the books I obtained in the public library" (cited in LN, 1).

AUDEN, W[YSTAN] H[UGH] (1907–1973), English poet.

"Some books are undeservedly forgotten, none are undeservedly remembered" (*The Duyer's Hand and Other Essays*, New York: Random House, 1962).

BACON, FRANCIS (1561–1626), English philosopher and author.

"Some books are to be tasted, others to be swallowed, and some few to be chewed and digested" ("Of Studies" in *Essays II*, 1625).

BALZAC, HONORÉ DE (1799–1850), French novelist.

"Nowadays we are attracted to a book much more by the style than by the material" ("Introduction" to *Physiologie du Mariage*, 1828).

BARTHOLINI, ALEXANDER (1597–1643), Danish physician and author.

"Without books, God is silent, justice dormant, natural science at a stand, philosophy lame, letters dumb, and all things involved in darkness" (*De Libris Legendis*, cited in NDT, 53).

BELINSKIĬ, VISSARION GRIGOR'EVICH (1811–1841), Russian literary critic and author.

"Children's books are written for upbringing . . . but upbringing is a great thing; it decides the fate of the human being" (cited in SOK, 219).

BEN GURION, DAVID (1886–1973), Israeli statesman, labor leader, and author.

"We have preserved the Book, and the Book has preserved us" (cited in TJQ, 34).

BERENSON, BERNARD (1865–1959), American art expert and critic.

"My house is a library with living rooms attached" (cited in WOJ, 16).

BIRRELL, AUGUSTINE (1850–1934), English essayist and public officer.

"Good as it is to inherit a library, it is better to collect one" ("Book Buying" in *Obiter Dicta*, 1884).

BOILEAU, NICHOLAS (1636–1711), French poet and literary critic.

"It may be agreeable and charming in a book, but one has also to know how to read it and live it" (L'Art Poétique, 1674).

BONALD, LOUIS GABRIEL (1754–1840), French philosopher and author.

"From the 'Bible' until the 'Social Contract' the books are the ones that made the revolution" (cited in SOK, 34).

BORGES, JOSÉ LUIS (1899–1986), Argentinian author, Nobel Prize winner in literature.

"Beginning with the vedas and bibles, we have welcomed the notion of sacred books. In a certain way, every book is sacred" (cited in TDE, 34).

BRADBURY, RAY DOUGLAS (1920–   ), American science fiction author.

"You must live feverishly in a library. Colleges are not going to do any good unless you are raised and live in a library every day of your life" (cited in WD, February 1976, 25).

BRAINE, JOHN GERARD (1922–   ), English author.

"Being a writer in a library is rather like being a eunuch in a harem" (cited in *New York Times*, 7 October 1962, p. VII, 5).

BUAST, PIERRE CLAUDE (1765–1824), French lexicographer.

"Book publishing is the artillery of thought" (cited in SOK, 34).

BULGARIAN SAYING

"He who knows books has four eyes" (cited in RP, 86).

BURROUGHS, JOHN (1837–1921), American naturalist and author.

"I go to books and to nature as the bee goes to a flower, for a nectar that I can make into my own honey" (cited in TGAQ, 187).

BURY, RICHARD DE (1287–1345), French illuminist and author.

"All the glory of the world would be buried in oblivion, unless God had provided mortals with the remedy of books" (*Philobiblon*, cited in LOC, as motto).

CARLYSLE, THOMAS (1795–1881), English philosopher and publicist.

"The true University of these days is a collection of books" ("The Hero as a Man of Letters" in *On Heroes and Hero Worship*, 1841).

CHINESE SAYING

"To read a book for the first time is to make an acquaintance with a new friend; to read it for a second time is to meet an old one" (cited in RP, 351).

CHOATE, RUFUS (1799–1859), American statesman and lawyer.

"A book is the only immortality" (cited in TGAQ, 83).

CICERO, MARCUS TULIUS (106–43 B.C.), Roman orator, politician, and philosopher.

"A room without books is like a body without a soul" (cited in BDZ, 57).

COOKE, TERENCE (1921–1983), American cardinal and bishop of the Diocese of New York.

"The reflections and histories of men and women throughout the world are contained in books. . . . America's greatness is not only recorded in books, but it is also dependent upon each and every citizen being able to utilize public libraries" (cited in LN, 1).

COURIER, PAUL-LOUIS (1772–1825), French scholar and philosopher.

"Let people talk, let them blame you, condemn you, even hang you, publish what you think . . . to speak is a good thing, to write is better, to print is an excellent thing" (*Pamphlet de Pamphlets*, 1824).

COUSINS, NORMAN (1915–), American editor.

"A library . . . is the delivery room for the birth of ideas—a place where history comes to life" (cited in *ALA Bulletin*, October 1954, 475).

DAUDET, ALPHONSE (1840–1897), French philosopher.

"Books are the best friends. You can turn to them in difficult moments of your life. They will never betray you" (cited in PK, 89).

DAWSON, GEORGE MERCER (1849–1901), Canadian geologist and author.
"A great library contains the diary of human race" (cited in NDT, 340).

DE AMICIS, EDMONDO (1846–1908), Italian author.
"The destiny of many men depends on the fact whether their parents' house had or did not have a library" (cited in DDC, 84).

DE ASIS, MACHADO (1839–1908), Brazilian author.
"Nothing can be remedied in confused books, but everything can be put in omitted books" (cited in EDC, 484).

DESCARTES, RENÉ (1596–1650), French philosopher, mathematician, and scientist.
"To read a good book is like conversing with the noblest minds of bygone ages" (*Discours de la Méthode*, 1637).

DIDEROT, DENIS (1713–1784), French philosopher and encyclopedist.
"People cease to think when they cease to read" (cited in PK, 162).

DISRAELI, ISAAC (1766–1848), English author.
"Some will read old books, as if there were no valuable truth to be discovered in modern publications" (cited in WOJ, 28).

DOUGLAS, KIRK (1916–), American actor.
"My mother and my father were illiterate immigrants from Russia. When I was a child they were constantly amazed that I could go to a building and take a book on any subject. They couldn't believe this access to knowledge we have here in America. They couldn't believe that it was free" (cited in LN, 1).

DOWNS, ROBERT (1903–), American author, librarian, and administrator.
"My lifelong love affair with books and reading continues unaffected by automation, computers, and all other forms of the twentieth-century gadgetry" (*Books in My Life*, Washington, D.C., write for info., Library of Congress, 1985).

DYER, WILLIAM (1636–1696), English clergyman.
"Libraries are the wardrobes of literature, whence men, properly informed may bring forth something for ornament, much for curiosity, and more for use" (cited in NDT, 339).

EDWARDS, TRYON (1809–1894), American author and clergyman.
"My books are my tools, and the greater their variety and perfection the greater the help to my literary work" (cited in NDT, 340).

EHRENBURG, IL'IÂ GRIGOR'EVICH (1891–1967), Soviet author and journalist.

"Books are changing people, but it is a long and latent process" (cited in PK, 175).

EMERSON, RALPH WALDO (1803–1882), American philosopher, poet, and essayist.

"Consider what you have in the smallest chosen library. A company of the wisest and wittiest men that could be picked out of all civil countries, in a thousand years, have set in best order the results of their learning and wisdom" ("Books" in *Society and Solitude*, 1870).

ERASMUS OF ROTERDAM, DESIDERIUS (1466–1536), Dutch scholar, humanist, and author.

"When I get a little money, I buy books, and if any is left, I buy food and clothes" (cited in NDT, 54).

FENELON, FRANÇOIS DE SAVIGNAC DE LA MOTHE (1651–1715), French theologian and author.

"If all the crowns of Europe were placed at my disposal on condition that I should abandon my books and studies, I should spurn the crowns away and stand by the books" (cited in NDT, 54).

FRANCE, ANATOLE (1844–1924), French author.

"Never lend books, for no one ever returns them; the only books I have in my library are books that other folks have lent me" (cited in H. Prochnow, *A Treasury Chest of Quotations for All Occasions*, New York: Harper and Row, 1983, 473).

FRANK, ANNE (1929–1945), Dutch Jewish teenager, victim of Nazi regime, and author.

"If I read a book that impresses me, I have to take myself firmly in hand, before I mix with other people; otherwise they would think my mind is queer" (*Anne Frank: The Diary of a Young Girl*, New York: Pocket Books, 1972).

GIBBON, EDWARD (1737–1794), English historian.

"From this slender beginning I have gradually formed a numerous and select library, the foundations of all my works, and the best comfort of my life, both home and abroad" (cited in NDT, 340).

GIDE, ANDRÉ (1869–1951), French author and philosopher.

"May my book teach you to be concerned more with yourself than with it—and then with everything more than with yourself" (*Les Nourritures Terrestres*, 1897).

GIUDEO (IMMANUEL, BEN SOLOMON), **MANOLO** (1260–1328), Italian Jewish poet and philosopher.

"Spend your money on good books, and you'll find its equivalent in gold and intelligence" (cited in TJQ, 35).

GOETHE, JOHANN WOLFGANG VON (1749–1832), German poet, playwright, and novelist.

"Some books seem to be written not to instruct, but rather to show that the author knows something" (cited in BDZ, 57).

GONCOURT, EDMOND DE (1822–1896), French author and literary critic.

"A book is never a masterpiece; it becomes one" (cited in H. Davidoff, *World Treasury of Proverbs*, New York: Random House, 1946, 36).

GORKY (PESHKOV), **MAKSIM** (ALEXEĬ MAKSIMOVICH) (1868–1936), Soviet novelist and playwright.

"Two forces are successfully influencing the education of a cultivated man: art and science. Both are united in the book" (cited in PK, 20).

GRIGGS, SUTTON ELBERT (1872–1930), American black minister, orator, and publisher.

"It often requires more courage to read some books than it does to fight a battle" (cited in A. King, *Quotations in Black*, Westport, Conn.: Greenwood Press, 1981, 115).

GRISWOLD, WHITNEY (1906–1963), American educator and historian.

"Books won't stay banned. They won't burn. Ideas won't go to jail. In the long run of history, the censor and the inquisitor have always lost. The only sure weapon against bad ideas is better ideas" (cited in GQ, 291).

GUEDALLA, PHILIP (1889–1944), English historian, biographer, and essayist.

"The preface is the most important part of the book. Even reviewers read a preface" (cited in DDC, 383).

HALEY, ALEX (1921–1992), American black novelist.

"My parents were teachers and they went out of their way to see to it that I had books. We grew up in a home that was full of books. And so I learned to read. I loved to read" (cited in WD, August 1980, 21).

HEINE, HEINRICH (1797–1856), German poet and publicist.

"Where books are burned, at the end people are burned too" (cited in BDZ, 57).

HESSE, HERMANN (1877–1962), German novelist and poet.

"A house without books is poor, even if it has beautiful carpets on the floor, and expensive tapestries and paintings cover the walls" (cited in BDZ, 57).

HOLMES, OLIVER WENDELL (1809–1894), American physician and author.

"Old books . . . are books of the world's youth, and new books are fruits of its age" (*The Professor at the Breakfast Table*, 1858).

HUGO, VICTOR (1802–1885), French poet, novelist, and dramatist.

"The discovery of the art of bookprinting is the greatest possession of world history" (cited in BDZ, 56).

IBN EZRA, MOSES (1055–1135), Spanish Hebrew poet.

"A book is the most delightful companion. . . . It will join you in solitude, accompany you in exile, serve as a candle in the dark and entertain you in loneliness" (cited in TJQ, 35).

ITALIAN SAYING

"A man has lived to no purpose unless he has either built a house, begotten a son, or written a book" (cited in RP, 288).

JAPANESE SAYING

"If you tread on a book, you will receive divine retribution" (cited in D. Buchanan, *Japanese Proverbs and Sayings*, New York: Norman, 1965, 224).

JEFFERSON, THOMAS (1743–1826), American president and author.

"A library book . . . is not, then, an article of mere consumption but fairly of capital, and often in the case of professional men, setting out in life, is their only capital" (cited E. Brussell, *Dictionary of Quotable Definitions*, New York: Prentice-Hall, 1970, 55).

JESUS, CAROLINA MARIA DE (1923?–), Brazilian author.

"The book is man's best invention so far" (*Child of Dark: The Diary of Carolina Maria de Jesus*, New York: New American Library, 1962).

JONG, ERICA (1942–), American author and poet.

"Books go out into the world, travel mysteriously from hand to hand, and somehow find their way to the people who need them at times when they need them" (*How to Save Your Own Life*, New York: Holt, Rhinehart & Winston, 1977).

JONSON, BEN (1573–1637), English Dramatist.

"So books are faithful repositories, which may be a while forgotten, but when opened again, will again impart instruction" (cited in NDT, 54).

JOUBERT, JOSEPH (1754–1824), French author.

"There was a time when the world acted on books; now books act on the world" (cited in NDT, 55).

KAFKA, FRANZ (1883–1924), German author.

"A book ought to be an icepick to break up the frozen sea within us" ("Letter to Pollak," 1904, in *Letters to Friends, Family, Editors*, New York, 1953).

KOREAN SAYING

"In a good book every letter is gold" (cited in SOK, 283).

LANDFORD, JOHN ALFRED (1823–1903), American author and journalist.

"No possession can surpass, or even equal a good library, to the lover of books. Here are treasured up for his daily use and delectation, riches which increase by being consumed, and pleasures that never cloy" (cited in NDT, 340).

LANDOR, WALTER SAVAGE (1775–1805), English poet and novelist.

"He who first praises a good book becomingly is next in merit to the author" (cited in DDC, 246).

LASH, JOSEPH (1909–1987), American author.

"The library vied with the local school in triggering fancy and imagination and populating them with experiences and histories. Even after I entered college the use of the latter's library did not replace the reference and reading room of the 42nd Street" (cited in LN, 1).

LINCOLN, ABRAHAM (1809–1865), American president.

"Everything I want to know is in the books. My best friend is the man who gives me a book which I did not read" (cited in PK, 59).

LONGFELLOW, HENRY WADSWORTH (1807–1882), American poet and modern languages professor.

"The student has his Rome, his Florence, his whole glowing Italy, within four walls of his library. He has in his books the ruins of an antique world and the glories of a modern one" (cited in NDT, 339).

MADARIAGA, JAVIER SOLANA (1945–), Spanish lawyer, politician, and minister of culture.

"In Spain, books have always been our enlightenment. But the penalties, hardships and sufferings for enlightenment have been the penalties of books, and in turn the sorrows and penalties of books have been the hardships of enlightenment" (cited in TDE, 8).

MAILER, NORMAN (1923–), American author.

"In my day the library was a wonderful place. . . . We didn't have visual aids and didn't have various programs . . . it was a sanctuary. . . . So I tend to think the library should remain a center of knowledge" (cited in AL, July/August 1980, 411–12).

MALLARMÉ, STEPHANE (1848–1898), French poet and symbolist.

"Everything in the world exists to end up in a book" (*Le Livre*, cited in R. Collison, *Dictionary of Foreign Quotations*, New York: Facts on File, 1980, 34).

MANN, HEINRICH (1871–1950), German author.

"A house without books is like a room without windows. No man has a right to bring up his children without surrounding them with books. . . . Children learn to read being in the presence of books" (cited in NDT, 341).

MARTIALIS, MAURUS VALERIUS (40–104), Latin author.

"My books have stayed within these bounds: to spare the person, to denounce vice" (cited in N. Guterman, *Book of Latin Quotations*, New York: Doubleday, 1966, 293).

MÉLANCON, ROBERT (1947–), Canadian French author and scholar.

"A great public library, in its catalogue and its physical disposition of its books on shelves, is the monument of literary genres" (cited in *World Literature Today* [Spring] 1982, 231).

MILTON, JOHN (1608–1674), English poet and publicist.

"A good book is the precious life blood of a master spirit, embalmed and treasured up on purpose to a life beyond life" (*Aeropagitica*, 1644).

MITCHELL, MARIA (1818–1889), American astronomer and educator.

"A book is a very good institution! To read a book, to think it over, and to take out notes is a useful exercise; a book which will not repay some hard thought is not worth publishing" (*Life, Letters, and Journals*, 1896).

MONGOLIAN SAYING

"When the sun rises, nature wakes up; when a book is read, the mind is enlightened" (cited in SOK, 284).

MONTAIGNE, MICHEL EYQUEM (1553–1592), French philosopher, author, and magistrate.

"There are more books about books than about any other subject" (*Essays, III*, 1588).

MOROCCAN SAYING
"Just the sight of the book takes away the sadness of the heart" (cited in SOK, 284).

al-MUTANNABI, ABU al-TAYIB (910–965), Arab poet.
"The most valuable place in the world is the saddle on the horse; the best conversation companions in our time are books" (cited in PK, 81).

NIGER (CHARNEY), SAMUEL (1883–1956), American Yiddish author.
"A good library is a place, a palace where the lofty spirits of all nations and generations meet" (cited in TJQ, 35).

NORRIS, KATHLEEN (1947–), American author.
"Just the knowledge that a good book is waiting one at the end of a long day makes that day happier" (*Hands Full Of Living*, cited in CTRQ, 104).

ORIENTAL SAYING
"The traveler who feels lonely should always take a book as his companion, there is never a better traveler; the sick and suffering should take a book, there is no better medicine in the world" (cited in PK, 80).

ORTEGA Y GASSET, JOSÉ (1883–1955), Spanish philosopher and author.
"The librarian's mission should be, not like up to now, a mere handling of the book as an object, but rather a know how (mise au point) of the book as a vital function" (*Mission del Bibliotecario*, Madrid: Revista de Occidente, 1962).

OVID (OVIDIUS), PUBLIUS NASO (43 B.C.–18 A.D.), Latin poet.
"Books are the index of the writer's mind" (*Tristia*).

PALEY, WILLIAM SAMUEL (1901–), CBS founder and chairman.
"I had an early passion for reading, especially for Horatio Alger stories. I went to the public library almost every day, and when I found a Horatio Alger book I had not read before, it was like finding a gold mine" (*As it Happened: A Memoir*, New York: Doubleday, 1979).

PARKER, THEODORE (1810–1860), American minister and author.
"The books which help us most are those which make us think the most" (cited in NDT, 56).

PASCAL, BLAIZE (1623–1662), French scientist and philosopher.
"The last thing we discover in writing a book is the knowledge of how to begin it" (*Pensées*, 1670, posthumous).

PLINY THE ELDER (23–79), Latin naturalist and author.
"There is no book so bad that we cannot get something useful from it" (*Historia Naturalis*).

PLUTARCH (46–120), Greek biographer and essayist.
"Books have more courage to tell the truth to the rulers, even more than the rulers' friends" (cited in PK, 159).

POLISH SAYING
"Old truths, old laws, old friends, an old book and old wine are the best (cited in RP, 248).

POWELL, LAWRENCE CLARK (1906–), American librarian and author.
"Believers and doers are what we need—faithful librarians who are humble in the presence of books. . . . To be in a library is one of the purest of all experiences. This awareness of library's unique, even sacred nature, is what should be instilled in our neophites" (*A Passion for Books*, Westport, Conn.: Greenwood Press, 1958).

PROUST, MARCEL (1871–1922), French author.
"The reader's recognition of what is said in this book is proof of its truth" (*Le Temps Retrouvé*, Paris, 1954).

RICHTER, JEAN PAUL R. (1793–1825), German novelist.
"Only through men are men subdued and surpassed, not by books and superior qualities" (cited in L. Dalbiac, *Dictionary of Quotations* [German], New York: Ungar, 1958, 264).

ROGERS, HENRY (1806–1877), English essayist.
"Upon books the collective education of the race depends; they are the sole instruments of registering, perpetuating and transmitting thought" (cited in NDT, 56).

ROMANIAN SAYING
"A good book can take the place of a friend, but a friend cannot replace a good book" (cited in V. Wertsman, *Romanians in America: 1748–1974*, Dobbs Ferry, N.Y.: Oceana, 1975, 111).

ROOSEVELT, FRANKLIN DELANO (1882–1945), American president.
"No man and no force can take from the world the books that embody men's eternal fight against tyranny of every kind" ("Statement at the American Bookseller Association," April 23, 1941, cited in L. Spinard, *Treasury of Great American Sayings*, West Nyack, N.Y.: Parker, 1975, 53).

ROUSSEAU, JEAN-JACQUES (1712–1778), French philosopher and author.
"The abuse of books is the death of knowledge" ("Livre V" in *Emile*, 1762).

RUSKIN, JOHN (1819–1900), English art critic and sociologist.
"All books are divisible into two classes: the books of the hour, and the books of all times" ("Of King's Treasures" in *Sesame and Lilies*, 1865).

RUSSELL, JOHN (1921–   ), American journalist.

"I cannot think of a greater blessing than to die in one's own bed, without warning and discomfort, on the last page of the new book that we most wanted to read" (cited in *New York Times*, 19 April 1986, C10).

RUSSIAN SAYING

"Gold is digged out from earth, and knowledge—from books" (cited in SOK, 283).

SADOVEANU, MIHAIL (1880–1961), Romanian author.

"The book not only fulfills the mission of mediating between us and our fellow beings remote in time and space; the book also fulfills the miracle of making us live free of lies, injustice, prejudices" (motto of *Romanian Books*, periodical).

SALIBA, JAMIL (1902–   ), Syrian author.

"The books in the nation are the flame of the light, the measurement of thought, the criterium of renaissance, and the fine flower of its originality and glory" ("Abdel Amalek," cited in F. Montreynaud, *Dictionnaire de Citations du Mond Entier*, Paris; Les Usuels de Robert, 1979, 666).

SCHLESINGER, ARTHUR MEIR (1888–1965), American historian.

"The public library has been historically a vital instrument of democracy and opportunity in the United States. . . . Our history has been greatly shaped by people who read their way to opportunity and achievements in public libraries" (cited in LN, 4).

SENECA, LUCIUS ANNAEUS (3 B.C.–65 A.D.), Roman philosopher, dramatist, and statesman.

"It does not matter how many books you may have, but whether they are good or not" (*Epistolae Morale*).

SHAKESPEARE, WILLIAM (1564–1616), English dramatist and poet.

"Knowing I loved my books, he furnished me, from my own library with volumes I prize above my dukedom" (*The Tempest*, 1611, Act I, Scene II).

SHAW, GEORGE BERNARD (1856–1950), Irish playwright and critic.

"Ten generations will come one after the other, and during this time only once an immortal book is born" (cited in PK, 127).

SPINOZA, BENEDICTUS (BARUCH) (1632–1677), Dutch philosopher.

"Books which teach and speak of whatever is highest and best are equally sacred, whatever be the tongue in which they are written, or the nation to which they belong" (*Tractatus Politicus* 1670, Chapter X).

STEINBECK, JOHN ERNST (1902–1968), American author.
"A book is somehow sacred. A dictator can kill and maim people, can sink to any kind of tyranny and only be hated, but when books are burned the ultimate in tyranny has happened . . . this we cannot forgive" (cited in GQ, 661).

STEVENSON, ROBERT LOUIS (1850–1894), English author and poet.
"There is no quite a good book without a good morality, but the world is wide, and so are morals" ("A Gossip on a Novel of Duma's" in *Memoirs and Portraits*, cited in CTRQ, 103).

STONE, IRVING (1903–1989), American author.
"If it is noticed that much of my outside work concerns itself with libraries, there is an extremely good reason for this. I think that the better part of my education, almost as important as that secured in the schools and the universities, came from libraries" (cited in LN, 4).

SWIFT, JONATHAN (1667–1745), English author.
"Books, like men their authors, have no more than one way of coming into the world, but there are ten thousand to go out of it, and return no more" (cited in PK, 57).

TROLLOPE, ANTHONY (1815–1882), English novelist.
"Of all needs a book has, the chief need is to be readable" (*Autobiography*, Berkeley; University of California Press, 1978).

TVARDOVSKIĬ, ALEKSANDR TRIFONOVICH (1910–1971), Soviet poet.
"Man's relationship with the book is the highest and irreplaceable form of intellectual development" (cited in PK, 79).

VALERY, PAUL (1871–1945), French poet and critic.
"Books have the same enemies as people: fire, humidity, animals, weather, and their own content" (cited in J. Dissère, *Dictionnaire Encyclopédique des Citations*, Paris: Editions de la Renaissance, 1970, 223).

WALLACH, ELI (1915–   ), American actor.
"America means books—opening the floodgate to intelligence, insights and growth" (cited in LN, 4).

WARE (IRONQUILL), EUGENE FITCH (1841–1911), American poet.
"Man builds no structure which outlives the book" ("The Book," cited in TGAQ, 200).

WEBER, CARL JULIUS (1767–1832), German author.

"A book that is not worth reading twice at least, is also not worth reading once" (*Democritos*, 1832–1840).

WILDE (O'FLAHERTIE WILLS), **OSCAR** (FINGALL) (1854–1900), English author.

"There is no such thing as a moral or an immoral book. Books are well written or badly written" ("Preface" to *The Picture of Dorian Gray*, 1891).

4
Librarian's Belle Lettres

This section has two subsections: (1) Librarians, Publishers, and Booksellers in Novels and Plays, with 95 entries; (2) Librarians and Libraries in Poetry, with 33 entries. The majority of selected authors and poets are from the United States and Great Britain. The entries cover adult as well as juvenile literature and refer to women and men belonging to various generations, positive and negative images, various geographical regions.

Each entry provides the author's name, dates of birth and death (if it is the case), main area of writing, brief description of the character (in fiction or plays) or title of poem, and the source (title of book or journal, plus publication data) in parentheses. Whenever the date of birth is unknown, the letters n.d. are mentioned after the author's (poet's) name, meaning *no data* are available in standard library catalogs (book, card, or computer form) or in standard reference sources.

Bibliography

Librarians, Publishers, and Booksellers in Novels and Plays

Barzun, Jacques, and Wendell H. Taylor. *A Catalogue of Crime.* New York: Harper & Row, 1971.

Burke, W.J., and Will D. Howe. *American Authors and Books.* New York: Crown, 1972.

Contemporary Authors: A Biographical Guide to Current Authors and Their Work. Detroit: Gale Research Company, 1967–1986.

Contemporary Authors: Permanent Series. Detroit: Gale Research Company, 1975–1986.

Fiction Catalog. New York: H.W. Wilson Company, 1950–1986.

Heylman, Katherine M. "Librarians in Juvenile Literature." *School Library Journal* (May 1975): 25–28.

McReynolds, Rosalee. "A Heritage Dismissed." *Library Journal* 110, no. 18 (November 1985): 25–30.
Moynahan, Julie. "Libraries and Librarians: Novels and Novelists." *American Libraries* (November 1974): 550–53.
Play Index. New York: H.W. Wilson Company, 1950–1986.
Ward, Martha, and Dorothy Marquardt. *Authors of Books for Young People.* Metuchen, N.J.: Scarecrow Press, 1971.

Librarians and Libraries in Poetry

American Poetry Index. Great Neck, N.Y.: Poetry Index Press, vols. 1984–1986.
Annual Index to Poetry in Periodicals. Great Neck, N.Y.: Poetry Index Press, 1985.
Poetry Index Annual. Great Neck, N.Y.: Poetry Index Press, vols. 1980–1993.
Roth's American Poetry Annual. Great Neck, N.Y.: Roth Publishing, vols. 1980–1982.

Librarians, Publishers, and Booksellers in Novels and Plays

ALDIS, DOROTHY KEELEY (1861–1962), American author of juvenile literature.

Miss Quinn's Secret—An intelligent and pretty woman librarian in a small town gets young readers involved in a local project (New York, 1949).

ALLINGHAM, MARGERY (1904–1966), American author of mysteries.

Flowers for the Judge—A murder and mysterious disappearance of a family of English publishers (New York, 1936).

AMIS, KINGSLEY WILLIAM (1922–   ), British author.

One Fat Englishman—A bad-tempered and child-hating English publisher is a successful woman's conqueror (New York, 1964).

The Uncertain Feeling—A young Scottish assistant librarian in a public library pursues a promotion on the basis of an affair with the wife of an official (New York, 1956).

ANGELO, VALENTI (1897–   ), American author of juvenile literature.

Big Little Island—Two women librarians, both working for the New York Public Library, assist a young immigrant reader (New York, 1965).

BASSO, HAMILTON (1904–1966), American author.

The Greenroom—Relationship between an editor of a publishing company and its most important author of memoirs (New York, 1949).

BERKMAN, EVELYN (b. n.d.), American author.

The Fourth Man on the Rope—A young woman librarian, divorced and mother of a teenage son, leaves the capital of England to work as a cataloger in a small town (New York, 1972).

BETTS, DORIS WAUGH (1932–   ), American author.

Heading West—A young female librarian in her thirties is kidnapped by a psychopath while on vacation (New York, 1981).

BIGGERS, EARL DERR (1884–1933), American author.

The Black Camel—A young and bright woman librarian involved in solving a mystery (New York, 1928).

BLAKE (DAY-LEWIS), **NICHOLS** (CECIL) (1904–   ), American author of mysteries.

End of a Chapter—Deletions in libelous manuscript shortly before printing, and the murder of an author on the publisher's premises (New York, 1957).

BLUE, ROSE (1931–   ), American author of juvenile literature.

A Quiet Place—A young and pretty black woman librarian uses tact and politeness in a conversation with a young reader who is disappointed with the closing of the library (Danbury, Conn. 1969).

BLUME (SUSSMAN), **JUDY** (1938–   ), American author of juvenile literature.

Forever—A forty-year-old librarian, mother of a teenage girl, is in charge of a children's room in a public library (New York, 1975).

BÖLL, HEINRICH (1917–), German novelist.

The Safety Net—An owner of a newspaper chain in Germany is affected by terrorism (New York, 1982).

BONHAM, FRANK (1914–   ), American author of juvenile literature.

Mystery of the Fat Cat—A library director and a young woman librarian help members of a local youth gang solve a mystery (New York, 1968).

BRAINE, JOHN GERARD (1922–   ), British author.

The Jealous God—A would-be Catholic priest falls in love with a pretty woman librarian and divorcee (Boston, 1965).

BRAUTIGAN, RICHARD GARY (1935–1984), American novelist.

The Abortion: A Historical Romance—A young male librarian, manuscript curator, flies with his pregnant girlfriend to Mexico for an abortion (New York, 1971).

BRODERICK, DOROTHY (1929–   ), American author of juvenile literature.

Leete's Island Adventure—A woman librarian uses books to help a teenager solve his problems, and she encourages his girl friend to become a librarian (New York, 1962).

BROOKNER, ANITA (1938–   ), American author.

Look at Me—A young woman, curator of illustrations for a medical research group, and her environment (New York, 1983).

BURR, ANNA ROBESON (1873–1941), American author.

The Jessop Bequest—The librarian is a man beset by problems, and he is assisted by a young man and a young woman (Boston, 1907).

CANFIELD (FISHER), **DOROTHY** (DOROTHEA) (1879–1958), American author.

"Hillsboro Is Good Luck"—A young librarian who loves his work tries to enlighten the inhabitants of a small town, and after a fire destroys the library, the librarian marries a local woman (in *Atlantic Monthly*, July 1908, 131–39).

CAUDILL, REBECCA (1899–   ), American author of juvenile literature.
Did You Carry the Flag Today?—A young and attractive woman librarian has a positive influence on readers of a public library; she skillfully communicates her ideas (New York, 1971).

CHURCHILL, WINSTON (1871–1947), American novelist.
Coniston—A woman librarian advocating intellectual freedom for American women (New York, 1906).

CLEARY, BEVERLY (1916–   ), American author of juvenile literature.
Beezus and Ramona—One woman librarian is patronizing and distant from readers, while her colleague, also a woman, is understanding and helpful to young readers (New York, 1955).
Emily's Runaway Imagination—A warm and pleasant woman librarian shows understanding for readers, both young and adult (New York, 1961).

CLEWES, DOROTHY MARY (1907–   ), English author.
The Library—A young woman librarian is pleasant, smiling, and hard working; she helps a group of young readers from a London slum (New York, 1970).

COOPER, KENT (1880–1965), American author.
Anna Zenger, Mother of Freedom—Fictionalized story of the first newspaper in New York, and the battle for freedom of the press (New York, 1946).

DALY, ELIZABETH (1878–1967), American author of mysteries.
Arrow Pointing Nowhere—A murder connected to a picture torn from a book of views, and the involvement of a bibliophile detective eager to solve the crime (New York, 1944).
Book of the Dead—The bibliophile detective from the previous book is in great mortal danger (New York, 1944).
Book of the Lion—The bibliophile detective is involved in an apparent discovery of a rare book by Chaucer (New York, 1948).
Night Walk—A village librarian is one of the murdered victims, and the suspect is lured to the library (New York, 1947).

DASKAM (DODGE), **JOSEPHINE BACON** (1876–1961), American author.
''Little Brother of the Books''—A crippled child inspires love and compassion from people at large, and from three rigid librarians (in *Whom the Gods Destroyed*, New York, 1902).

DRURY, ALLEN (1918–   ), American novelist.
Anna Hastings; The Story of a Washington Newspaper Person—A successful woman publisher writes her biography, but a friend journalist retraces her life story in a different manner (New York, 1977).

EBERHART, MIGNON GOOD (1899–   ), American author of mysteries.
Witness at Large—A double murder and nearly a third murder of a survivor, all related to a would-be sale of a publishing house (New York, 1966).

ENRIGHT, ELIZABETH (1909–1968), American author of juvenile literature.
Thimble Summer—A short and fat woman librarian shows love and understanding for two young readers who were locked up in the library for one night (New York, 1938).

ESTES, ELEANOR (1906–   ), American author of juvenile literature.
Rufus M—A middle-aged, plumpish woman librarian spends most of her time with catalog cards, punching books or carrying books; she is helpful to a young reader (New York, 1943).

FOLEY (DENNISTON), **RAE** (ELINORE) (1900–1978), American author.
Girl on a High Wire—A woman librarian inherits an estate of over $15 million and confronts enemies (New York, 1969).

FRANKLIN (HENSINGER), **CLAY** (CLAYTON) **FRANKLIN** (1907–   ), American playwright.
''No Sweet Revenge''—A man from a small town in the South tries to blackmail a librarian who did not overlook his forgery (in *Two for a Happening*, New York, 1969).

FRAYN, MICHAEL (1933–   ), English playwright and fiction author.
Alphabetical Order—A new assistant librarian brings order into his arid and colorless office (London, 1976).

FREEMAN, DON (1922–   ), American author of juvenile literature.
Quiet, There's a Canary in the Library—A young woman librarian, pleasant but keeper of discipline in a public library, raises a warning finger when a young dreaming reader starts shouting (San Francisco, 1969).

GAGLIANO, FRANK (1931–   ), American playwright.
Night of the Dance—Battle between library staff and the members of a youth gang who want to destroy the library (New York, 1969).

GEORGE, JEAN CRAIGHEAD (1919–   ), American author of juvenile literature.

My Side of the Mountain—A young woman librarian from a small town is attractive, discreet, tactful, and helpful to readers (New York, 1959).

GILBERT, EDWIN (1907–1976), American author.
The Hour Glass—Censorship of books, and its various aspects, examined in the last section of the volume (Philadelphia, 1959).

GOODRUM, CHARLES ALVIN (1923–   ), American author.
Dewey Decimated—A retired librarian helps to investigate the murder of a curator of rare books in the library stacks (New York, 1977).

GUARE, JOHN (1938–   ), American playwright.
"A Day of Surprises"—A comedy deriding librarians who act more like lifeless books, rather than human beings (in *Best Short Plays*, Philadelphia, 1970).

HAGGARD, HENRY RIDER (1856–1925), English author of mysteries.
Mr. Meeson's Will—Love and murder, set in a publishing house with 2,000 employees who edit and sell books by cheating the authors (New York, 1888).

HILL, DONNA MARIE (1921–   ), American author of juvenile literature.
Catch a Brass Canary—A young librarian gets involved in a conflict between teenagers in a branch library in New York City (Philadelphia, 1965).

HODGINS, ERIC (1899–   ), American author.
Blanding's Way—A publisher of a local newspaper tries to integrate into a new community (New York, 1950).

JAMES, HENRY (1843–1916), American novelist.
The Bostonians—A young and refined cataloger at Harvard University (New York, 1886).

JOHNSON (BISHOP), **W. BOLINGBROKE** (MORRIS) (1893–1973), American author.
The Widening Stain—Two murders in an academic library, with a woman librarian solving the case (New York, 1941).

JOYCE, JAMES (1882–1941), Irish novelist.
Ulysses—Three male librarians, including the dean of the National Library of Ireland, show kindness and understanding (Dublin, Ireland, 1922).

KELLOGG, MARYONE (1922–   ), American author.
Like the Lion's Tooth—Two librarian types run a school for disturbed asth-

matic children and are involved in endless psychological interpretations of the children's acts and gestures (New York, 1972).

KONIGSBURG, ELAINE (1930–   ), American author of juvenile literature.
Jennifer, Hecate, Macbeth, William McKinley and Me, Elizabeth—A young woman librarian loves readers even if they don't greet her, because they are good readers (New York, 1967).

LEWIS, SINCLAIR (1855–1951), American novelist.
Main Street—A younger woman librarian, independent and revolutionary, is contrasted with another woman librarian, more rigid, of the older generation (New York, 1920).

LINCOLN, JOSEPH CROSBY (1870–1944), American author.
Galusha the Magnificent—A scholarly author of books and librarian in Boston (New York, 1921).

MAGGI, CARLOS (1922–   ), Uruguayan playwright.
"The Library"—A satire of the bureaucracy and stagnation for several decades in a Latin American library (in W.I. Oliver, *Voices of Change in the Spanish American Theater*, Austin, Tex., 1971).

MARCHANT, WILLIAM (1923–   ), American author and playwright.
The Desk Set—A reference librarian with an encyclopedic knowledge is changed by an electronic brain (New York, 1956).

MERWIN, SAMUEL (1910–   ), American author.
Anabel at Sea—A woman librarian searches for a husband on a cruise around the world (Boston, 1927).

MILLER, HELEN LOUISE (n.d.), American playwright on juvenile subjects.
"The Library Circus"—In this play, animals step out from books to present a circus for children (in *First Plays for Children*, Boston, 1971).

MITCHELL, SILAS WEIR (1829–1914), American author
The Guillotine Club—A medical student is temporarily employed in a library with the purpose to solve mysteries; His supervisor is a very fussy man (New York, 1910).

MOELLER, PHILIP (1880–1958), American playwright and librettist.
"Helena's Husband"—Play, in which the king's librarian is over seventy years old, wise and good speaker, but with a shabby appearance (in *Five Somewhat Satirical Plays*, New York, 1918).

MOJTABI, ANNE GRACE (1938–   ), American author and librarian.
Mundome—A male librarian who works in a kind of Kafkaesque environment in a public library in New York, shows deep compassion for his mentally ill sister (New York, 1974).

MORLEY, CHRISTOPHER DARLINGTON (1890–1957), American author.
The Haunted Bookshop—A bookseller keeps a secondhand bookshop in Brooklyn, New York, and trains a young girl, with whom he discusses the value of books and reading (New York, 1919).
Parnassus on the Wheels—A spinster in her thirties, who was trained by the bookseller from the previous books, looks for adventures and buys a van of books to sell them in the countryside (New York, 1917).

MOYNAHAN, JULIAN LANE (1925–   ), American author.
Pairing Off—A young male cataloger working for the Boston Free Library, and his adventures with women (New York, 1969).

NAIPAUL, VIDIADHAR SURAJPRASAD (1932–   ), American author, originally British, born in Trinidad Tobago.
Stone and the Knight's Companion—An aging and lonely male librarian working for a London private company (New York, 1964).

NEUFELD, JOHN (1938–   ), American author of juvenile literature.
Freddy's Book—Two women librarians from the children's section of a public library, even though nice with readers, are not helpful in a case when a boy wanted a book on sex (New York, 1973).

NICHOLSON, MEREDITH (1866–1941), American author and diplomat.
''The Susiness of Susan''—A young and clever woman librarian befriends an explorer and archeologist, who was invited as guest speaker (in *Best Laid Schemes*, New York, 1922).

NORRIS (GILMAN), **KATHLEEN** (1880–1966), American author.
Martie the Unconquered—A young woman is unsuccessfully married, leaves her husband, and starts a new life, with her child, as a librarian in a public library (New York, 1917).

PARKER, RICHARD (1915–   ), American author of juvenile literature.
A Time to Choose: A Story of Suspense—A young and pretty woman librarian and male librarian who talks a lot, viewed by English teenagers (New York, 1973).

PHILLIPS, DAVID GRAHAM (1867–1911), American author.
Golden Fleece—All library workers are polite and obliging, except one li-

brarian, a man who likes to gossip and does not have a pleasant appearance. (New York, 1903).

PHILLIPS, ETHEL CALVERT (1947–   ), American author.
Pyxie—A woman librarian from New Jersey helps a reader to find the right book (New York, 1932).

PHILLIPS, MARGUERITE (n.d.), American juvenile playwright.
"The Man Behind the Book"—A play portraying a young male librarian who must solve the problem of misplaced letters by a pseudonym author (in A.S. Burack, *A Treasury of Holiday Plays for Teenagers*, Boston, 1963).

PIRANDELLO, LUIGI (1867–1936), Italian dramatist.
The Late Matia Pascal—A male librarian, tired of his monotonous life, assumes a new personality after an accident, but at the end he is disappointed (New York, 1964, originally published in 1904).

POWELL, ANTHONY (1905–   ), English author.
What's Become of Waring—The fate of an English book publishing house, and its best-seller author, rendered in a humorous manner (Boston, 1963).

PRINCE, MARJORIE (n.d.) American author.
The Cheese Stands Alone—Two old-maidish school teachers, who become summer librarians on a vacation island, are suspicious of young boys and girls, and one of them likes to catch people with overdue books (Boston, 1973).

PURDY (ALBEE)**, JAMES** (EDWARD) (1928–   ), American author.
Cabot Wright Begins—A group of publishers and writers put together various segments of a convicted rapist's life to commercialize it into a best-seller (New York, 1964).

PYM (CRAMPTON)**, BARBARA** (MARY) (1913–1980), English author.
An Unsuitable Attachment—An older librarian gets attached to a young man (New York, 1982).

RAYMOND, ERNEST (1888–1974), American author.
Gentle Graves—A retired publisher leaves to his daughters the love story of his two cousins, set in London before World War II (New York, 1985).

ROMAINS, JULES (1885–1972), French author of mysteries.
Men of Good Will—A bookbinder gets involved—for mere curiosity—in the activities of a murderer (New York, 1933).

ROTH, PHILIP MILTON (1933–   ), American novelist.
Goodbye, Columbus—A young library aid in the reading room of a public library, and his relations with readers of various ethnic backgrounds: blacks, Jews, Irish (Boston, 1959).

ROTHBERG, ABRAHAM (1922–   ), American author and critic.
The Thousand Doors—An American literary agent tries to smuggle a manuscript of a former Communist leader in Yugoslavia (New York, 1965).

SACHS, MARILYN (1927–   ), American author of juvenile literature.
Veronica Ganz—A round-faced woman librarian, knowledgeable and well read, is challenged by a nasty young reader (New York, 1968).

SEDGES (BUCK)**, JOHN** (PEARL) (1892–1973), American author.
Long Love—A young man, supported by his wife, persuades his father to invest money in book publishing and builds a successful business (Fresno, Calif., 1949).

SEGAL, ERICH (1937–   ), American author.
Love Story—A Yale University student falls in love with a young woman librarian who suffers from leukemia and dies (New York, 1970).

SIMENON, GEORGE (1903–   ), Belgian author of mysteries.
"The Little Man from Archangel"—A bookstore owner is in despair because of his wife's infidelity and the neighbors' hostility (in *Sunday and the Little Man from Archangel*, New York, 1966).

SMITH, BETTY WEHNER (1904–1972), American author.
A Tree Grows in Brooklyn—A woman librarian working for a public library in Brooklyn hated children, never smiled, made unfriendly comments, and never noticed a little girl who took out books every day (New York, 1943).

STEVENSON, DOROTHY EMILY (1892–1972), English author.
Miss Buncle's Book—A young woman, who writes a book about her village, marries the publisher (New York, 1937).
Miss Buncle Married—The woman from the previous books is happily married, and she writes a new book, but this time the book is never published (New York, 1937).

STRONG, L[EONARD] A[LFRED] (1896–1958), English author.
Which I Never—Activities of a company of vanity publishers, murder, espionage, and disappearances (New York, 1952).

SYMONS, JULIAN GUSTAVE (1912–   ), English author of mysteries.

The Narrowing Circle—Murder in a large publishing company (New York, 1954).

The Plain Man—Murder in a publishing company, solved by its editor (New York, 1952).

TAYLOR, SYDNEY (1904–1978), American author of juvenile literature.

All-of-a-Kind Family—A young and attractive woman librarian is sensitive and sympathetic to readers of an immigrant family (Chicago, 1951).

More All-of-a-Kind Family—A middle-aged woman librarian in the adult room overlooks library rules in order to accommodate younger readers (Chicago, 1954).

THIRKELL (MACKAIL), **ANGELA** (1890–1961), English author of mysteries.

Pomfret Towers—A young publisher marries a woman who produces for him a new manuscript (New York, 1938).

TULY, JIM (1891–1947), American author.

Emmett Lawler—Women librarians help young readers in the library (New York, 1922).

VAN VECHTEN, CARL (1880–1964), American black author.

Nigger Heaven—A young black woman works in a public library in Harlem (New York, 1926).

VOLODIN (LIFSHITŜ), **ALEKSANDR** (1919–   ), Soviet playwright.

"The Idealist"—A Soviet librarian's work and life (in V.D. Mihailovich, *White Stones and Fir Trees*, Lewisburg, Pa., 1971).

WALLACE, IRVING (1916–   ), American novelist and biographer.

The Almighty—An heir to an owner of a newspaper wants to upgrade circulation by hiring terrorists whose acts shock the world and make big headlines (New York, 1982).

WEIDMAN, JEROME (1913–   ), American author.

The Center of the Action—An enterprising young man takes over a closed New York publishing company and develops it into a prosperous business (New York, 1969).

WHARTON, EDITH (1862–1937), American author.

Summer—A young and rather dim woman librarian works in a local public library and, at the end, marries the custodian of the library (New York, 1917).

WHITE, THEODORE HAROLD (1915–   ), American author.
The View from the Fortieth Floor—The president of a new publishing company fights to save some magazines from failure, having in mind the fate of thousands of employees (New York, 1960).

WIDDEMER, MARGARET (1880–1978), American novelist and poet.
The Rose Garden Husband—A young woman assistant librarian, with a very low salary, dreamed of being married and having a house and money (Philadelphia, 1915).

WOOLEY, CATHERINE (1904–   ), American author of juvenile literature.
Ginnie and Geneva—A woman librarian who is pleasant and nice, with deep interest in children (New York, 1948).

ZINDEL, PAUL (1936–   ), American author of juvenile literature.
The Pigman—A young woman librarian in a high school is very helpful to young readers (New York, 1968).

Librarians and Libraries in Poetry

ANDERSON, NINA DUVAL (n.d.-   ).
"The Benson Branch," in Zydek, Frederick, ed., *Close to Home: Poems.* Omaha: Creative Writing Program, University of Nebraska at Omaha, 1981.

ARVIO, SARAH (n.d.-   ).
"Library at Los Milagros," in *The Yale Review*, 76, 1987.

BLUNDEN, EDMUND (1896–1974), British poet.
"In a Library," in Alan Taylor, ed., *Long Overdue: A Librarian's Reader.* Edinburgh: Library Association, 1993.

CHAR, RENE (1907–1988).
"The Library is on Fire," in Sonia Raizis, ed., *Chelsea Retrospective 1958–1983.* New York: Chelsea Associates, 1984.

COLINAS, ANTONIO (1946–   ).
"Giacomo Casanova Accepts the Position of Librarian," in Kay Pritchett, ed., *Four Post Modern Poets of Spain.* Little Rock: The University of Arkansas Press, 1991.

EBERHART, RICHARD (1904–   ).
"Reading Room, The New York Public Library," in Paul Janeczko, ed.,

Going Over to Your Place: Poems for Each Other. Minneapolis: Bradbury Press/ Macmillan, 1987.

ESCHNER, SISTER MAURA (1915–   ).
"The Library: South Stair," in author's *Hope is a Blind Heart.* Wheaton, Ill.: Harold Shaw Publications, 1989.

FINLEY, MICHAEL (MIKE) (1950–   ).
"The Browsers," in Robert Wallace, ed., *Light Years '84.* Cleveland: Bits Press, 1983.

FLEMING, RAY (1945–   ).
"Daydreaming in the Bodleian Library," in author's *Diplomatic Relations.* East Lansing, Mich.: Lotus, 1982.

HEARN, MICHAEL PATRICK (1950–   ).
"In the Library," in author's *Breakfast, Books and Dreams: A Day in Verse.* New York: Frederick Warne, 1981.

HESS, SONYA (n.d.).
"The Library is Showing Art Ful of a Breaze of Shadow," in *West Branch Journal*, 24, 1989 (Bucknell University).

HOLLINGSWORTH, JOHN (1916–   ).
"I fell in Love with a Librarian," in Ian Dury, ed., *Hard Lines: New Poetry and Prose.* Winchester, Mass.: Faber & Faber, 1983.

HUFF, BARBARA (1929–   ).
"The Library," in Jack Prelutsky, ed., *The Random House Book of Poetry for Children.* New York: Random House, 1983.

JAECH, STEPHEN (n.d.).
"Library Night Assignment," in *Seattle Review*, 8, no. 2. Seattle: University of Washington, 1985.

JARRELL, RANDALL (1914–1965).
"A Girl in the Library," in Richard Ellman, *Modern Poems.* New York: W.W. Norton, 1989.

JOHNSON, PYKE JR. (n.d.).
"Take a Librarian to Lunch," in Robert Wallace, ed., *Light Years '85.* Cleveland: Bits Press, 1984.

KNOX, CAROLINE (1938–   ).
"The Crybaby at the Library," in Charlotte Mandel et al., eds., *Saturday's Women: Eileen W. Barnes Award Anthology.* Upper Montclair, N.J.: Saturday Press, 1982.

KYLE, CHRISTIAN J. (n.d.).
"Six Poetry Anthologies in the High School Library," in Ronet McFarland et al., eds., *Deep Down Things: Poems of the Pacific North West.* Seattle: Washington State University Press, 1990.

LAYTON, IRVING (1912–   ).
"Letter to a Librarian," in X. J. Kennedy, *Tygers of Wrath: Poems of Hate, Anger and Invective.* Atlanta: University of Georgia Press, 1981.

LIFSHIN, LYN (1949–   ).
"The Librarian," in author's *Kiss the Skin Off.* Silver Springs, Md.: Cherry Valley, 1985.

MCDANIEL, WILMA ELIZABETH (n.d.).
"Library Patrons," in *Hanging Loose* (Journal), no. 52, 1988. Brooklyn, N.Y.

MCDOWELL, ROBERT (1953–   ).
"The Librarian after Hours," in author's *Quiet Money.* New York: Henry Holt, 1987.

MCILVANNEY, WILLIAM (1936–   ), British author.
"In the Library," in Alan Taylor, ed., *Long Overdue: A Library Reader.* Edinburgh: Library Association, 1993.

MANNING, NICHOLA (n.d.).
"Library Books," in *Wormwood Review*, 25, no. 1, 1985, Stockton, Calif.

NIMS, JOHN FREDERICK (n.d.).
"The Library," in *American Libraries*, February 1991.

OCHESTER, ED (1939–   ).
"In the Library," in Paul Janeczko, ed., *Poetspeak: In their Work, About their Work.* Portland, OR: Bradbury Press, 1983.

OLSON, CHARLES (1910–1970).
"The Librarian," in A. Poulin, ed., *Contemporary American Poetry* (4th ed.). Boston: Houghton Mifflin, 1985.

PALMER, MICHAEL (1942–   ).
"The Library is Burning," in Douglas Meserli, ed., *Language Poetries: An Anthology.* New York: New Directions, 1987.

RUBIN, LARRY (1930–   ).
"A Note on Library Policy," in *Light Years '85.* Cleveland Bits Press, 1984.

SCOTT, DENNIS (1939–   ), British Poet.
"Hatch: or the Revolution Viewed as an Exploding Library," in E. Markham, ed., *Hinterland: Caribbean Poetry from the West Indies and Britain.* New Castle, England: Bloodaxe Books, 1989.

SKILLMAN, JUDITH (n.d.).
"The Librarian Decides on Cryonics," in author's *Worship of the Visible Spectrum.* Portland, Ore.: Breitenbush Books, 1988.

SMITH, DAVE (1942–   ).
"A Quilt in the Bennington College Library," in Jack Myers et al., eds., *New American Poets of the 90s.* Boston: David R. Godine, 1991.

TOWLE, TONY (1939–   ).
"The Morgan Library," in *New and Selected Poems, 1963–1983.* New York: Kulchur Foundation, 1983.

WAGONER, DAVID (1926–   ).
"After the Speech to the Librarians," in Peter Wild et al., eds., *New Poetry of the American West.* Durango, Colo.: Logbridge-Rhodes, 1982.

WILLIAMS, WILLIAM CARLOS (1883–1963).
"The Library," in author's *The Collected Poems of William Carlos Williams.* New York: New Directions, 1986.

5

Librarian's Philately: Books, Newspapers, and Libraries on Stamps, by Country

This section has 127 entries, presenting a selection of stamps—issued by over 100 countries from all continents, and by the United Nations—with books, newspapers, and libraries as a topic, but also honoring various cultural and educational events in the historical development of each country. It may serve as a checklist for those who are already involved in collecting this special topic or as an incentive to start collecting stamps as a recreational-educational hobby.

Each entry provides the country's name, the year of issue, a short description of a specific stamp (book, newspaper, library), the event honored by the stamp (anniversary, International Book Year, campaign against illiteracy, for example), and the source (catalog symbol and identification number) in parentheses. In some cases, there is an annotation reading "part of a set with other themes," which means that a specific stamp or stamps are part of a set with other subjects (for instance, a stamp with a library building may be part of a set with various architectural constructions other than libraries).

Bibliography

Brooks, Arthur E. *Education on Stamps*. Milwaukee, Wis.: American Topical Association, 1969.

Eberhart, George M. "Biblio-Philately: Libraries and Librarians on World Stamps." *American Library* (June 1982): 382–86.

Krol, Hans. "Libraries and Archives on Postage Stamps." *Topical Time* (September–October 1976): 81–83 and (November–December 1979): 28–31.

Minkus World Wide Postage Stamp Catalog. New York: Minkus Publications, 1995.

Richter, John Henry. "Librarians and Archives on Stamps." *Topical Time* (reprint) 6–7 (1955–1956): 20–23.

Scott Standard Postage Stamp Catalogue (vols 1–5). New York: Scott Publishing Company, 1995.

Yvert & Telier Catalogue de Timbre-Poste. Amiens, France: Yvert & Telier, 1995.

ALBANIA

1967—Open book with Albanian alphabet letters and children reading, 60th anniversary of the adaptation of the unified Albanian alphabet at the Congress of Monastyr (S/1191–1192). 1972—Newspapers, 30th anniversary of the Albanian press (S/1432–1434).

ALGERIA

1965—Library of Algiers burning, third commemoration of the fire set by French colonial troops before retreating (S/B-98 1972—Open book with International Book Year emblem (S/477). 1980—Open book and library, Science Day (S/640).

ANDORRA

1987—Catalan old manuscript (S/182).

ANGUILLA

1972—Public Library of the Valley, part of a set with other themes (S/153). 1976—same stamp with overprint ''New Constitution'' (S/239).

ARGENTINA

1980—Buenos Aires Gazette, 1810, Journalism Day honored (S/1270).

ARMENIA

1992—Runic message from the 7th century B.C., part of a set (S/435-A).

AUSTRALIA

1960—Open Bible, 350th anniversary of King James Bible (S/339). 1961—Page from the *Book of Hours*, 350th anniversary of King James Bible (S/342). 1967—Hands and Bible, 150th anniversary of the British and Foreign Bible Society (S/424).

AUSTRIA

1929—National Library, part of a set with other themes (S/338). 1931—Same stamp, with an overprint of the 1931 Rotary Convention (S/B-29). 1933—same stamp, with overprint ''Interhilfe'' (S/B-121). 1947—National Library, part of a set with other themes (S/B-215). 1966—rare books, picture and archive collection and noted illustrations, National Library honored (S/733–776).

BAHAMAS

1962—Nassau Public Library, part of a set celebrating city's 100th anniversary. (S/179). 1978—Nassau Public Library, part of set honoring architectural heritage (S/420).

BARBADOS
1970—Open book and a child reading, part of a set devoted to the 25th anniversary of the International Year of Education and the United Nations (S/344). 1972—Public Library of Bridgetown, part of a set devoted to the International Book Year (S/378).

BELGIUM
1915—Library of Louvain, part of a set with various views (S/118). 1918—Same stamp, with a red cross overcharge and additional values (S/B-43). 1928—Same library, new building, part of a set intended to combat tuberculosis (S/B-83). 1962—Royal Library, part of a set intended to help cultural and philanthropic organizations (S/B-706). 1966—Royal Archives and Royal Library, part of a set honoring the national scientific heritage (S/619–620). 1972—Newspaper and pen, freedom of the press (S/770). 1975—Library of Louvain, 25th anniversary of Bible Colloquium (S/931). 1977—Open book painting by Van Eyck Brothers, 50th anniversary of the International Federation of Library Associations (S/993).

BERMUDA
1962—Public Library and Historical Society of Hamilton, part of a set with various buildings (S/182). 1970—Same stamp, surcharged with new value (S/244). 1984—Newspaper, 200th anniversary of the press and postal service (S/446).

BOLIVIA
1977—Mastheads of several newspapers, Bolivian press honored (S/604–608). 1992—Newspaper *Los Tiempos* front page, 25th anniversary of the paper (S/850).

BRAZIL
1938—National Archives, 100th anniversary of this institution (S/464). 1975—*O Estado de Sao Paolo*, 100th anniversary of this newspaper (S/1375). 1987—National Archives 150th Anniversary, illuminated Georgian canticle and computer terminal (S/2125). 1988—Abolition of slavery, official declaration and quill pen, maps with African coastline and slave routes between Africa and South America (S/2132–2133). 1988—100th anniversary of two famous books—*O Ateneu* by Raul Pompeia, and *Poesias* by Olavo Bilac (S/2150–2151). 1989—Public Library of Bahia building (S/2162). 1990—Centennial anniversary of Bahia State Public Archives, building (S/2228). 1990—180th anniversary of Brazilian National Library, set depicting building (S/2288–2290).

BULGARIA
1953—Kolarov Library, 75th anniversary of this library (S/854). 1956—Open book and Ivan Vazov National Library, 100th anniversary of this library (S/

926–928). 1964—Title page of *Bukvar' Poucheniia*, 140th anniversary of the Bulgarian Primer (S/1341). 1977—Newspaper masthead, 50th anniversary of the newspaper *Rabotnichesko Delo* and 100th anniversary of Bulgarian daily press (S/2422). 1978—Manuscript books from the 13th to 16th centuries, 100th anniversary of Cyril and Methodius National Library (S/2544–2548). 1982—Public libraries and reading rooms, 125th anniversary (S/2810). 1987—60th anniversary of newspaper *Rabotnichesko Delo*, mast of newspaper (S/3255). 1987—95th anniversary of newspaper *Rabotnik*, 90th anniversary of newspaper *Rabotnicheski Vstnik*, and 60th anniversary of newspaper *Rabotnichesko Delo*, front pages of the three papers (S/3287-A). 1988—30th anniversary of journal *Problems of Peace and Socialism*, cover titles (S/3356). 1991—100th anniversary of *Philatelic Press* magazine, title pages (S/3611).

BURKINA FASO
1990—International Literacy Year, open book (S/804–805).

BURMA
1976—Three open books and students, International Literacy Year (S/257–260).

CAMBODIA
1960—Open book and a girl with a book in her hand, fight against illiteracy (S/82). 1972—Open book, International Book Year honored (S/272–274).

CANADA
1930—Library of the Parliament, part of a set with other themes (S/173). 1958—Newspapers, Canadian press honored (S/375). 1964—Confederation Memorial and Library, 100th anniversary of the Charlestown Conference (S/431). 1966—Library of the Parliament, 12th Conference of the Parliamentary Association (S/450).

CENTRAL AFRICAN REPUBLIC
1972—Open book and emblem of the International Book Year, this event honored (S/156). 1977—Bible and people, Bible Week (S/316).

CHILE
1969—Open Bible, 400th anniversary of the translation of the Bible in Spanish (S/380). 1972—Book and young people, International Book Year (S/429).

CHINA, PEOPLE'S REPUBLIC OF
1979—Central Archives Hall, International Archives Week (S/1544–1546). 1992—10th anniversary of Constitution, book (S/2422).

CHINA, REPUBLIC OF (TAIWAN)
1992—Books and bookbinding, scrolls, fold binding, butterfly binding, string binding (S/2830–2833).

COLOMBIA
1941—National Library, Bogota, part of a set with other buildings (S/C-131, S/C-133). 1948—Same library, with stamp values changed (S/C-161, S/C-163). 1950—Same library, with new stamp values (S/C-183, S/C-185, S/C-196, S/C-198). 1951—Same stamp, with values changed again (S/C-205, S/C-207, S/C-214, S/C-216). 1973—Bogota University Library, 350th anniversary (S/C-581, 582). 1977—Charter of National Library, 200th anniversary of this institution (S/C-651, 652). 1988—National anthem, text and score (S/974).

CONGO, REPUBLIC
1972—Open book, International Book Year honored (S/C-140). 1990—International Literacy Year, open book and two youngsters (S/848).

COSTA RICA
1959—National Library, part of a set with other themes (S/C-280). 1967—Various flowers, revenues to help university library (S/C-443 to 450). 1972—Open book and National Library, International Book Year honored (S/C-545 to 548). 1976—Open book and tree, publishing in Costa Rica (S/C-658 to 660). 1978—A reader with book and map of the country, National Five Year Literacy Program (S/275).

CUBA
1957—First publication in Cuba, Jose Marti National Library honored (S/582, S/C-167, 168). 1958—*Diario de la Marina*, newspaper building (S/C-179). 1978—Alfredo M. Aguayo University Library, 150th anniversary honored (Y/443) Yvert & Telier Catalogue (see Bibliography).

CYPRUS
1974—Title page of a history book, part of a set honoring the Second International Congress of Cypriot Studies (S/419). 1976—Children and a library, part of a set with other themes (S/149). 1977—Library of Sultan Mahmud II (M/49) Minkus Catalog (see Bibliography). 1978—Municipal Library of Paphos, part of a set with other themes (S/497).

CZECHOSLOVAKIA
1966—State Science Library of Olomovc, 400th anniversary of this library (S/1412). 1972—Open book, International Book Year honored (S/1804). 1989—12th Biennial of Children's Book Illustrations, illustrations from books of various countries (S/2754–2757).

DENMARK

1973—Royal Library of Copenhagen, 300th anniversary (S/525). 1982—Printing press, 500th anniversary of printing (S/730). Danish University Library, 500th anniversary of this institution (S/731).

DOMINICA

1975—Public Library of Rousseau, part of a set honoring country's national day (S/443).

DOMINICAN REPUBLIC

1936—Noted personalities of the country, set issued to collect funds for the erection of a National Library and Archives building (S/310–322). 1970—Children reading books, First World Exhibit of Books and Culture Festival in Santo Domingo (S/677, S/C-181, 182). Book and sun, International Education Year (S/RA-48). 1972—Open book, International Book Year (S/689–690, S/C-191).

ECUADOR

1956—Title page of first book printed in Ecuador, 200th anniversary of printing (S/C-302 to 305). 1958—Municipal Library and Museum of Guayaquil, part of a set publicizing philately (S/C-333). 1959—Front page of *El Telegrafo*, 75th anniversary of country's oldest newspaper (S/C-342).

EGYPT

1966—Printed page and torch, 100th anniversary of national press (S/691). 1968—Open *Koran*, 1400th anniversary of this book (S/C-118, 119). 1976—Front page of *Al-Ahram*, 100th anniversary of this newspaper (S/1010). 1979—Open book, reader and globe, Cairo International Book Fair (S/1099). 1980—Golden goddess of writing and open book, Cairo International Book Fair (S/1129). 1991—50th anniversary of Syndicate of Journalists, quilt pen, manuscript, and globe (S/1437).

ETHIOPIA

1966—Press building, opening honored (S/455-457). 1972—Open Bible and first Amharic Bible, World Assembly of United Bible Societies (S/634–636). 1990—UNESCO World Literacy Year, illiterate man holding newspaper upside down, adults learning alphabet in school, literate man holding newspaper upright (S/1271/1273).

FAROE ISLANDS

1978—National Library, old and new buildings publicizing this institution (S/39–40).

FINLAND
1932—Helsinki University Library, part of a set with other themes (S/B-9). 1935—Bards reciting from the *Kalevala* and heroes from this national epic, 100th anniversary of publication (S/207–209). 1982—Periodical *Om Konsten atT Ratt Behaga*, 200th anniversary (S/662). *Abckiria*, first Finnish book, part of a set devoted to education (S/668). 1988—500th anniversary of *Missale Aboense*, the first printed book in Finland (S/775). 1990—Illustrations from various fairy tale books (S/820–825).

FRANCE
1937—Books *Discours sur la Méthode* and *Discours de la Méthode*, by R. Descartes, 300th anniversary of publication (S/330–331). 1959—Books and symbols of learning, 150th anniversary of the Palm Leaf Medal of the French Academy (S/905). 1981—Bookbinding process, no annotation (S/1739). Newspaper *La Gazette*, 350th anniversary (S/1743).

GERMANY, BERLIN (WEST) (before unification of both Germanys)
1978—National Library, building opening (S/9 N-421).

GERMANY, EAST (DEMOCRATIC REPUBLIC) (before unification with West Germany)
1958—Newspaper *Rote Fahne*, 40th anniversary (S/418). 1971—Berlin old library, part of a set with other themes (S/1289). 1975—Dictionary of Jacob and Wilhelm Grimm, part of a set honoring the German Academy of Science 275th anniversary (S/1661). 1976—Library, part of a set devoted to the Leipzig Fall Fair (S/1755). 1977—Leipzig Book Fair building, event honored (S/1801). 1981—Egyptian papyrus, Maya manuscript, French manuscript, East German literary treasures honored (S/2207–2209). 1990—Treasures in the German State Library of Berlin, rare books from the 13th through 18th centuries (S/2828/ 2831).

GERMANY, WEST (FEDERAL REPUBLIC) (before unification with East Germany)
1972—Open book, International Book Year honored (S/1095). Lithography press, 175th anniversary of lithography printing (S/1088). 1980—Duden dictionaries, old and new editions, 100th anniversary (S/1325). Title page of Moravian Brothers Bible, 250th anniversary (S/1333).

GERMANY, WORLD WAR II
1939—Johannes Gutenberg and the Leipzig Library, part of a set honoring the Leipzig Fair (S/494).

GHANA
1972—Books for children and students, and Accra Central Library, International Book Year (S/445–449).

GIBRALTAR
1971—Gibraltar Commercial Library, part of a set with other topics (S/255).

GREECE
1976—Greek grammar of 1478, 500th anniversary of printing in this country. 1980—Open book, energy conservation manual, part of a set with other themes (S/1354). 1982—Byzantine religious books and illuminated manuscripts, set honoring printing (S/1427–1431).

GREENLAND
1980—Training College Library and teacher Rasmus Bertheln, 150th anniversary of public library service (S/140).

GRENADA
1981—Open book, pencil, adult education, part of a set marking the Second Festival of the Revolution (S/1034).

GUATEMALA
1973—*Libro Nacional de Guatemala* and its translator and discoverer Francisco Ximenez, International Book Year (S/424–427).

GUINEA
1964—Eleanor Roosevelt with an open book, reads to children, set honoring the first lady and the 15th anniversary of the Universal Declaration of Human Rights (S/613–617). 1972—Open books, man and woman readers, International Book Year honored (S/613–617).

GUYANA
1968—Open *Koran*, 1400th anniversary of this book (S/60–63).

HUNGARY
1948—Book and emblem of Athenaeum Press, 100th anniversary of this publishing house, part of a set with other themes (S/830). 1954—National Museum and Library, part of a set with other themes (S/1085). 1960—Municipal libraries, 60th anniversary, part of a set with other themes (S/1578). 1970—Bibliotheca Corvina, interiors, 100th anniversary of Hungarian postal stamps (S/B-279 to 282). 1972—Girl reading, International Book Year (S/2144). 1987—125th anniversary of Hungarian printing, paper and worker's union, woodcuts from the 18th century (S/3074).

ICELAND
1925—Reykjavik Museum Building, housed the National Library and still housing the National Archives (S/25). 1953—Icelandic manuscript books of the 15th century (S/278–282). 1968—Reading room in the National Library, 150th anniversary (S/400–401). 1970—Icelandic manuscript books of the 14th century (S/417–419).

INDIA
1976—Excerpt from *Vande Mataram*, national song of the country (S/746). 1979—Old Buddhist text, National Archives honored (S/829). Boy and alphabet book, International Book Fair in New Delhi (S/831).

INDONESIA
1972—Books and readers, International Book Year (S/818).

IRAN
1965—Open book, Book Week honored (S/1360). 1966—Book cover, Book Week publicity (S/1414). 1978—Books, International Book Year honored (S/1691–1692). 1991—1st Asian Biennial of Children's Books, illustrations from various children's books (S/2480). 1993—14th anniversary of the country's Islamic Republic, open book (S/2581).

IRAQ
1969—Open book and hands reaching it, campaign against illiteracy (S/519–520). Newspaper front page, 100th anniversary of Iraqi press (S/521). 1979—Book, pencil and flame, compulsory education law (S/908–910). Open book and world map, Arab achievements (S/917–918).

IRELAND
1949—Leinster House building, originally headquarters of the National Library (S/139–140). 1977—Irish manuscript of the 16th century, 100th anniversary of the National Library and Museum (S/411–412).

ISLE OF MAN
1975—Man and Bible and various religious personalities, 200th anniversary of the *Manx Bible* (S/74–77). 1978—James Ward Public Library, part of a set with other themes (S/137). 1982—*The Principles and Duties of Christianity*, first book printed in Manx in 1707, and its author T. Wilson (S/213).

ISRAEL
1963—Hebrew typesetter of the 19th century, 100th anniversary of Hebrew press in Palestine (S/241–241a). 1967—Page from *Shulhan Arukh*, 400th anniversary of this Jewish religious and civil code book (S/340). 1972—Printed page, International Book Year honored (S/495). 1974—Elias Sourasky Library

of the Tel-Aviv University, part of a set with other themes (S/545). 1975—Illuminated page, 400th anniversary of Hebrew printing in the city of Safad (S/645). 1991—150th anniversary of newspaper *Jewish Chronicle*, front page (S/1092). 1993—Centennary of Hebrew magazines for children, front pages (S/1179).

ITALY

1972—*Divina Comedia* by Dante, various editions, 500th anniversary of publication (S/1077–1079). 1975—State Archives building, 100th anniversary of unification of all state archives (S/1200). 1988—500th anniversary of first printed Bible in Hebrew (Sonino Bible), bible book from the 15th century (S/1733).

IVORY COAST

1972—Children reading, International Book Year honored (S/326). 1975—National Library, first anniversary (S/387).

JAPAN

1948—School children reading a book, reorganization of country's educational system (S/406). 1961—National Diet and book, opening of the National Diet Library (S/739).

JORDAN

1968—Open book and hands reaching for knowledge, fight against illiteracy campaign (S/548–549). 1973—Open book, International Book Year (S/737–738).

KENYA

1980—National Archives and Mc Millan Library, part of a set with other themes (S/175, 179).

KENYA, UGANDA, TANGANYIKA (before gaining independence)

1963—Open book and scholars, inauguration of the University of East Africa (S/140–141).

KOREA, NORTH (DEMOCRATIC REPUBLIC)

1973—Kim-Il-Sung University Library in Pyongyang (Y/1178).

KOREA, SOUTH (REPUBLIC OF)

1962—Library of early Buddhist scriptures, part of a set with other themes (S/370). 1966—Same as above (S/394). 1967—Same as above (S/583). 1969—Same as above (S/650), all with changed values. 1970—Open book, International Education Year (S/700). 1972—Open book and globe, International Book Year (S/808). 1976—Books and children, juvenile literature (S/1044).

KUWAIT
1967—Open book and hands reaching for knowledge, literacy campaign (S/368–369). 1968—Open book and flags, Education Day (S/374–375). Open book and emblem, Teacher's Day (S/382–384). 1971—Open book, readers and UNESCO symbol, International Literacy Day (S/533–534). 1972—Open book and emblem, International Book Year (S/539–540).

LAOS
1950—Wat Sisaket Library, near Vientiane, postage due set (S/J-1 to 7). 1970—Same library, different values (S/C-65).

LIBERIA
1950—Hand, open book and sun, National Literacy Campaign (S/329, S/C-66).

LIBYA
1972—Open book, International Book Year (S/437–438). 1975—Woman and man in a library, Libyan Arab Book Exhibition (S/570–572). 1976—Arabic scroll, Arab Regional Branch of the International Council of Archives (S/639–641). 1977—Colonel Muammar Qadhafi's *Green Book*, outline on Libyan society (S/707).

LIECHTENSTEIN
1987—125th anniversary of Constitution, text of handwritten Constitution (S/872). 1993—Caligraphic Christmas texts by various authors (S/1013–1015).

LUXEMBOURG
1981—National Library building, part of a set with other themes (S/655).

MALDIVE ISLANDS
1970—Teacher, adult readers and classroom, International Education Year (S/338–342). 1972—Open book, International Book Year (S/381–382).

MALI
1972—People, book and pencil, World Literacy Day (S/181). 1972—International Book Year (S/C-157).

MAURITIUS
1980—Helen Keller reading a Braille book, part of a set with other themes (S/504).

MEXICO
1939—First printing shop in Mexico and printer J. Zumárraga, 400th anniversary of printing in this country (S/748–750). 1972—Library, International Book Year (S/1048). 1989—10th International Book Fair, open books (S/1606).

MONACO
1982—Open book, reader and globe, International Bibliophile Association (S/1343).

MONGOLIA
1960—Newspaper *Unen*, 40th anniversary of the press (S/212–213). 1968—*Das Kapital* by Karl Marx, death commemoration of the author (S/486–487). 1990—70th anniversary of *Unen* newspaper, first page (S/1811).

NETHERLANDS
1977—*Delft Bible*, oldest book printed in Dutch, 500th anniversary (S/368).

NEW ZEALAND
1968—*Maori Bible*, 100th anniversary of publication in the Maori language (S/408).

NICARAGUA
1972—mystery books by various authors, 50th anniversary of Interpol (S/C-801 to 812).

NORWAY
1966—Open *Bible*, 150th anniversary of the Bible Society (S/490–491). 1974—Gulating Law, manuscript of the 13th century and the king lawmaker (S/635–636).

PAKISTAN
1958—Open book, 10th anniversary of the Declaration of Human Rights (S/99–100). 1964—Bengali and Urdu alphabet books, Universal Children's Day (S/211). 1976—Children reading a book, juvenile literature (S/428).

PANAMA
1956—National Archives, 100th anniversary of President B. Porras' birth (S/406–407). 1953—Newspaper *La Estrella*, 100th anniversary of the country's first newspaper (S/C-138 to 139).

PAPUA AND NEW GUINEA
1967—Book and pen, symbol on country's university, part of a set with other themes (S/232).

PARAGUAY
1966—*Paraguay de Fuego* by Ruben Dario, set honoring the author (S/C-366 to 370).

PERU
1988—Newspapers and newspapermen, issued for Journalists' Fund (S/938).

PHILIPPINES
1949—Title pages of rare books and noted librarians, aimed to collect funds and restore war-damaged libraries (S/B-1 to B-3). 1976—Book and emblem, 75th anniversary of National Archives (S/1292).

POLAND
1935—E. Raczynski Public Library of Poznan, part of a set with other themes (S/302). 1936—Same as above, overprinted "Gordon-Bennett, August 30, 1936" (S/307). 1991—200th anniversary of Polish Constitution, front page (S/3035–3036).

PORTUGAL
1931—Woman symbolizing Portugal holding the book *Luisiadas* by Luis de Camoens (S/497–519). Reissued in subsequent years. 1962—Children reading, part of a set devoted to a congress of pediatrics (S/891). 1978—Books, bookcase and postal cards, printing press, 100th anniversary of Postal Museum and Postal Library (S/1414). 1979—Children reading books, 50th anniversary of the International Bureau of Education (S/1433–1434). 1987—150th anniversary of Portuguese Royal Library building in Rio de Janeiro, building depicted (S/1708).

QATAR
1971—Boy reading, International Literacy Day (S/256–258). 1972—Open book, International Book Year (S/299–302). 1978—Man learning to read, International Literacy Day (S/534–535).

ROMANIA
1945—*Gazeta Matematica*, 50th anniversary of this mathematics journal (S/596–597). 1948—Various newspapers, week of democratic press (S/695). Government printing plant and press, 75th anniversary of state printing (S/679–680). 1965—*Scînteia*, 25th anniversary of this newspaper (S/1109). 1967—Romanian Academy Library, 100th anniversary (S/1960). Book *Das Kapital* by Karl Marx, 100th anniversary of publication (S/1961).

RYUKYU ISLANDS
1968—Young man, library, book and map, 10th International Library Week (S/169).

SAAR REGION
1952—Saar University Library, part of a set with other themes (S/244). 1955—Same as above with overprint "Volksbefragung 1955" (S/259).

SAINT PIERRE AND MIQUELON ISLANDS
1986—450th anniversary of discovery of the two islands, geography books depicted (S/476).

EL SALVADOR
1970—National Library, 100th anniversary (S/819). Same as above with overprint "Año del Centenario de la Biblioteca Nacional/1970" (S/C-297).

SAMOA, WESTERN
1962—Apia Public Library, no annotations (S/225). 1969—*Treasure Island* and other books by Robert L. Stevenson, 75th anniversary of this author (S/308–311).

SAN MARINO
1943—Printing press and various newspapers, press honored (S/203–212). 1990—Drawings from book *Pinocchio* in a cartoon style (S/1212–1215).

SAUDI ARABIA
1963—Open *Koran*, Islamic Institute anniversary (S/252–254). 1992—Documents and scrolls regarding the Royal Consultative Council (S/1169–1170).

SENEGAL
1989—3rd Francophone Summit on the Arts and Culture, one stamp depicts children reading a book (S/825–828). 1989—75th anniversary of country's National Archives, building and documents depicted (S/837–840).

SOMALIA
1973—Somali script, set publicizing this script (S/400–402).

SOUTH AFRICA
1970—*Bible*, 150th anniversary of the South African Bible Society (S/362). 1975—*Afrikaanse Patriot*, title page of this first newspaper of the country (S/449).

SOVIET UNION (before the fall of Communism)
1939—V.I. Lenin Library in Moscow, part of a set with other themes (S/708). 1949—Men reading newspaper *Pravda* and other publications, Soviet Press Day celebration (S/1355–1356). 1950—Newspapers *Iskra* and *Pravda*, 50th anniversary of the first title (S/1532–1533). 1954—Various books by V.I. Lenin, 50th anniversary of the Communist Party (S/1678–1679). 1957—V.I. Lenin Library, Moscow philatelic exhibition (S/1979); *Kolokol;* 100th anniversary of this newspaper's first issue (S/1949). 1962—V.I. Lenin Library, 100th anniversary (S/2609–2610). 1964—Soviet Academy of Science Library, 250th anniversary (S/2980). 1967—*Izvestiîa*, 50th anniversary of this newspaper (S/3308). Book

Das Kapital by Karl Marx, 100th anniversary of publication (S/3360). 1975—
Komsomol'skaîa Pravda, 50th anniversary of this newspaper for youth (S/4282).
Pionerskaîa Pravda, 50th anniversary of this newspaper for children (S/4283).
1982—*Pravda*, 70th anniversary of this Communist Party newspaper (S/5309).
1988—30th anniversary of journal *Problems of Peace and Socialism*, journal
cover (S/5703). 1989—Folk tale books from various Soviet republics, illustrated
pages (S/5789–5793).

SPAIN
1916—National Library, part of a set collecting war taxes (S/O-14, O-18).
1930—Newspapers, press building and book *Don Quijote de la Mancha*, 40th
anniversary of Madrid Press Association (S/C-73 to 87). 1977—Earliest known
Catalan manuscript, 1000th anniversary of the Catalan language (S/2056).
1979—Children in a library, International Year of the Child (S/2146). 1990—
500th anniversary of novel *Tirant Lo Blanch*, illuminated page from novel (S/
2630).

SRI LANKA
1968—Open *Koran*, 1400th anniversary of this book (S/419). 1970—Ola leaf
manuscript, International Education Year (S/451). 1972—Open book International Book Year (S/472).

SURINAME
1990—UNESCO International Literacy Year, adult and child with an open book
(S/852–854).

SWEDEN
1941—Reformers presenting *Bible* to Gustavus Vasa, 400th anniversary of the
first authorized version of this book in Swedish (S/316–318). 1961—Printer of
the 17th century and a reader in the library, 300th anniversary of the Royal
Library as a depository library (S/600–602). 1983—Printing press and various
books, 500th anniversary of printing in Sweden (S/1448–1452). 1990—Newspaper mastheads, set devoted to paper production (S/1837–1840).

SWITZERLAND
1961—Book of history with symbols of time and eternity, no annotations (S/
B-303).

SYRIA
1970—Open book and radar, International Telecommunications Day (S/C-458,
C-459). 1972—Open book, International Book Year (S/606–607). 1968—Old
man and woman reading, literacy campaign (S/C-406 to 409).

THAILAND
1987—International Literacy Day, children and adults in front of an open book (S/1185).

TOGO
1969—Books and map of Africa, 12th anniversary of the International Association for the Development of Libraries in Africa (S/709).

TONGA
1983—Printing press, newspaper *Tonga Chronicle* and missionary W. Woon, 150th anniversary of printing in this country (S/551–554). 1984—*Tonga Chronicle*, 20th anniversary of this newspaper (S/580–581).

TUNISIA
1960—Presidential Library and President Habib Bourguiba (S/384–386). 1989—Open book with young readers, stamp honors education (S/958). 1992—African Human Rights Conference, open book with French and Arabic inscriptions "Human Rights" (S/1016).

TURKEY
1969—*Kutadgu Bilig*, a law book written in 1069, 900th anniversary of publication (S/1827).

TURKISH REPUBLIC OF NORTHERN CYPRUS
1989—*Saded* newspaper centennary, one stamp part of a set (S/258–262).

UNITED ARAB EMIRATES
1980—Open book and sun, Arab achievements symbols (S/109–111). 1989—20th anniversary of newspaper *Al Ittihad*, front page of newspaper (S/285–286).

UNITED NATIONS
1955—Open book, 10th anniversary of the United Nations Charter (S/35–38). 1969—Books and United Nations emblem, publicity for U.N. Institute for Training and Research (S/192–193).

UNITED STATES
1939—Stephen Day press, 300th anniversary of printing in Colonial America (S/857). 1952—*Gutenberg Bible*, 500th anniversary of the printing of this book (S/1014). 1954—Columbia University Memorial Library, 200th anniversary of the founding of this university (S/1029). 1955—Open book and symbols of various disciplines, 100th anniversary of Michigan State College (S/1065). 1957—*Bible*, quill pen and hat, 300th anniversary of Flushing Remonstrance (S/1014). 1975—Early American printing press, part of a set with other themes (S/1593). 1981—New York University Library, part of a set with other themes

(S/1928). 1982—The Library of Congress, this institution honored (S/2004). Letters of the alphabet and words "American Libraries," second stamp devoted to Library of Congress (S/2015).

Note: In October 1985, the U.S. Postmaster General approved new standards, developed by the Citizen's Stamp Advisory Committee, which eliminate the honoring of libraries and other non-profit institutions on stamps. (*Stamp Collector*, October 14, 1985, p. 39.)

URUGUAY
1945—*La Educacíon del Pueblo*, a book by José P. Varela, part of a set honoring this author (S/534). 1960—National Printing House, no annotations (S/Q-91). 1982—Open book and two readers, National Literacy Campaign (S/1131). 1993—75th anniversary of newspaper *Diario El Pais*, newspaper mast (S/1476).

VATICAN
1961—*L'Oservatore Romano*, 100th anniversary of this newspaper's publication (S/310–312). 1972—Illuminated medieval manuscripts, International Book Year (S/521–525). 1975—Investiture of Vatican's first librarian, Bartolomeo Sacchi, by Pope Sixtus IV, and Pope visiting the library, 300th anniversary of the founding of the Vatican Apostolic Library (S/582–584). 1980—Illuminated letters, codices, Vatican Apostolic Library honored again (S/668–672). 1991—Centenary of Papal Encyclical *Rerum Novarum*, title page (S/882–884).

VENEZUELA
1968—*Correo del Orinoco* and printing press, 150th anniversary of this newspaper (S/915).

VIETNAM
1972—Book and globe, International Book Year (S/441–443). 1974—National Library Building in Saigon, this institution honored (S/480–481).

YEMEN, NORTH (before unification with the South)
1979—Open book, sun and map, Arab achievements honored (S/354–355).

YEMEN, SOUTH (DEMOCRATIC REPUBLIC) (before unification with the North)
1972—Open book, International Book Year (S/124–125).

YUGOSLAVIA (before the secession of Bosnia-Herzegovina, Croatia, Macedonia, and Slovenia; presently Yugoslavia consists of Serbia and Montenegro)
1947—*Gorski Vijenac*, a national epic book of Montenegro by Peter Nyegosh, 150th anniversary of this book's publication (S/215–217). 1972—Serbian National Library in Belgrade, 140th anniversary (S/1119). 1974—National University Library in Ljubljana, 200th anniversary (S/1225). 1975—*Matica Srpska*,

150th anniversary of this first Serbian literary journal (S/1232). 1979—*Politika*, 75th anniversary of this newspaper's publication (S/1416). 1981—Serbian printing office, 150th anniversary of printing in Serbia (S/1543). 1982—*Borba*, 60th anniversary of this Communist Party newspaper (S/1562). 1986—Ancient manuscripts from 14th through 18th centuries (S/1792–1795). 1989—800th anniversary of *Kulin Ban* charter, text on stamp (S/1976). 1990—500th anniversary of enthronement of King Dzuradz Crnojevic, illuminated manuscript (S/2036). 1990—50th anniversary of newspaper *Vjesnik*, pages from paper (S/2063).

ZAIRE
1971—Open book and man reading, fight against illiteracy (S/747–749).

___ 6 ___
Librarian's Latin Expressions

This section comprises 145 entries with Latin words/expressions related to books, publishers, and libraries. Like many other professionals (e.g., lawyers, doctors, pharmacists, botanists, etc.) who have special terms and expressions in their professions, librarians and publishers have their own Latin terms and vocabulary. These words and phrases are encountered in books, in daily activities, during the research process, and in correspondence with other librarians or with American and/or foreign institutions.

The expressions included in this section were compiled on a selective basis, and those which have an asterisk(*) in front are mottos of various American colleges or universities.

Bibliography

Bills, A.J. *A Dictionary of Foreign Words and Phrases in Current English.* New York: E.P. Dutton, 1966.

Cassell's Latin Dictionary: Latin-English and English-Latin. New York: Macmillan, 1982.

Follett World-Wide Latin Dictionary: Latin-English and Latin-American English. Chicago: Follett, 1967.

Mawson, C.O. Sylvester. *Dictionary of Foreign Terms.* New York: Thomas Crowell, 1975.

Acta diurna (publica, urbana)—newspapers; three expressions for newspapers vary according to different historical periods.

Ad apertum librum—with an open book; to study without any preparation.

Ad finem—toward the end; usually speaking of pages, chapters, or passages of a book.

Ad usum Delphini—for the use of the Dolphin; refers to books of Latin classical authors with censored texts, especially prepared for the son of King Louis XIV of France.

Ad usum scholarum—books with censored texts, prepared for the use of students.

Addenda et corrigenda—additions and corrections; usually mentioned at the end of a book and intended to modify the erroneous words.

Adversaria—memoranda; things written on the opposite page of a book; comments.

Albus liber—white book; usually devoted to important events.

Apocrypha—writings of doubtful authorship; refers to parts of the Bible excluded by the reformers.

Apparatus criticus—critical notes assisting in the study of a text printed from a manuscript.

Ars artium omnium conservatrix—the art of preserving all arts; expression referring to printing books.

*Artes, scientia, veritas—art, science, truth; motto of the University of Michigan.

Auctor—author of a book.

*Aut disce, aut discede; manet tertia caedi—either learn or leave, the third choice is to be flogged; motto of Winchester College, England.

Aut liberi aut libri—or songs or books; refers to the fact that similar songs have different meanings.

Avete—greetings; expression used in school magazines as a heading for a list with new members or subscribers. *See also Salvete* and *Valete*.

Bibliopola—bookseller.

Bibliotheca, bibliothecae—library, libraries.

Bibliothecae processe—librarian; early Latin.

Bibliothecarius—librarian; late Latin.

Breviarium—book of laws; compilation of laws.

Breviora—short editions by the same author; expression mostly used in English-speaking countries.

Caestrum—etching, needle, stylus, used for writing manuscript books in the Middle Ages.

Caetera desideratur—the rest is to be desired; means that the manuscript is not complete.

Caetera dessunt—the manuscript or another document is missing.

Cancel—the substituted part of a manuscript; *See Cancellandum.*

Cancellandum—part of a leaf (page) of a book for which another is substituted.

Capita selecta—main parts of a written work.

Caret—missing; typographical expression or symbol indicating that some words are missing; usually the missing words are written above the line or on a margin.

Codex, codices—book, books written on parchment; it also means a collection of laws (e.g., Codex Justinianus).

Colophon—an inscription or device at the end of a manuscript or printed book, similar to a modern title page.

Collectanea—collection of notes and quotations, gathered from various sources.

Confer—compare, consult (abbreviated cf. or cfr.); it means to insert in a book or writing, or determine a passage or page.

Corpus—body; collection of works on a given subject or by a certain author (e.g., Corpus Iuris Civilis, etc.).

Crambe repetita—cabbage dished up again; redundant text in a book.

Crux, cruces—a difficult point; usually in a text which editors find hard to explain.

Crescat scientia, vita excolatur—let knowledge grow, let life be perfected; motto of University of Chicago.

Cursus litteratum—the true reading of a manuscript or book text is deformed in copying it. *See also Ductus litteratum.*

DDD (*dat donat, dicat or dat, dicat, dedicat*)—given, offered, dedicated, or given, devoted and dedicated; inscription on a book by its author.

De omnibus rebus et quibusdam aliis—concerning all things and other matters; refers to books with vague subjects.

Dei sub numine vegit—it flourishes under the will of God; motto of Princeton University.

Dele (atur)—instruction given to a printer to correct galleys, usually by using the letter delta.

Disecta membra—fragment of a literary work not put in order.

Domini illuminatio mea—God is my light; motto of Oxford University.

Dramatis personae—list of characters in a play or story.

Ductus literatum—the process by which the true text, corrupted in the course of copying, is reestablished by its editor. *See also Cursus literatum.*

Editio princeps—the first printed edition of a book.

Emollit mores nec sinit esse feros—makes gentle the character and does not permit to be unrefined; motto of University of South Carolina.

Erratum, errata—error, errors; a list of corrected words or phrases, usually at the end of a book.

Et discere et rerum exquirere causa—both to learn and investigate things; motto of University of Georgia.

Et sequentes, et sequentia (abbr. et seq.)—and the following pages, chapters, etc.

Ex dono—as a gift; inscription made on a book, mentioning that it is a gift of the specified person.

Ex libris—from the book of; book label indicating the name of the book owner.

Excerpta—collection of copies of main works by an author, or gist of books (texts) by the same author.

Explicit—last word of a manuscript or document, having the same meaning as *Finis*, and the opposite of *Incipit*. *See Finis* and *Incipit.*

Expurganda—text (passages) to be eliminated from the books before printing.

Exudit—published, issued; expression used by publishers.

Facetiae—short, humorous paragraphs or jokes; expression used in book cataloging.

Farrago libeli—miscellaneous content of a book.

Fasciculus, fasciculi—a single-volume book issued in parts, sections; section of a book divided in smaller parts.

Fiat lux—let there be light; motto of Clark University.

Finis—end, limit; an expression indicating the end of a book.

Florea Etona—flourish Eton; motto of Eaton College, England.

Florilegium—gathering of flowers; also an expression used for an anthology of writings.

Folio verso (f.v.)—the back of a page.

Folium—leaf, page of a book.

Format—size of a book, external makeup, style, paper.

Gesta Romanorum—collection of tales related to the times of the Roman Empire.

Glutinator—book binder.

Glossa—explanation, interpretation, commentary, annotation of a text.

Gradus ad Parnasum—dictionary of phrases and poetical words, facilitating the writing of Latin poetry.

Grammaticus—concerned with reading and writing; a grammarian or philologist.

Helluo librorum—a book worm, a passionate reader of books.

Hinc lucem et polula sacra—from where we receive the lights and sacred rights; motto of Cambridge University.

Homo unius libro—a man of one book, ignoring the writings of others; an expression attributed to St. Thomas D'Aquino.

Ignotus—person unknown; expression used in catalogs of works of art when the author of the art piece is unknown.

Impensis—publisher.

In extenso—amply; usually referring to bibliographic quotations.

In quarto—in four leaves; book consisting of sheets folded twice to give four leaves.

Incipit—beginning of a manuscript or book; expression recorded for the purpose of identifying the beginning; opposed to *Explicit*.

Incunabulum, incunabula—cradle book or books; volumes printed before the 16th century, shortly after the invention of printing.

Index Expurgatorium—books marked with an asterisk in the *Index Librorum Prohibitorum* (see this title separately), and referring to books that cannot be read before correction. The index was first published in 1571 by the Vatican.

Index Librum Prohibitorum—Index of Prohibited Books, issued by the Vatican under the threat of excommunication for those who don't abide by it; authorized in 1564 by the Council of Trent.

Index locorum—index of passages cited in a book.

Index nominum—name index in a book.

Index rerum—subject index in a book.

Index Translationum—list of translated works in the world; a biannual publication of UNESCO since 1950.

Index verborum—Index of words, studies, quoted in a book.

Inedita—unpublished work by an author.

Legenda—things to be read; often mentioned in atlases and other reference works.

Legere—to read.

Legimus, ne legentur—we read that others may not read; refers to reviewers of books.

Libelus famosus—defamatory publications.

Libelus, libeli—book, books: *see also Liber.*

Liber, libri—book, books; general terms. *See also Codex* and *Volumen.*

Limae labor—work of the file; careful correction and revision of a work.

Loco citato (abbr. l.c.)—a cited passage from a book, to demonstrate a point.

Locus desperatus—a passage of a text mentioned in a manuscript with a completely changed meaning compared to the original.

Lux and veritas—light and truth; motto of Yale University.

Magnum opus—great work, main work of an author.

Marginalia—marginal notes in a printed work or manuscript.

Medicina animi—the medicine of the soul; an inscription on the door of the library of King Osimandias of Egypt.

Ne variatur—it may not vary; indicates that the text of a book or manuscript remain unchanged to become an authoritative source.

Nihil obstat—there is no objection; expression used by a religious censor indicating that the book does not contain unorthodox ideas.

Nonum editus—not yet edited.

Nota—an abbreviation or special sign made by medieval scribes.

Novella, novelle—short story, short stories, realistic or satirical.

Opera minora—minor works by an author.

Opera omnia—all works by another.

Operculum—works of small size.

Pegma—book case. *See also Scrinium.*

Pharmacopaea—book containing authoritative formulas for the preparation of drugs or medicine.

Punctum deletis—a dot written under a letter of a manuscript to indicate deletion.

Qui librum edendum curat—book publisher.

Qui scribit, bis legit—he who writes reads twice; Latin saying.

Quod bene notandum—to be especially noticed in a book or manuscript text.

Recensio—critical review of a book or manuscript.

Recitator—reader with a loud voice.

Redivivus—living again; a restored text of a book.

Repertorium—a catalog of writings or a program of a show.

Rubric—illuminated initial letter in a medieval manuscript or title (caption) of a chapter.

Salvete—greetings; title of a column in a school magazine, with new members. *See also Avete* and *Valete.*

Saeculum—mirror; title of many ancient books and compilations.

*Scientia sol mentis es—science is the sun of mind; motto of the University of Delaware.

Scrinium—case for books, or box for books.

Scriptum—written.

Scriptor classicus—classical writer; writer of books for the few.

Scriptor proletarius—writer for the masses.

Stet—let it stand; a deletion or correction in a manuscript to remain as it is.

Stilus—sharp instrument for writing on wax tablets.

Subjectum—subject of a book.

Summa—a summary treatise; a single work.

*Studiis et rebus honestis—for studies and noble achievements; motto of the University of Vermont.

Symposium—a collection of opinions of scholars.

Tablinum—archives room in an ancient Roman house.

Textus receptus—the standard text of a book or other writing.

Trivium, trivia—less serious work or works of a writer.

Vade mecum—goes with me; a handbook with ready reference.

Valete—farewell; heading of a column in a school magazine, with departing members. *See also Avete* and *Salvete.*

Variorum notae—with various notes of different commentators.

Vita sine litteris mors es—life without literature (books) is death; Latin saying.

Volumen, volumena—volume, volumes; referring to books in a roll form.

7

Librarian's Job-Finding Sources
of Information

This section lists 56 entries regarding state agencies, library organizations, and periodicals where library vacancies are announced. The job-hunting process is a hardworking and time-consuming period; sometimes it takes several weeks, but very often it may take several months to find a suitable job or change the place of work. In addition to a well-prepared resumé, the librarian seeking a job should be equipped with patience; have a positive attitude; be enthusiastic and never discouraged by setbacks; be well organized, polite, tactful, and respectful during the interview; and persuasively demonstrate the skills, intelligence, and competence to prospective employers. Job hunters should also keep in mind that the American Library Association's annual conferences (midwinter and summer) are excellent opportunities for studying the job market, for being interviewed, and for eventually getting the desired job. During these conferences, ALA's Placement Center organizes a special section with folders for employers (listing vacancies, requirements, salaries) and job seekers (listing resumés, with professional experience, desired jobs, etc.), and thus facilitates speedy and productive interviews. (*Note:* some of the telephone and fax numbers provided in this section may have changed during the time that this work was in production.)

Bibliography

Bielfield, Arlene. *Library Employment within the Law.* New York: Neal-Schuman, 1993.
Dewey, Barbara. *Library Jobs: How to Fill Them, How to Find Them.* Phoenix: Oryx Press, 1987.
Garoogian, Rhoda, and Andrew Garoogian. *Careers in Other Fields for Librarians.* Chicago: American Library Association, 1985.

Heim, Kathleen, and Margaret Myers. *Opportunities in Information Science Careers.* Lincolnwood, Ill.: VGM Career Horizons, 1992.

Moen, William, and Kathleen M. Heim. *Librarians for the New Millenium.* Chicago: American Library Association, 1988.

Organizations and State Agencies

American Association of Law Libraries
53 West Jackson, Suite 940
Chicago, IL 60604
Tel: 312-939-7877
Fax: 312-431-1097

American Society for Information Science
8720 Georgia Avenue, Suite #501
Silver Spring, MD 20910-3602
Tel: 301-495-0900
Fax: 301-495-0810

Arizona Department of Libraries, Archives & Public Records
1700 W. Washington, Room 300
Phoenix, AZ 85007
Tel: 602-275-2325
Fax: 602-255-4312

British Columbia Library Association
110-6545 Bonsor Avenue
Burnaby, BC V51 1HB, Canada
Tel: 604-430-6411

California Library Association
717 K St., Suite 300
Sacramento, CA 95814-3477
Tel: 916-447-8541; 916-443-1222; 818-797-4602 (identical listing)

California Media and Library Educators Association
1499 Old Bayshore Highway, Suite 142
Burlingame, CA 94010
Tel: 415-692-2350; 415-697-8832

California South Chapter, Special Libraries Association
2244 Walnut Grove Boulevard
Mail Stop G-55, GO 1
Rosemead, CA 91770
Tel: 818-302-8966
Fax: 818-302-8966

Colorado State Library
201 East Colfax, 3rd Floor
Denver, CO 80203-1704

Tel: 866-6741; 303-866-6732
Fax: 303-866-6940

Connecticut Library Association
Box 1046
Norwich, CT 06360
Tel: 203-645-8090

Delaware Division of Libraries
43 South Dupont Highway
Dover, DE 19901
Tel: 1-800-282-8696 (in-state); 302-739-4748 (out-of-state)

Drexel University College of Information Studies
Philadelphia, PA 19104
Tel: 215-895-1672; 215-895-2478

Florida State Jobline
R.A. Gray Building
Tallahassee, FL 32399-0251
Tel: 904-488-5232 (in-state); 904-487-2651 (out-of-state)

Illinois Jobline, Illinois Library Association
33 West Grand St., Suite 301
Chicago, IL 60610
Tel: 312-828-0930 (professionals); 312-828-9198 (support staff)

Indiana Statewide Library Jobline
Central Indiana ALSA
1100 West 42 St.
Indianapolis, IN 46208
Tel: 317-926-6561

Institutional Library Mail Jobline
G. Spooner, Consultant
State Library of Louisiana, POB 131
Baton Rouge, LA 70821-0131
Fax: 504-342-3547

Iowa State Library
East 12 and Grand Streets
Des Moines, IA 50319
Tel: 515-281-6788

Kansas State Library Jobline
c/o Jana Renfro, 3rd Floor State Capitol
Topeka, KS 66612
Tel: 913-296-3296

Kentucky Job Hotline
Department of Library Archives, Box 537

Frankfort, KY 40602
Tel: 502-564-3008; 502-875-7000

Long Island (NY) Library Resources
Melville Library Building, Suite E5310
Stony Brook, NY 11794-3399
Tel: 516-632-6650
Fax: 516-632-6662

Maryland Library Association Jobline
115 West Franklin Street
Baltimore, MD 21201
Tel: 410-685-5760; 410-727-7422

Medical Library Association Jobline
North Michigan Avenue, Suite 300
Chicago, IL 60602
Tel: 312-553-4636; 312-419-9094

Michigan Library Association
1000 Long Boulevard, Suite 1
Lansing, MI 48911
Tel: 517-694-7440; 517-694-6615

Missouri Library Association Jobline
1306 Business 63 S, Suite B
Columbia, MO 65201-8404
Tel: 314-442-6590; 314-449-4627

Mountain Plains Library Association
c/o Weeks Library, University of South Dakota
Vermillion, SD 57069
Tel: 605-677-5757; 605-677-6082
Fax: 605-677-5488

Music Library Association Placement Services
Placement Officer, 240 Morrison Hall
University of California
Berkeley, CA 94720
Tel: 510-643-5198
Fax: 510-641-8237

Nebraska Job Hotline
Nebraska Library Commission
1200 North Street, Suite 120
Lincoln, NE 68508-2023
Tel: 402-471-2045; 800-307-2665 (in-state only)

New England Library Jobline
GSLIS, Simmons College
300 The Fenway
Boston, MA 02115
Tel: 617-738-3148

New Jersey Library Association, Box 1534
Trenton, NJ 08607
Tel: 609-695-2121

New York Library Association
252 Hudson Avenue
Albany, NY 12210-1802
Tel: 518-432-6952; 800-232-6952 (in-state only)

New York Special Libraries Association
NYPL, Donnell Library, 4th Floor
20 West 53rd Street
New York, NY 10019
Tel: 212-740-2007
Fax: 212-247-5848

North Carolina State Library
Division of State Library
109 East Jones Street
Raleigh, NC 27601-2807
Tel: 919-733-6410; 919-733-2570

Ohio Library Council Jobline
35 East Gay Street, Suite 305
Columbus, OH 43215
Tel: 614-221-9057
Fax: 614-221-6234

Oklahoma Department of Libraries Jobline
200 N.E. 18th Street
Oklahoma City, OK 73105
Tel: 405-521-4202; 405-521-2502

Oregon Library Association
Oregon State Library
Salem, OR 97310
Tel: 503-585-2232; 503-378-4243

Pacific Northwest Library Association
c/o Graduate School of Library
University of Washington FM-30
Seattle, WA 988195
Tel: 206-543-2890; 206-543-1794

Pennsylvania Jobline
Pennsylvania Library Association
1919 North Front Street
Harrisburg, PA 17102
Tel: 717-234-4646; 717-233-3113

Pratt Institute SLIS Job Hotline
School of Library & Information Science
Brooklyn, NY 11205
Tel: 718-636-3742

Special Libraries Association
Headquarters, 1700 18th Street, NW
Washington, DC 20009
Tel: 202-234-3632; 202-234-4700

Special Libraries Association, New York Chapter
David Fank, 625 Avenue of the Americas
New York, NY 10011
Tel: 212-740-2007
Fax: 212-645-7681

Special Libraries Association, San Andreas–San Francisco Bay Chapter
(telephone information only)
Tel: 415-528-7766

Special Libraries Association, Southern California Chapter (no address)
Tel: 818-795-2145; 818-302-8966
Fax: 818-302-8015

Texas Library Association Job Hotline
3355 Bee Cave Road, Suite 401
Austin, TX 78746
Tel: 512-328-0651; 512-328-1518

Texas State Library Jobline
Library Development, Box 12927
Austin, TX 78711
Tel: 512-463-5470; 512-463-5447

University of South Carolina
College of Library and Information Science
Columbia, SC 29208
Tel: 803-777-8443; 803-777-3858

University of Western Ontario
School of Library & Information Science
London, ON N6G 1H1, Canada
Tel: 519-661-3543; 519-661-2111, ext. 8494

Virginia Library Association Jobline
669 South Washington Street
Alexandria, VA 22314
Tel: 703-519-8027

Washington–Metropolitan Government Library Council
1875 I Street, Suite 200
Washington, DC 2006
Tel: 202-962-3712; 202-223-6800, ext. 458

West Virginia Jobline
Call Pennsylvania Jobline

Periodical Job Announcements

American Libraries
American Library Association
50 East Huron Street
Chicago, IL 60611-2795
Tel: 312-944-6780
Fax: 312-440-9374

Chronicle of Higher Education
Chronicle of Higher Education, Inc.
1255 23rd St. NW
Washington, DC 20037-1190
Tel: 202-466-1000
Fax: 202-296-2691

College and Research Libraries
American Library Association
Same address, telephone, and fax as *American Libraries*

Journal of Academic Librarianship
JAI Press
55 Old Post Road, #2
Greenwich, CT 06836
Tel: 203-661-7602
Fax: 203-661-0792

Library Hotline
Cahners Publishing
249 West 17th Street
New York, NY 10011
Tel: 212-645-0067
Fax: 212-463-6530

Library Journal
Cahners Publishing
Same address, telephone, and fax as *Library Hotline*

New York Times
New York Times Company
229 West 43rd Street
New York, NY 10036
Tel: 212-556-1934; 212-556-1234

Using the Internet for Job Opportunities

AALL Placement WWW: [http://washburnlaw.wuac.edu/aallnet/aallplace.htm]

ALA College & Research Libraries: [http://www.jefferson.lib.co.us.71/00/jobline]

American Libraries Career Leads: [http://www.ala.org]

Internet Public Library: [http://www.ipl.org]

Library Support Staff Resource Center: [http://roden.lib.rochester.edu/ssp.default.htm]

The Riley Guide (various job banks): [http://www.jobtrack.com/jobguide]

For other opportunities and for background on the above, please consult Paula Azar, "Job Opportunities Glitter for Librarians Who Surf the Net," *American Libraries* (September 1996): 66–69.

APPENDIXES

___ Appendix 1 ___
The Librarian's Ten
Golden Rules

A Library User is the most important person in any library.

A Library User is not dependent on us—we are dependent on him.

A Library User is not an interruption of our work—he is the purpose of it.

A Library User does us a favor when he calls—we are not doing him/her a favor when he/she calls.

A Library User is a part of the library—not an outsider.

A Library User is not someone to argue or match withs with.

A Library User is a person who brings us his wants—it is our job to fill those wants.

A Library User is deserving of the most courteous and attentive treatment we can give him.

A Library User is the life-blood of the library and any parts or sections of it.

A Library User is not a cold statistic—he/she is a flesh-and-blood human being with feelings and emotions like our own.

Appendix 2
The Library Supervisor's Ten Golden Rules

The Supervisor *must always* be cheerful (if he/she is miserable it will make the whole office miserable).

The Supervisor *should never allow* two people to do what can be done by one person only (George Washington advised that a job that can be done by one is worse done by two, and scarcely done by three or more).

The Supervisor *should encourage staff* to be candid with him/her, should stimulate innovations and honest and constructive criticism, and permit staff members to voice disagreement face-to-face.

The Supervisor *should be fair* in dealing with staff members (unfairness at the top can demoralize office workers).

The Supervisor *should hire* people who are capable, hardworking, and with even better qualifications than the supervisor—this would build an agency of giants; if mediocre people are hired, then there will an agency of midgets.

The Supervisor *should make working fun*, encourage exuberance, and avoid sad people who spread gloom and doom.

The Supervisor *should never forget* that the most priceless asset of any agency has been, remains, and will always be respect for the library patron.

The Supervisor *should try* to be active in the community he/she serves and become a personage of the local community.

The Supervisor *should spot* people of unusual promise early in their careers, and move them up the ladder fast (otherwise they will leave the agency; their loss is as damaging as the loss of library patrons).

The Supervisor *should exude* self-confidence, and never be petty or a buck-passer; and—at the same time—be resilient and able to pick himself/herself up after a defeat very quickly.

___ Appendix 3 ___
Library Bill of Rights

The American Library Association affirms that all libraries are forums for information and ideas, and that the following basic policies should guide their services.

1. Books and other library resources should be provided for the interest, information, and enlightenment of all people of the community the library serves. Materials should not be excluded because of the origin, background, or views of those contributing to their creation.

2. Libraries should provide materials and information presenting all points of view on current and historical issues. Materials should not be proscribed or removed because of partisan or doctrinal disapproval.

3. Libraries should challenge censorship in the fulfillment of their responsibility to provide information and enlightenment.

4. Libraries should cooperate with all persons and groups concerned with resisting abridgment of free expression and free access to ideas.

5. A person's right to use the library should not be denied or abridged because of origin, age, background, or views.

6. Libraries which make exhibit spaces and meeting rooms available to the public they serve should make such facilities available on an equitable basis, regardless of the beliefs or affiliations of individuals or groups requesting their use.

Adopted by the American Library Association, June 18, 1948. Amended February 2, 1961, June 27, 1967, and January 23, 1980, by the ALA Council.

_____ Appendix 4 _____
Library Main Book
Classifications

DEWEY DECIMAL CLASSIFICATION

Classification	Subject	Classification	Subject
000	General Works	600	Applied Science
100	Philosophy	700	Fine Arts and Recreation
200	Religion	800	Literature
300	Social Sciences	900	History
400	Language	920	Collected Biography
500	Pure Science	B	Individual Biography

LIBRARY OF CONGRESS CLASSIFICATION

Classification	Subject	Classification	Subject
A-AZ	General Works	HM-HX	Sociology
B-BD, BH, BJ	Philosophy	J	Political Science
BF	Psychology	K	Law
BL-BX	Religion	L	Education
C, D	History—General	M	Music
DA	History—Great Britain	N	Art and Architecture
DB-DR	History—Europe	P	Philology, Linguistics
DS-DT	History—Asia, Africa	PA	Classics
DU	History—Australia, Oceania	PB-PD	Modern European Languages
E	History—U.S.—General	PE	English Language
F	History—Canada, Latin America	PF-PL, PM	German, Slavic, Oriental Languages
G-GC	Geography	PN	Literature—General
GF-GT	Anthropology	PQ	Romance Literature
GV	Sports	PR-PS	English and American Literature
H-HA	Social Sciences—General		
HB-HJ	Economics	PT	Germanic Literature

LIBRARY OF CONGRESS CLASSIFICATION (continued)

Classification	Subject	Classification	Subject
Q	Science—General	R	Medicine
QA	Mathematics	S	Agriculture
QB	Astronomy	T	Engineering and Technology
QC	Physics		
QD	Chemistry	U-V	Military and Naval Science
QE	Geology		
QH-QR	Life Sciences	Z	Bibliography

NATIONAL LIBRARY OF MEDICINE CLASSIFICATION

Classification	Subject	Subject	Classification
QS	Human Anatomy	WF	Respiratory System
QT	Physiology	WG	Cardiovascular System
QU	Biochemistry	WH	Hemic and Lymphatic Systems
QV	Pharmacology		
QW	Bacteriology and Immunology	WI	Gastrointestinal System
		WJ	Urogenital System
QX	Parasitology	WK	Endocrine System
QY	Clinical Pathology	WL	Nervous System
QZ	Pathology	WM	Psychiatry
W	Medical Profession	WN	Radiology
WA	Public Health	WO	Surgery
WB	Practice of Medicine	WP	Gynecology
WC	Infectious Diseases	WQ	Obstetrics
WD 100	Deficiency Diseases	WR	Dermatology
WD 200	Metabolic Diseases	WS	Pediatrics
WD 300	Diseases of Allergy	WT	Geriatrics, Chronic Disease
WD 400	Animal Poisoning		
WD 500	Plant Poisoning	WU	Dentistry, Oral Surgery
WD 600	Diseases Caused by Physical Agents	WV	Otorhinolaryngology
		WW	Opthalmology
WD	Aviation and Space Medicine	WX	Hospitals
		WY	Nursing
WE	Musculoskeletal System	WZ	History of Medicine

___ Appendix 5 ___
UNESCO Public
Library Manifesto

A Gateway to Knowledge

Freedom, prosperity, and the development of society and of individuals are fundamental human values. They will only be attained through the ability of well-informed citizens to exercise their democratic rights and to play an active role in society. Constructive participation and the development of democracy depend on satisfactory education as well as on free and unlimited access to knowledge, thought, culture, and information.

The public library, the local gateway to knowledge, provides a basic condition for lifelong learning, independent decision making, and cultural development of the individual and social groups. This Manifesto proclaims UNESCO's belief in the public library as a living force for education, culture, and information, and as an essential agent for the fostering of peace and spiritual welfare through the minds of men and women.

UNESCO therefore encourages national and local governments to support and actively engage in the development of public libraries.

The Public Library

The public library is the local center of information, making all kinds of knowledge and information readily available to its users.

The services of the public library are provided on the basis of equality of access for all, regardless of age, race, sex, religion, nationality, language, or social status. Specific services and materials must be provided for those users who cannot, for whatever reason, use the regular services and materials—for example, linguistic minorities, people with disabilities, or people in hospital or prison.

All age groups must find material relevant to their needs. Collections and services have to include all types of appropriate media and modern technologies as well as traditional materials. High quality and relevance to local needs and conditions are fundamental. Material must reflect current trends and the evolution of society, as well as the memory of human endeavor and imagination.

Collections and services should not be subject to any form of ideological, political or religious censorship, nor commercial pressures.

Missions of the Public Library

The following key missions, which relate to information, literacy, education, and culture, should be at the core of public library services:

1. creating and strengthening reading habits in children from an early age;
2. supporting both individual and self-conducted education as well as formal education at all levels;
3. providing opportunities for personal creative development;
4. stimulating the imagination and creativity of children and young people;
5. promoting awareness of cultural heritage, appreciation of the arts, scientific achievements and innovations;
6. providing access to cultural expressions of all performing arts;
7. fostering intercultural dialogue and favoring cultural diversity;
8. supporting the oral tradition;
9. ensuring access for citizens to all sorts of community information;
10. providing adequate information services to local enterprises, associations, and interest groups;
11. facilitating the development of information and computer literacy skills;
12. supporting and participating in literacy activities and programs for all age groups, and initiating such activities if necessary.

Funding, Legislation, and Networks

The public library shall in principle be free of charge. The public library is the responsibility of local and national authorities. It must be supported by specific legislation and financed by national and local governments. It has to be an essential component of any long-term strategy for culture, information provision, literacy, and education.

To ensure nationwide library coordination and cooperation, legislation and strategic plans must also define and promote a national library network based on agreed standards of service.

The public library network must be designed in relation to national, regional, research, and special libraries as well as libraries in schools, colleges, and universities.

Operation and Management

A clear policy must be formulated, defining objectives, priorities, and services in relation to the local community needs. The public library has to be organized effectively and professional standards of operation must be maintained. Cooperation with relevant partners—for example, user groups and other professionals at the local, regional, and national, as well as international level, has to be ensured.

Services have to be physically accessible to all members of the community. This requires well-situated library buildings, good reading and study facilities, as well as relevant technologies and sufficient opening hours convenient to the users. It equally implies outreach services for those unable to visit the library.

The library services must be adapted to the different needs of communities in rural and urban areas.

The librarian is an active intermediary between users and resources. Professional and continuing education of the librarian is indispensable to ensure adequate services.

Outreach and user education programs have to be provided to help users benefit from all the resources.

Note: This manifesto was presented at IFLA's 61st conference in Istanbul, Turkey (August 20–26, 1995). *Source: American Libraries* (October 1995). Reprinted with American Library Association's permission.

Appendix 6
American Library Association (ALA) Awards

ALA AWARDS

More than 100 awards are sponsored by ALA and its units to honor distinguished service and foster professional growth.

Please submit your application or nomination. The deadline for most awards is around December 1.

For more information and application forms, contact the ALA unit cited in parentheses for each award.

American Library Association
50 E. Huron St.
Chicago, IL 60611
Toll-free: 1-800-545-2433
Fax: 312-280-3224

Achievement/ Distinguished Service

AASL Distinguished School Administrators Award. For expanding the role of the library in elementary and/or secondary school education. Donor: Social Issues Resources Series, Inc., $2,000 and plaque. (American Association of School Librarians)

AASL Distinguished Service Award. For outstanding contribution to school librarianship and school library development. Donor: Baker & Taylor Books, $3,000 and plaque. (American Association of School Librarians)

Academic or Research Librarian of the Year Award. For outstanding contribution to academic and research librarianship and library development. Donor: Baker & Taylor, $3,000 and citation. (Association of College and Research Libraries)

ACRL/EBSS Distinguished Education and Behavioral Sciences Librarian Award. To an academic librarian who has made an outstanding contribution as an education and/or behavioral sciences librarian through accomplishments and service to the profession. Citation. (Association of College and Research Libraries)

ALA/Mecklermedia Library of the Future Award. To a library, consortium, group of librarians, or support organization for information technology in a library setting. Donor: Mecklermedia Corp., $2,500 and Tiffany crystal. (ALA Awards Committee)

The May Hill Arbuthnot Honor Lectureship. To invite an individual of distinction to prepare and present a paper that will be a significant contribution to the field of children's literature and that will subsequently be published in *The Journal of Youth Services in Libraries*. The host site will be selected from applications submitted after the announcement of the chosen lecturer. (Association for Library Service to Children)

Armed Forces Libraries Round Table Certificate of Merit. Presented to an individual or group in recognition of special contributions to Armed Forces libraries. Recipients need not be librarians or members of the association. Certificate. (Armed Forces Libraries Round Table)

Armed Forces Libraries Round Table Achievement Citation. Presented to a member of the Armed Forces Libraries Round Table for significant contributions to the development of armed forces library services and to organizations encouraging an interest in libraries and reading. Citation. (Armed Forces Libraries Round Table)

ASCLA Leadership Achievement Award. For leadership in consulting, multitype library cooperation and state library development. Citation. (Association of Specialized and Cooperative Library Agencies)

ASCLA Professional Achievement Award. A citation presented to one or more ASCLA members for professional achievement within the areas of consulting, networking, statewide services, and programs. (Association of Specialized and Cooperative Library Agencies)

ASCLA Service Award. A Citation presented to recognize an ASCLA personal member for outstanding service and leadership to the division. The award recognizes sustained leadership and exceptional service. (Association of Specialized and Cooperative Library Agencies)

(Hugh C.) Atkinson Memorial Award. For outstanding achievement (including risk-taking) by academic librarians that has contributed significantly to improvements in library automation, management, and/or development or research. Citation and $2,000 cash award. (Interdivisional award sponsored by ACRL, ALCTS, LAMA, LITA)

Beta Phi Mu. For distinguished service in library education. Donor: Beta Phi Mu International Library Science Honorary Society, $500 and citation. (ALA Awards Committee)

> **December 1 is the deadline for most awards. Contact the sponsoring unit for more information.**

Bowker/Ulrich's Serials Librarianship Award. Presented by the Serials Section for distinguished contributions to serials librarianship. Such contributions may be demonstrated by leadership in serials-related activities through participation in professional associations and/or library education programs, contributions to the body of serials literature, research in the area of serials, or development of tools or methods to enhance access to or management of serials. Bowker/Ulrich's. $1,500 and citation. (Association for Library Collections & Technical Services)

> **Toll-free: 1-800-545-2433.**
>
> **Fax: 312-280-3224**

(Francis Joseph) Campbell Citation. For contribution of recognized importance to library service for the blind and physically handicapped. Citation and medal. (Association of Specialized and Cooperative Library Agencies)

(James Bennett) Childs Award. To a librarian or other individual for distinguished lifetime contributions to documents librarianship. Plaque. (Government Documents Round Table)

(Melvil) Dewey Medal. To individual or group for recent creative professional achievement in library management, training, cataloging and classification, and the tools and techniques of librarianship. Donor: OCLC/Forest Press, Inc., citation and medal. (ALA Awards Committee)

Distinguished Service Award. To honor an ALSC member who has made significant contributions to, and an impact on, library service to children and/or ALSC. $1,000 award plus service pin. (Association for Library Service to Children)

Documents to the People Award. To individual, library, organization or noncommercial group that most effectively encourages or enhances the use of government documents in library services. Donor: Congressional Information Service, Inc., $2,000. (Government Documents Round Table)

(Miriam) Dudley Bibliographic Instruction Librarian Award. For contribution to the advancement of bibliographic instruction in a college or research institution. Donor: Mountainside Publishing Co., $1,000. (Association of College and Research Libraries)

EBSCO Community College Learning Resources/Library Achievement Awards. Two awards to individuals, groups, or institutions to recognize significant achievement in the areas of (1) programs and (2) leadership. Donor: EBSCO Subscription Services, $500 plus citation for each award. (Association of College and Research Libraries)

Equality Award. To individual or group for outstanding contribution that promotes equality of women and men in the library profession. Donor: Scarecrow Press, Inc., $500 and citation. (ALA Awards Committee)

Federal Librarians Achievement Award. For leadership or achievement in the promotion of library and information science in the federal community. Citation. (Federal Librarians Round Table)

(Federal Librarians) Distinguished Service Award. To honor a FLRT member for outstanding and sustained contributions to the association and to federal librarianship. Citation. (Federal Librarians Round Table)

Gale Research Award for Excellence in Business Librarianship/BRASS. To an individual for distinguished activities in the field of business librarianship. Donor: Gale Research, Inc., $1,000 and a citation. (Reference and Adult Services Division)

(Bernadine Abbott) Hoduski Founders Award. To recognize documents librarians who may not be known at the national level but who have made significant contributions to the field of state, international, local, or federal documents. Plaque. (Government Documents Round Table)

(Paul) Howard Award for Courage. To a librarian, library board, library group, or an individual who has exhibited unusual courage for the benefit of library programs or services. Donor: Paul Howard, $1,000 and a citation, given every other year. (ALA Awards Committee)

(The John Ames) Humphry/ OCLC/Forest Press Award. To individual for significant contributions to international librarianship. $1,000. Donor: OCLC/Forest Press. (ALA International Relations Committee)

LAMA Recognition of Achievement Awards. To honor notable contributions to leadership and demonstrated commitment to LAMA and its goals. Certificate of Appreciation presented for significant contributions to the goals of LAMA over a period of several years; Certificate of Special Thanks presented for a single, significant contribution to the goals of LAMA. Citation. (Library Administration and Management Association)

LITA/Gaylord Award for Achievement in Library and Information Technology. For achievement in library and information technology. Donor: Gaylord Bros., Inc., $1,000. (Library and Information Technology Association)

(Joseph W.) Lippincott Award. To a librarian for distinguished service to the profession. Donor: Joseph W. Lippincott, Jr., $1,000 and citation. (ALA Awards Committee)

(Margaret) Mann Citation. Presented by the Cataloging and Classification Section for outstanding professional achievement in cataloging or classification through publication of significant professional literature, participation in professional cataloging associations, or valuable contributions to practice in individual libraries. This achievement generally is to have culminated within the last five years. Citation. (Association for Library Collections & Technical Services)

(Allie Beth) Martin Award. Honors a librarian who, in a public library setting, has demonstrated extraordinary range and depth of knowledge about books or other library materials and has distinguished ability to share that knowledge. Donor: Baker & Taylor, $3,000 and plaque. (Public Library Association)

(Margaret E.) Monroe Library Adult Services Award. To a librarian for impact on library service to adults. Citation. (Reference and Adult Services Division)

(Isadore Gilbert) Mudge - R. R. Bowker Award. For distinguished contributions to reference librarianship. $1,500 and a citation. (Reference and Adult Services Division)

National Achievement Citation. To public libraries to give national recognition to their significant, innovative activities that improve their organization, management or services. Any public library may apply and the chief officer of the library must authorize the application; $30 application fee. Citation. (Public Library Association)

(Esther J.) Piercy Award. To recognize the contribution to those areas of librarianship included in library collections and technical services by a librarian with not more than ten years of professional experience who has shown outstanding promise for continuing contribution and leadership. Donor: Yankee Book Peddler, Inc., $1,500. (Association for Library Collections & Technical Services)

RASD Genealogical Publishing Co./History Section Award. To encourage and commend professional achievement in historical reference and research librarianship. Donor: The Genealogical Publishing Company, $1,000 and a citation. (Reference and Adult Services Division)

(Louis) Shores-Oryx Press Award. To an individual, team or organization for excellence in book reviewing and materials for libraries. Donor: Oryx Press. $1,000 and a citation. (Reference and Adult Services Division)

(ALA) Trustee Citations. To recognize public library trustees for distinguished service to library development on the local, state, regional or national level. Two awards. Citation. (American Library Trustee Association)

Authors/Illustrators/Publishers

(Mildred L.) Batchelder Award. To American publisher of an English-language translation of a children's book originally published in a foreign language in a foreign country. Citation. (Association for Library Service to Children)

(Randolph) Caldecott Medal. To a U.S. illustrator of the most distinguished picture book for children published in the U.S. in the preceding year. Donor: family of Daniel Melcher, medal. (Association for Library Service to Children)

(Andrew) Carnegie Medal. To U.S. producer of the most distinguished video for children in the previous year. Donor: Carnegie Corp. of New York, medal. (Association for Library Service to Children)

Gay/Lesbian Book Award. To authors of fiction and non-fiction book(s) of exceptional merit relating to gay/lesbian experience. Donor: Gay Book Award Committee. (Social Responsibilities Round Table)

(Coretta Scott) King Awards. To Black author and illustrator to promote understanding and appreciation of culture and contributions of all people. Donors: Johnson Publishing Co. and Encyclopaedia Britannica to the author; and World Book to the illustrator, $250 and a set of encyclopedias each. (Social Responsibilities Round Table)

(John) Newbery Medal. To U.S. author of the most distinguished contribution to American literature for children published in the United States in the preceding year. Donor: Family of Daniel Melcher, medal. (Association for Library Service to Children)

K. G. Saur Award for Best C&RL Article. To author(s) to recognize the most outstanding article published in *College and Research Libraries* during the preceding volume year. Donor: K. G. Saur donates $500 to each author. (Association of College and Research Libraries)

(Laura Ingalls) Wilder Medal. To author or illustrator whose works have made a lasting contribution to children's literature. Medal, triennially. (Association for Library Service to Children)

Margaret A. Edwards Award. To author whose book or books have provided young adults with a window through which they can view their world and which will help them to grow and to understand themselves and their role in society. Citation and $1,000. Donor: School Library Journal. (Young Adult Library Services Association)

Buildings

Library Buildings Award Program. Biannual. To all types of libraries for excellence in architectural design and planning by an American architect. Donor: American Institute of Architects and LAMA, citations to architectural firms and libraries. (Library Administration and Management Association)

Children's/Young Adult Services

Grolier Award. For stimulation and guidance of reading by children and young people. Donor: Grolier Educational Corporation, $1,000 and citation. (ALA Awards Committee)

Econo-Clad/YALSA Literature Program Award. To YALSA member for development and implementation of outstanding library program for young adults, ages 12 - 18, involving reading and the use of literature. Donor: Econo-Clad Books, $1,000. (Young Adult Library Services Association)

Exhibits

Kohlstedt Exhibit Award. To companies or organizations for the best single, multiple, and island booth displays at the Annual Conference. Citation. (Exhibits Round Table)

Funding

Gale Research Company Financial Development Award. To library organization for financial development project to secure new funding resources for public or academic library. Donor: Gale Research Inc., $2,500. (ALA Awards Committee)

Major Benefactors Honor Award. To individual(s), families or corporate bodies who have made major benefactions to public libraries. Citation. (American Library Trustee Association)

Intellectual Freedom

AASL Intellectual Freedom Award. To a school library media specialist who has upheld the principles of intellectual freedom. Donor: Social Issues Resources Series, Inc., $2,000 to recipient, $1,000 to media center of recipient's choice and plaque. (American Association for School Librarians)

(John Phillip) Immroth Memorial Award for Intellectual Freedom. For notable contribution to intellectual freedom fueled by personal courage. Citation and $500. (Intellectual Freedom Round Table)

(Eli M.) Oboler Memorial Award. To author of a published work in English, or in English translation dealing with issues, events, questions or controversies in the area of intellectual freedom. Donor: Providence Associates, Inc. biennially, $1,500. (Intellectual Freedom Round Table)

State and Regional Achievement Award. To state library association intellectual freedom committee, state library media association intellectual freedom committee, or state or regional intellectual freedom coalition, for the most successful and creative project during the calendar year. Donor: Social Issues Resources Series, Inc., $1,000 and citation. (Intellectual Freedom Round Table)

Literacy

Advancement of Literacy Award. Honors a publisher, bookseller, hardware and/or software dealer, foundation or similar group that has made a significant contribution to the advancement of adult literacy. Donor: Library Journal, plaque. (Public Library Association)

Literacy Award. To a library trustee or an individual who in a volunteer capacity has made a significant contribution to addressing the illiteracy problem in the United States. Citation. (American Library Trustee Association)

Public Relations

(John Cotton) Dana Library Public Relations Awards. To libraries or library organizations of all types for public relations programs or special projects ended during the preceding year. Donor: The H. W. Wilson Company. Citation. (Library Administration and Management Association)

Publications/Articles

AASL Emergency Librarian Publication Award. For outstanding publication in school librarianship to be given to a school library association that is an affiliate of AASL. Donor: Emergency Librarian, $500 and certificate. (American Association of School Librarians)

Best of "LRTS" Award. Given to the author or authors of the best paper published each year in the official ALCTS journal, *Library Resources & Technical Services.* Citation. (Association for Library Collections & Technical Services)

BIS Bibliographic Instruction Publication of the Year Award. Recognizes outstanding publication related to bibliographic instruction published in a given year. Citation. (Association of College and Research Libraries)

Blackwell North America Scholarship Award. To honor the author or authors of the year's outstanding monograph, article or original paper in the field of acquisitions, collection development and related areas of resources development in libraries. Donor: Blackwell/North America, will donate a $2,000 scholarship to the U.S. or Canadian library school of the winning author's choice. (Association for Library Collections & Technical Services)

Dartmouth Medal. For creating current reference works of outstanding quality and significance. Donor: Dartmouth College, medal; certificate for honorable mention. (Reference and Adult Services Division)

Denali Press Award. For creating reference works of outstanding quality and significance that provide information specifically about ethnic and minority groups in the United States. Donor: The Denali Press, $500 and a plaque. (Reference and Adult Services Division)

Katharine Kyes Leab and Daniel J. Leab American Book Prices Current Exhibition Catalogue Awards. For three best catalogs published by American or Canadian institutions in conjunction with exhibitions of books and/or manuscripts. Citations. (Association of College and Research Libraries)

G.K. Hall Award for Library Literature. For outstanding contribution to library literature issued during the three years preceding presentation. Donor: G.K. Hall & Co., $500 and citation. (ALA Awards Committee)

Library Video Award. To a public library demonstrating excellence and innovation in library programming with video and the ability to market and promote the use of these services to library users. Donor: Baker & Taylor, plaque and $1,000 honorarium. (Public Library Association)

Oberly Award for Bibliography in Agricultural Sciences. For the best English-language bibliography in the field of agriculture or a related science in the preceding two-year period. Donor: Eunice R. Oberly Fund, biennially, in odd-numbered years, cash and citation. (Association of College and Research Libraries)

Rare Books & Manuscripts Librarianship Award. Recognizes articles of superior quality published in the ACRL journal, *Rare Books & Manuscripts Librarianship.* Donor: Christie, Manson & Woods, $1,000 and citation. (Association of College and Research Libraries)

Reference Service Press Award. To author of the most outstanding article published in RQ during the preceding two volume years. Donor: Reference Service Press, Inc., $1,000 and a plaque. (Reference and Adult Services Division)

(The H.W.) Wilson Library Periodical Award. To library, library group or association for a periodical making a contribution to librarianship. Donor: The H. W. Wilson Company; $1,000 and certificate. (ALA Awards Committee)

Research

(Phyllis) Dain Library History Dissertation Award. To author of a dissertation treating history of books, libraries, librarianship, or information science. Given every two years; deadline November 1 of even-numbered years. $500 and certificate. (Library History Round Table)

(Jesse H.) Shera Award for Research. For an outstanding and original paper reporting the results of research related to libraries, $500. Deadline: February 1, 1995. (Library Research Round Table)

(Justin) Winsor Prize Essay. To author of an outstanding essay embodying original historical research on a significant subject of library history. $500 and essay published, if desired, in *Libraries and Culture.* (Library History Round Table)

Scholarships

AASL Information Plus Continuing Education Scholarship. To a school library media specialist, supervisor or educator for attendance at an ALA or AASL continuing education event. Donor: Information Plus, $500. (American Association of School Librarians)

AASL School Librarian's Workshop Scholarship. To full-time student preparing to become school library media specialist at the preschool, elementary or secondary level. Donor: Jay W. Toor, President, Library Learning Resources, $2,500. (American Association of School Librarians)

Armed Forces Libraries Round Table NewsBank Scholarship. To a member of the Armed Forces Libraries Round Table who has given exemplary service in the area of library support for off-duty education programs in the armed forces. Donor: NewsBank, Inc., $1,000 to the school of the recipient's choice and a certificate. (Armed Forces Libraries Round Table)

Bound to Stay Bound Books Scholarships. For study in field of library service to children toward the MLS or beyond in an ALA-accredited program. Two awards. Donor: Bound to Stay Bound Books, Inc., $5,000 each. (Association for Library Service to Children)

(David H.) Clift Scholarship. To worthy U.S. or Canadian citizen to begin an MLS degree in an ALA-accredited program. Donor: Scholarship endowment interest, $3,000. (Office for Library Personnel Resources)

(Louise) Giles Minority Scholarship. To worthy U.S. or Canadian minority student to begin an MLS degree in ALA-accredited program. Donor: Scholarship endowment interest, $3,000. (Office for Library Personnel Resources)

NMRT EBSCO Scholarship. To U.S. or Canadian citizen to begin an MLS degree in an ALA-accredited program. Candidates must be members of NMRT. Donor: EBSCO Subscription Services, $1,000. (New Members Round Table)

David Rozkuszka Scholarship. To provide financial assistance to an individual who is currently working with government documents in a library and is trying to complete a master's degree in library science. $3,000. (Government Documents Round Table)

LITA/GEAC-CLSI Scholarship in Library and Information Technology. For work toward MLS Degree in an ALA-accredited program with emphasis on library automation. Donor: CLSI, Inc., $2,500. (Library and Information Technology Association)

LITA/OCLC Minority Scholarship in Library and Information Science. To encourage a qualified member of a principal minority group, with a strong commitment to the use of automation in libraries, to enter library automation. To be awarded annually to a master's student. Donor: OCLC. $2,500. (Library and Information Technology Association)

LITA/LSSI Minority Scholarship in Library and Information Science. To encourage a qualified member of a principal minority group, with a strong commitment to the use of automation in libraries, to enter library automation. To be awarded annually to a master's student. Donor: Library Systems & Services, Inc. $2,500. (Library and Information Technology Association)

(Frederic G.) Melcher Scholarship. To students entering the field of library service to children for graduate work in an ALA-accredited program. $5,000 each. (Association for Library Service to Children)

School Library Media Center

AASL Microcomputer in the Media Center Award. To library media specialists for innovative approaches to microcomputer applications in the school library media center. Two categories: (A) elementary (K-6) and (B) secondary (7-12). Donor: The Follett Software Company, $1,000 to the specialist and $500 to the library for each. Citation, and travel expenses to ALA Annual Conference. (American Association of School Librarians)

AASL National School Library Media Program of the Year Award. To school districts (large and small categories) and a single school, for excellence and innovation in outstanding library media programs. Three categories, up to $3,000 each and plaque. (American Association of School Librarians)

Special Services

ASCLA/National Organization on Disability Award for Library Service for Persons with Disabilities. To institutions or organizations for development of program or services that have made the library's total service more accessible through changing physical and/or additional barriers. Donor:

National Organization on Disability, funded by J. C. Penney, $1,000. (Association of Specialized and Cooperative Library Agencies)

EMIERT/Gale Research Multicultural Award. Recognition of outstanding achievement and leadership in serving the multicultural/multiethnic community with significant collection building, public and outreach services to culturally diverse populations and creative materials and programs. Donor: Gale Research Company, $1,000 and citation. (Ethnic Materials Information Exchange Round Table)

Excellence in Small and/or Rural Public Library Service Award. Honors a library serving a population of 10,000 or less that demonstrates excellence of service to its community as exemplified by an overall service program or a special program of significant accomplishment. Donor: EBSCO Subscription Services, $1,000, plaque. (Public Library Association)

Exceptional Service Award. To recognize effective programming, pioneering activity, or significant research in service to special populations. Citation. (Association of Specialized and Cooperative Library Agencies)

Gale Research Award for Excellence in Reference and Adult Services. To a library or library system for developing an imaginative and unique library resource to meet patrons' reference needs. Donor: Gale Research, $1,000 and a citation. (Reference and Adult Services Division)

(Bessie Boehm) Moore Award. Presented to a public library that has developed an outstanding and creative program for public library services to the aging. $1,000 and citation. (ALA Awards Committee)

(John) Sessions Memorial Award. To a library or library system in recognition of work with the labor community. Donor: AFL/CIO, plaque. (Reference and Adult Services Division)

SIRS/Peace Award. To honor library or librarian who has contributed to advancement of knowledge related to issues of international peace. $500. Donor: Social Issues Resources Series, Inc. (Social Responsibilities Round Table)

(Leonard) Wertheimer Multilingual Award. To a person, group or organization for work that enhances and promotes multilingual public library service. Donor: NTC Publishing Group, $1,000 and plaque. (Public Library Association)

ALA Units

World Book - ALA Goals Awards. To American Library Association units for the advancement of public, academic, or school library service and librarianship through support of programs that implement the goals and priorities of ALA; one grant of up to $10,000 or two smaller grants totalling up to $10,000. Donor: World Book, Inc. (ALA Awards Committee)

Children's/Young Adult Services

ALSC/Book Wholesalers Summer Reading Program Grant. To an ALSC member for implementation of an outstanding public library summer reading program for children. Donor: Book Wholesalers, Inc, $3,000. (Association for Library Service to Children)

ALSC/Econo-Clad Literature Program Award. To ALSC member who has developed and implemented an outstanding library program for children involving reading and the use of literature, to attend ALA conference. Donor: Econo-Clad Books, $1,000. (Association for Library Service to Children)

Professional Development

AASL ABC/CLIO Leadership Grant. For planning and implementing leadership programs at state, regional, or local levels to be given to school library associations that are affiliates of AASL. Donor: ABC/CLIO, up to $1,750. (American Association for School Librarians)

AASL (Frances) Henne Award. To school library media specialist with five or fewer years in the profession to attend an AASL national conference or ALA Conference for the first time. Donor: R. R. Bowker, $1,250. (American Association for School Librarians)

ALTA/GALE Outstanding Trustee Conference Grant. To an ALTA member, currently serving on a local public library board, for first attendance at an ALA Annual Conference. Two awards. Donor: Gale Research, Inc., $750 each. Annually. (American Library Trustee Association)

Baker & Taylor/YALSA Conference Grants. To young adult librarians in public or school libraries to attend an ALA Annual Conference for the first time. Candidates must be members of YALSA, have one to ten years of library experience. Donor: Baker & Taylor, $1,000. (Young Adult Library Services Association)

Book Wholesaler's/YALSA Collection Development Grant. To YALSA members (up to two a year) who represent a public library and work directly with young adults for collection development of materials for young adults. Donor: Book Wholesalers, Inc., $1,000. (Young Adult Library Services Association)

(Louise Seaman) Bechtel Fellowship Award. For librarians, with at least twelve years of work at a professional level in a children's library collection, to read and study at the Baldwin Library of the George Smathers Libraries, University of Florida. Must be an ALSC member and have an MLS from ALA accredited program. Donor: Bechtel Fund, $3,750. (Association for Library Service to Children)

Bogle International Library Travel Fund. To ALA member(s) to attend first international conference. Donor: Bogle Memorial Fund, $500. (International Relations Committee)

Disclosure Student Travel Award/ BRASS. To enable a student in an ALA-accredited master's program interested in a career as a business librarian to attend an ALA Annual Conference. Donor: Disclosure, Inc., $1,000. (Reference and Adult Services Division)

EBSCO ALA Conference Sponsorship. To allow librarians to attend ALA's Midwinter Meetings and Annual Conferences. Five awards for Midwinter and five awards for Annual Conference each year. Donor: EBSCO Subscription Services, winners will be reimbursed up to $1,000 in actual expenses. (ALA Awards Committee)

First Step Award-Wiley Professional Development Grant. Offered by the Serials Section to provide librarians new to the serials field who have not previously attended an ALA Annual Conference with the opportunity to broaden their perspectives and to encourage professional development in ALA Annual Conference and participation in Serials Section activities. Donor: John Wiley & Sons, $1,500. (Association for Library Collections & Technical Services)

LITA/Library Hi Tech Award. To an individual or institution for a work that shows outstanding communication for continuing education in library and information technology. Donor: Pierian Press, $1,000 and plaque. (Library and Information Technology Association)

New Leaders Travel Grant. Designed to enhance the professional development and improve the expertise of public librarians by making their attendance at major professional development activities possible. Travel grant up to $1,500 per applicant.Donor: GEAC, Inc. (Public Library Association)

(Martinus) Nijhoff International West European Specialist Study Grant. Supports research pertaining to West European studies, librarianship, or the book trade. Travel funding for research in Europe for up to 14 days. (Association of College and Research Libraries)

(Shirley) Olofson Memorial Award. To individuals to attend their second ALA Annual Conference. Cash. (New Members Round Table)

(3M/NMRT) Professional Development Grant. To New Members Round Table members to encourage professional development and participation in national ALA and NMRT activities. Donor: 3M, cash to attend ALA Annual Conference. (New Members Round Table)

Putnam & Grosset Group Award. To children's librarians in school or public libraries with ten or fewer years of experience to attend ALA Annual Conference for the first time. Must be member of ALSC. 4 awards. Donor: Putnam & Grosset Group, $600 each. (Association for Library Service to Children)

Readex/GODORT/ALA Catharine J. Reynolds Grant. Grants to documents librarians for travel and/or study in the field of documents librarianship or area of study benefiting performance as documents librarian, $2,000. Donor: Readex Corporation. (Government Documents Round Table)

(The H.W.) Wilson Library Staff Development Grant. To a library organization for a program to further its staff development goals and objectives. Donor: The H. W. Wilson Company, $2,500. (ALA Awards Committee)

Public Libraries

(Loleta D.) Fyan Award. To a library, library school, association, unit or chapter of ALA, or an individual for the development and improvement of public libraries and the services they provide. One or more grants. Donor: Estate bequest, up to $10,000 total. (ALA Awards Committee)

Public Relations

Grolier National Library Week Grant. To libraries or library associations of all types for a public awareness campaign in connection with National Library Week in the year the grant is awarded. Donor: Grolier Educational Corporation, $2,000. (Public Information Office)

Publications/Articles

Carnegie Reading List Awards. To ALA units for preparation and publication of reading lists, indexes and other bibliographical and library aids useful in U.S. circulating libraries. Donor: Andrew Carnegie Fund, amount varies. (ALA Publishing Committee)

Whitney-Carnegie Awards. For the preparation of bibliographic aids for research, with scholarly intent and general applicability. Donor: James Lyman Whitney and Andrew Carnegie Funds, $5,000 maximum. (ALA Publishing Committee)

Research

AASL/Highsmith Research Grant. To conduct innovative research aimed at measuring and evaluating the impact of school library media programs on learning and education, up to $5,000. Donor: The Highsmith Company, Inc. (American Association of School Librarians)

(Carroll Preston) Baber Research Grant. For innovative research that could lead to an improvement in library services to any specified group(s) of people. Donor: Eric R. Baber, up to $7,500. Deadline: January 15, 1995. (ALA Office for Research & Statistics)

Doctoral Dissertation Fellowship. To assist doctoral student in academic librarianship whose research has potential significance in the field. Donor: Institute for Scientific Information, $1,000 and citation. (Association of College and Research Libraries)

(Frances) Henne/VOYA/YALSA Research Grant. To provide seed money to an individual, institution or group for a project to encourage research on library service to young adults. Donor: Voice of Youth Advocates, $500 minimum. (Young Adult Library Services Association)

(Samuel) Lazerow Fellowship for Research in Acquisitions or Technical Services. To foster advances in acquisitions or technical services by providing librarians a fellowship for travel or writing in those fields. Donor: Institute for Scientific Information, $1,000 and citation. (Association of College and Research Libraries)

Special Services

Facts on File Grant. To a library for imaginative programming that makes current affairs more meaningful to an adult audience. Donor: Facts on File, Inc. $2,000. (Reference and Adult Services Division.)

_____ Appendix 7 _____
On-Line and Electronic Network "Smilie" Parlance

"Smilies," presently used by millions of people, including librarians, consist of keystrokes that usually indicate some form of emotion(s) expressed by the message sender. The following is a list of abbreviations in E(lectronic)-mail, TDDs, typewriters, computers, and so on, and shorthands of letters.

:-)	= Basic smilie	l-P	= Yuk
(-:	= Do you note?	:I	= Hmmm . . .
;-)	= Winky smilie	:-$	= Put your money where
)	= Cheshire Cat grin		your mouth is
:-(	= Frowning smilie	:-X	= Lips are sealed
>:->	= Devilish remark	:_)	= Tongue-in-cheek
:-O	= Uh-oh	:-!	= Foot in mouth
:,-(	= Crying	<:-)	= For dumb questions
:*	= Kisses	{:|	= Sounds like a duck
[Name]	= Hug [accompanied by	O:-)	= For innocent users
	name of sender]	~=	= Inflammatory language
:-/	= Skeptical	8-)	= User wears sunglasses
:-e	= Disappointed	::-)	= User wears normal glasses
(:-	= "Unsmilie" frowning	:-{)	= User has a mustache
>-:<	= Mad	{:-)	= User wears a toupée
:{ }	= Big mouth (ironically)	:-~)	= User has a cold
:-(O)	= Yelling		
*|	= Wince		**Shorthands**
:-@	= Screaming	LOL	= Laughing out loud
:Q	= What?	OTF	= On the floor (as in rolling
:-P	= Nyaah		on the floor with laughter)

B4	= Before	FWIW	= For what it's worth
+u	= Bless you	ILY	= I love you
BTW	= By the way	IMHO	= In my humble opinion
d/l	= download (u/l is for the corresponding upload)	IOW	= In other words
		OIC	= Oh, I see

Index

About the Author

VLADIMIR F. WERTSMAN graduated from University "A.I. Cuza" Law School (Romania) and earned his Master's degree in Library Science from Columbia University (1969). He served as Adult Services Librarian and Branch Librarian in various branches of the Brooklyn Public Library, was Russian and Romanian languages specialist at Donnell Foreign Language Library, New York, and worked as Senior Librarian at the Job Information Center, Mid-Manhattan Library, New York. He is a member of the American Romanian Academy of Arts and Sciences, International Social Science Honor Society, American Association for the Advancement of Slavic Studies, and the American Library Association. He chaired the PLA/Multilingual Library Service Committee and presently is Chair of Publishers & Multicultural Materials Committee of Ethnic Materials Round Table, American Library Association. He is the author of *The Romanians in America, 1748–1974* (Oceana, 1975), *The Ukrainians in America, 1608–1975* (Oceana, 1976), *The Russians in America, 1727–1976* (Oceana, 1977), *The Armenians in America, 1616–1976* (Oceana, 1978), *The Romanians in America and Canada* (Gale Research, 1980), *The Librarian's Companion* (Greenwood Press, 1987) as well as *Career Opportunities for Bilinguals and Multilinguals, (first edition)* (Scarecrow Press, 1991) (second edition, Scarecrow 1994) plus:—*What's Cooking in Multicultural America* (Scarecrow, 1996)—*New York City in 500 Memorable Quotations* (Scarecrow, 1996). And co-author of the *Ukrainians in Canada and the United States* (Gale Research, 1981) and *Free Voices in Russian Literature, 1950s–1980s* (Russica, 1987). He contributed to recently published *Gale Encyclopedia of Multicultural America* (Gale, 1995) and *The Encyclopedia of New York City* (Yale, 1995). His biography is included in *Who's Who in America* (47–51st editions) and *Contemporary Authors* (New Revision Series).

ISBN 0-313-29975-7